WHO'S YOUR CITY?

WHO'S YOUR CITY?

*How the Creative Economy Is Making
Where to Live the Most
Important Decision of Your Life*

RICHARD FLORIDA

BASIC
BOOKS

A MEMBER OF THE PERSEUS BOOKS GROUP
NEW YORK

International edition published by Basic Books,
A Member of the Perseus Books Group

Books published by Basic Books are available at special discounts for bulk purchases in the United States by corporations, institutions, and other organizations. For more information, please contact the Special Markets Department at the Perseus Books Group, 2300 Chestnut Street, Suite 200, Philadelphia, PA 19103, or call (800) 810-4145, ext. 5000, or e-mail special.markets@perseusbooks.com.

Designed by Timm Bryson

Library of Congress Cataloging-in-Publication data are available for this book.
ISBN: 978-0-465-01353-1

10 9 8 7 6 5 4 3 2

For Rana

If everything that exists has a place, place too will have a place, and so on ad infinitum.

—ARISTOTLE

How in the image of material man, at once his glory and his menace, is this thing we call a city.

—FRANK LLOYD WRIGHT

The large towns and especially London absorb the very best blood from all the rest of England; the most enterprising, the most highly gifted, those with the highest physique and the strongest characters go there to find scope for their abilities.

—ALFRED MARSHALL

Contents

PART IV: WHERE WE LIVE NOW

1
THE QUESTION OF WHERE

————

I F SOMEONE ASKED YOU TO LIST LIFE'S BIGGEST DECISIONS, what would you say? If you're like most people, you'd probably start with the "what factor," as I call it. Most will say that one of the key decisions in life is figuring out what you want to do for your career. Even if money can't buy happiness, many people believe that doing work you love is likely to give you a prosperous and fulfilling life. My father drilled that notion into me. "Richard," he would say, "you don't have to end up in a factory like me, working hard and punching a clock for modest pay. You need to be a lawyer or a doctor, so you can do something important and make good money."

Many would add that an essential prerequisite to financial and career success is getting a good education and attending the right schools. Graduate from Harvard, Oxford, the Sorbonne, or the University of Tokyo, so goes the theory, and the rest will take care of itself. A good education is the means to a great job, a solid financial future, and a happy life. My parents, like so many others, were education fanatics. Even though they struggled to make ends meet, they put my brother Robert and me in Catholic school—which required not only tuition but also regular contributions to the local parish—and impressed upon us day and night the importance of studying hard, getting good grades, and going to college. They inspected our report cards and gave us rewards for good marks. Like so many other hardworking and devoted parents of modest means, they saw education as the key to upward mobility.

Others, meanwhile, will argue that while jobs, money, and schooling are surely important, the most critical decision in life is picking the right life partner—someone who will support you in all your endeavors and love you unconditionally along the way, what I think of as the "who factor." Those who study human psychology agree that loving relationships are key to a happy life.[1] My mother knew this intuitively. She turned down many college-educated suitors to marry my dad, a factory worker and World War II veteran with an eighth grade education. "Richard," she would say, "it was the best decision of my life by far. Sure, some of those other guys made more money. But love is what is really important. I have been madly in love with your father every day of my entire life."

Without question, both of those decisions—the what and the who—mean a great deal to our lives. But there is another decision that has an equal, if not greater, effect on our economic future, happiness, and overall life outcome: the "where factor."

Maybe this seems so obvious that people overlook it. Finding the right place is as important as—if not more important than—finding the right job or partner because it not only influences those choices but also determines how easy or hard it will be to correct mistakes made along the way. Still, few of us actually look at a place that way. Our approach is haphazard at best, dictated by where we grow up, where we go to school, or where we find a job. Perhaps it's because so few of us have the under-standing or mental framework necessary to make informed choices about location.

The place we choose to live can determine the income we earn, the people we meet, the friends we make, the partners we choose, and the options available to our children and families. People are not equally happy everywhere, and some places do a better job of providing a high quality of life than others. Some places offer us more vibrant labor markets, better career prospects, higher real estate appreciation, and stronger invest-ment and earning opportunities. Some places offer more prom-ising "mating markets." Others are better environments for raising children.

Place also affects how happy we are in less palpable ways. It can be an island of stability in a sea of uncertainty and risk. Jobs end. Relationships break up. The right place can be a hedge against life's downsides. I hate to dwell on the negative, but you need to think about this. It's always terrible to lose a job, even worse to suffer a breakup with a significant other. As bad as those are, however, they are substantially worse if you happen to live somewhere with few options in the job market or the mat-ing market. It's exponentially easier to get back on your feet when your location has a vibrant economy with lots of jobs to choose from, or a lot of eligible single people in your age range to date.

The point is, where we live is a central life factor that affects all the others—work, education, and love. It can make or break work arrangements and personal relationships. It can open new doors. And regardless of what kind of life we envision for our-selves—whether we aspire to make millions, have a family, or cultivate a bachelor lifestyle—choosing where to live is a deci-sion we all must make at least once. A good number of us will make it multiple times. The average American moves once every seven years. More than 40 million Americans relocate each year, and some 15 million make significant moves to a new county or state.[2]

This is a global phenomenon. The United States may be the world's most mobile society, but around the world highly educated and skilled people are more mobile than ever before. As Chapter 7 will show, global cities are magnets for people—particularly those who are ambitious and highly skilled. Some three in four residents of fourteen large global cities—London, Paris, Tokyo, Sydney, Shanghai, Beijing, and others—report that they "chose" their city, according to a 2008 survey of more than 8,500 people in these cities, and didn't just end up there by accident.[3]

If you ask most people how they got to the place they live now, they'll say they just ended up there. They stayed close to family or friends, they got a job there or followed a love interest. Some don't even see that there's a choice to be made at all.

Still, many of us *can* and *do* make a deliberate choice. For the first time ever, a huge number of us have the freedom and economic means to find the place that fits us best. But this remarkable freedom forces us to decide among a large number of options. Today there are many types of communities out there, all with something different to offer.

With choice comes responsibility. The key is to find the place that makes you happy and enables you to achieve your life goals. For some people, career and wealth are big components of happiness, but that is far from everybody. Many of us know people who left good jobs and prosperous professional careers to do something they truly love. Others move back to their hometown after university perhaps to help run the family business or more likely to be closer to family and friends. They prefer family and community to wealth. And many people are very happy where they are. These people may know the real value of community better than others do. What they value about place is the opportunity to lead their lives in the town and among the people already familiar to them.

Remember, when it comes to place, we can't have it all. There are real trade-offs to be made. Many people who move for their career give up the joy of being near family and lifelong friends. Those who choose to stay close to family and friends may give up economic opportunities.

Before I go any further, I want you to think hard about the following questions.

- How do you feel about the place where you're living now? Is it somewhere you really want to be? Does it give you energy? When you walk out onto the street (or the country lane) in the morning, does it fill you with inspiration or stress? Does it allow you to be the person you really want to be? Are you achieving your personal goals? Is it a place you would recommend to your relatives and friends?
- Have you thought about moving? If so, what are the top three places on your radar screen? What do you like about them? What do they offer you? How would your life be different in these places?
- Have you ever sat down and compared where you're living now to the places you like? Honestly, have you given this a fraction of the thought and energy you've given to your job and career prospects, or if you're single, to your dating life?

If you have, you are part of a very small minority. For such an important life decision, it's remarkable how few of us explore all the options or sufficiently ponder all of these questions.

Maybe that is because we're not fully informed. It's a mantra of the age of globalization that where we live doesn't matter. We can work as efficiently from a ski chalet in the Alps or a country house in Provence as from an office in London, New York, or Tokyo, as long as we have wireless and a cell phone.

But impressive new technologies notwithstanding, the so-called death of place is hardly a new story. First the railroad revolutionized trade and transport as never before. Then the telephone made everyone feel connected. The automobile was invented, then the airplane, and then the World Wide Web—perhaps the quintessential product of a globalized world. All of these technologies carry the promise of freeing us from geography, allowing us to move out of crowded cities to lead bucolic lives of our own choosing. Forget the past, when cities and civilizations were confined to fertile soil, natural ports, or raw materials. In today's high-tech world, we are free to live wherever we want. Place, according to this increasingly popular view, is irrelevant.

It's a compelling notion, but it's wrong. Today's key economic factors—talent, innovation, and creativity—are not distributed evenly across the global economy. They concentrate in specific locations. Major innovations in communications and transportation allow economic activity to spread out all over the world. In today's creative economy, economic growth comes from the clustering and concentrating of talented and productive people, what I call the *clustering force*. New ideas are generated and our productivity increases when we locate close to one another in cities and regions. The clustering force makes each of us more productive, which in turn makes the places we inhabit more productive, generating great increases in output and wealth.

Because of the clustering force, cities and regions have become the true engines of economic growth. No wonder these locations continue to expand. Today, more than half the world's population lives in urban areas. A large and growing share of economic output is produced in cities and their surrounding metropolitan regions.

These metropolitan regions are morphing into megaregions, home to tens of millions of people producing hundreds of billions and even trillions of dollars in economic output. As Chapter 3 details, the world's forty largest megaregions, which account for about 18 percent of global population, produce two-thirds of global economic output and more than 8 in 10 of the world's innovations.

The trend is most pronounced in the emerging economies, particularly the BRIC nations (Brazil, Russia, India, and China), where megaregions literally are the economy. The Rio de Janeiro–São Paulo megaregion is home to 10 percent of Brazil's population but creates 40 percent of its output. China's megaregions account for more than two-thirds of the country's total economic output.[4]

Place remains the central axis of our time—more important to the world economy and our individual lives than ever before.

As the most mobile people in human history, we are fortunate to have an incredibly diverse menu of places—in our own country and around the world—from which to choose. That's important because each of us has different needs and preferences. Luckily, places differ as much as we do. Some have thriving job markets, others excel at the basics, like education and safety. Some are better for singles, others for families. Some are more about work, some play. Some lean conservative, others liberal. They all cater to different types, and each has its own personality, its own soul. The different personalities of places seem like hard variables to get a handle on. On your own, it might border on the impossible. But I have mapped them, and you can find the maps in Chapter 11.

It's not just that places have different personalities. What we need from a place also shifts with each stage of life. When we're young, just out of school and single, many of us want a place that offers lots of jobs and opportunities for career advancement, a great nightlife, and a vibrant mating market filled with single people to meet and date. As we get older, and certainly when we marry and have children, our priorities change. We want a place that offers good schools, safe streets, and better lives for our families. And when the children go off to college and leave the house, our needs and interests change yet again.

At each of these turning points, and at many others along the way, a growing number of us have the opportunity to choose a place that truly fits our needs.

But how do we begin to think about that choice? Some fifty years ago, the brilliant economist Charles Tiebout outlined a powerful framework for identifying the trade-offs involved in choosing our place.[5] Tiebout argued that communities specialize in the bundles of services or "public goods" they offer—such as education, police, fire, parks, and what not. Different bundles of services and different qualities of services come with a price, paid as taxes. So when we choose a place, we're not only selecting a physical location, we're also picking the bundle of goods and services that will be available to us there. As Tiebout famously argued, people will "vote with their feet," selecting the particular community which offers goods and services compatible with their particular preferences and needs. Tiebout's model provides a basic logic for thinking about what we value in our communities. When given a wide range of choices, we need to identify our key needs and priorities and then find a place that meets them at a price we are willing and able to pay.

For most of us, the place where we live is our single largest investment. Superstar cities like London, Paris, Tokyo, Shanghai, or New York come with a hefty price tag, and others such as San Francisco, Amsterdam, Chicago, Toronto, Vancouver, Copenhagen, Stockholm, and Sydney have also become extraordinarily expensive. People who work in finance may find that the cost of living in London, Hong Kong, or New York is offset by the economic success they can achieve there. The same might be said of filmmakers who choose to move to Los Angeles or fashion designers who need to be in Milan or Paris—and other places at the top of the pecking order in their given industries.

But what if you work in a field for which there is no single best location, or if you're the kind of person who simply doesn't aspire to be at the very pinnacle of your industry? Then there are plenty of lovely places out there where you can live for a fraction of the amount. It's absolutely essential that you weigh your career goals against the quality of life you'd like to achieve.

I wrote this book to help you pick the place that's right for you. I'll share with you more than twenty-five years of personal research, as well as the work and findings of other researchers. I've structured my advice around three key ideas.

- Despite all the hype over globalization and the "flat world," place is actually more important in the global economy than ever before.
- Places are growing more diverse and specialized—from their economic makeup and job market to the quality of life they provide and the kinds of people who live in them.
- We live in a highly mobile society, giving most of us more say over where we live.

Taken together, these three facts mean that where you choose to live will greatly affect everything from your finances and job options to your friends, your potential mate, and your children's future.

The first part of this book tackles the big picture. It looks at how and why place continues to matter to the global economy. It provides maps and statistics that chart the reality of globalization and the function of megaregions, the new economic units of what I call the "spiky world." Part I provides the information for understanding how to decide where to live, and it's the foundation for seeing how your decision will fit into the wider world.

Part II addresses how your location affects your economic situation—the new realities of the job market, trends in the housing market, and real estate appreciation, all of which are real pocketbook issues. It shows how economic advantage accrues in some places more than others, details the new migration of talented and skilled people to a small set of regions, and documents the forces driving the ups and downs of the housing market. It also describes the trend toward the clustering of jobs—high-tech in Silicon Valley, finance in New York, London, and Hong Kong, filmmaking in Hollywood, Los Angeles, and "Bollywood," India, and music in Nashville, Tennessee.

Part III confronts what is perhaps the biggest trade-off connected with picking a place to live: how to balance career goals against lifestyle and other needs. It looks at the relationship between people's location and their ability to live happy, fulfilled lives. It draws from a large-scale survey of 28,000 people that I conducted with the Gallup Organization. This study, the Place and Happiness Survey, found that location is as relevant to a person's well-being as are job, finances, and interpersonal relationships.

Part IV looks at how people's needs and preferences for where they live evolve and change as they go through three life stages—young and single, married with children, and empty nesters. This section features new rankings my team and I developed of the best places for each of these main life stages.

The last chapter gets practical. It provides the basic tools you need to identify the place that's best for you. Even if you're ecstatic about where you currently live, this chapter will help you better understand what you truly desire and need. If you're thinking about a move, it provides a detailed guide of what to look for and where to look for it. By the end of this book, you'll better understand the critical role of place in today's global economy, and how to maximize your chances for a happy and fulfilling life by picking the place that's right for you.

PART I

WHY PLACE MATTERS

2
SPIKY WORLD

T HE WORLD IS FLAT, SAYS *NEW YORK TIMES* COLUMNIST
Thomas Friedman.[1] Thanks to advances in technology, the
global playing field has been leveled, the prizes are there for the
taking, and all of us are players—no matter where on the surface of the earth we may reside. "When the world is flat," Friedman writes, "you can innovate without having to emigrate."

It's an old idea with a long history. Since the turn of the twentieth century, commentators have been writing about the leveling effects of trade and technology that make place unimportant. From the invention of the telegraph and the telephone, the automobile and the airplane, to the rise of the personal computer and the Internet, many have argued that technological progress has eroded the economic significance of physical location.

The same prophecies persist today. In 1995 *The Economist* proclaimed the death of distance. "Thanks to technology and competition in telecoms," journalist Frances Cairncross predicted, "distance will soon be no object." Four years later the same magazine proudly announced the conquest of location. "The wireless revolution is ending the dictatorship of place in a more profound way."[2] The new communications technologies were proving to be the great levelers in an increasingly global-ized world. Place, we've been led to believe, is no longer rele-vant. We should feel free to live wherever we please.

I've spent the better part of the past decade trying to square provocative concepts with the facts. With the help of my re-search team, I've sorted through mounds of studies, statistical evidence, and counterevidence on the critical role of place in the global economy, which the next two chapters will detail. The bottom line?

By almost any measure, the international economic landscape is not at all flat.

"There are many advantages that children can enter this world with—including intelligence, physical power and agility, good looks and caring parents," wrote UCLA economist and global trade expert Edward Leamer in a devastating review of Friedman's book *The World Is Flat* in the highly respected *Jour-nal of Economic Literature*: "It also matters where you live."[3] And while theoretically we can choose to live virtually any-where, the reality of the global economy is that certain places offer far more opportunity than others.

The most obvious challenge to the flat-world hypothesis is the explosive growth of cities and urban areas worldwide. More and more people are clustering in urban areas—and there's no evi-dence to suggest that they'll be stopping anytime soon. The share of the world's population living in urban areas increased from just 3 percent in 1800 to 14 percent in 1900. By 1950, it had reached 30 percent. Today, this number stands at more than 50 percent. In the advanced countries, three-quarters of people live in urban areas.[4]

Population growth isn't the only indicator that the world is anything but flat. In this chapter, I'll show detailed maps that illustrate the extreme concentrations of economic activity and innovation. In terms of sheer economic horsepower and cutting-edge innovation, today's global economy is powered by a surprisingly small number of places. What's more, the playing field shows no sign of leveling. The tallest spikes—the cities and regions that drive the world economy—are growing ever higher, while the valleys—places that boast little, if any, economic activity—mostly languish.

Globalization is powerful. Places that never had a chance to participate in the world economy are now seeing some action. In that sense, economic activity and innovation have spread to more places around the world. But not all places, just certain places. So not all places participate and benefit equally. Innovation and economic resources remain highly concentrated. As a result, the really significant locations in the world economy remain limited in number.

Globalization has two sides. The first and more obvious one is the geographic spread of routine economic functions such as simple manufacturing or service work (for example, making or answering telephone calls). The second, less obvious side to globalization is the tendency for higher-level economic activities such as innovation, design, finance, and media to cluster in a relatively small number of locations.

When thinkers like Friedman focus on how globalization spreads out economic activity, they miss the reality of this clustering. Michael Porter, Harvard Business School professor and expert on competitive strategy, dubs this the location paradox. "Location still matters," he told *Business Week* in August 2006. "The more things are mobile, the more decisive location becomes." And this point, he added, "has tripped up a lot of really smart people."[5]

The mistake they make is to see globalization as an either-or proposition. It's not. The key to our new global reality is that the world is flat and spiky at the same time.

The World at Night

I'm a big fan of maps. The ones on the following pages were developed by Timothy Gulden, a researcher at the University of Maryland's Center for International and Security Studies. They depict global economic activity on a fine spatial scale. When previous versions of these maps were published in the *Atlantic Monthly* in October 2005, they generated quite a stir.[6] Since then, we have updated them to reflect more comprehensive data. Based on traditional measures of population density and new measures of global economic production and innovation, these maps show the striking location-based spikiness of globalization. There are roughly two or three dozen places that dominate the global economy.

Figure 2.1 charts population distribution across the globe. It is based on existing data that my team and I collected in order to identify the world's megaregions (which I'll discuss in more detail in Chapter 3). The most populous region is India's Delhi-Lahore region, which is home to more than 120 million people. There are eight regions with more than 50 million people; another twelve are home to 25 to 50 million; and thirty-three more have between 10 and 25 million people.

Population density is a rudimentary measure of economic activity that does not fully convey the vast gulf separating the world's most productive regions from the rest. Relatively small cities like Helsinki, Stockholm, and Copenhagen can be immensely rich in per capita output. Conversely, some enormous urban settlements like those of the developing world do not generate a lot of economic output and remain quite poor. So it is

FIGURE 2.1. POPULATION IN A SPIKY WORLD

MAP BY TIM GULDEN

SOURCE: LANDSCAN GLOBAL POPULATION DATABASE, OAK RIDGE NATIONAL LABORATORY

important to identify megaregions not just in terms of their population but also in terms of their economic output.

Unfortunately, there exists no single comprehensive information source for the economic production of the world's regions. A rough proxy is available, though. The second map shows a variation on the widely circulated illustration of the world at night, with higher concentrations of light and thus higher energy use (and presumably stronger economic production) but in greater relief (see Figure 2.2).

To build these maps, Gulden used data from the U.S. Defense Meteorological Satellite Program at the National Oceanic and Atmospheric Administration (NOAA). He charted contiguous lighted areas, noting the sources behind the emissions—lit homes, powered factories, illuminated streets, and lively entertainment districts. Using a series of spatial and statistical techniques, Gulden was able to estimate the amount of economic activity from the amount of light emanating from these areas. I call Gulden's measure light-based regional product, or LRP for short.

Once Gulden had derived his estimates, he calibrated them against published figures on economic output of U.S. metropolitan regions and against World Bank estimates of gross domestic product by country. He then overlaid the light-based estimates with detailed population estimates from Oak Ridge National Laboratory to verify that the method produced plausible estimates of economic activity. Finally, Gulden checked his estimates of LRP against GDP estimates by William Nordhaus and his team at Yale University.[7] The final result (Figure 2.2) shows our estimates of light-based regional product for every square kilometer on the globe for the year 2000.

As this map shows, the world economy takes shape around a couple dozen megaregions. As the next chapter will detail, two of them produced more than $2 trillion in economic output—greater Tokyo ($2.5 trillion) and the giant megaregion stretching

FIGURE 2.2. ECONOMIC ACTIVITY IN A SPIKY WORLD

MAP BY TIM GULDEN

SOURCE: U.S. DEFENSE METEOROLOGICAL SATELLITE PROGRAM

from Boston through New York to Washington, D.C. ($2.2 trillion). These two megaregions would rank as the third and fourth largest economies in the world, about the same size as Germany; only the United States and Japan are larger. Four more megaregions produce more than $1 trillion in output—the great mega that runs from Chicago to Pittsburgh ($1.6 trillion), Europe's Am-Brus-Twerp ($1.5 trillion), Japan's Osaka-Nagoya region ($1.4 trillion), and the greater London region ($1.2 trillion). Each of them would place among the top ten national economies in the world; they are all bigger than Italy, Canada, India, South Korea, Russia, or Brazil. There are forty that produce more than $100 billion in economic output each. In addition to becoming the economic powerhouses behind national economies, megaregions are behind the global economy as well.

Although they do not yet rival those of the United States, Europe, or Japan, the economies of both India and China are also quite spiky. In China, according to Gulden's light emission calculations, 68 percent of economic output is produced in places that house just 25 percent of its people. In India, places with 26 percent of the population produce more than half (54 percent) of the nation's total output. Compare that to the United States, where regions produce economic output roughly in proportion to their population. The population and productive capacity of the United States, as spiky as it is, is spread over a relatively large number of places. China and India, which industrialized much later, have seen their resources and productive capability concentrate to a much greater degree. Our current round of globalization is making the world even spikier than before.

Smart Spots

Population and economic activity are both spiky. But it is innovation—the engine of economic growth—that is most concentrated. It's here that the playing field is least level. Our third map shows the world's innovation centers, as measured by patents granted worldwide (see Figure 2.3). Gulden developed these maps through another ingenious method. Using light emissions to define economic regions, he applied U.S. Patent and Trademark Office data that traces the geographic location of every inventor who files a patent in the United States. But because U.S. patent data is biased to U.S. inventors and those from firms and countries that obtain patents in the United States, he used data from the World Intellectual Property Organization to create more accurate estimates for every location in the world.[8]

The map of global innovation clearly shows a world composed of innovative peaks and valleys. The leaders—the tallest spikes— are the metropolitan regions around Tokyo, Seoul, New York, and San Francisco. Boston, Seattle, Austin, Toronto, Vancouver, Berlin, Paris, Stockholm, Helsinki, Osaka, Seoul, Taipei, and Sydney also stand out. Innovation is also cropping up in certain locations in China and India, as their economies develop. Though they are not nearly as tall as the biggest spikes, a number of cities in these countries are developing significant innovation capability. In India, Bangalore produces about as many patents as Syracuse, while Hyderabad is comparable to Nashville. In China, Beijing produces about as many patents as Seattle or Phoenix, while Shanghai produces about as many as Toronto or Salt Lake City. Our own estimates show that innovation in these cities increased fourfold between 1996 and 2001 and has likely grown at an even greater rate in recent years. Beijing and Shanghai appear poised to join the ranks of global innovators.

This trend may come at the expense of the United States, which has long depended on the innovative and entrepreneurial capabilities of Indian and Chinese immigrants. The detailed research of AnnaLee Saxenian, of the University of California–Berkeley, has

FIGURE 2.3. INNOVATION IN A SPIKY WORLD

MAP BY TIM GULDEN

SOURCES: THE WORLD INTELLECTUAL PROPERTY ORGANIZATION; UNITED STATES PATENT AND TRADEMARK OFFICE

shown that Indian and Chinese entrepreneurs ran roughly 25 percent of all Silicon Valley start-ups from 1980 to 1999, which generated $17 billion in annual revenue and about 58,000 jobs.[9] By 2005 that percentage had increased to 30 percent.

But as the map shows, there are at most two dozen places worldwide that generate significant innovation. These regions have ecosystems of leading-edge universities, high-powered companies, flexible labor markets, and venture capital that are attuned to the demands of commercial innovation—and there aren't many of them.

This spiky pattern for commercial innovation can also be seen in its financing. Venture capital—funds invested in high-tech companies—is also geographically concentrated. The United States boasts a major center in Silicon Valley, with smaller ones in Boston, New York, and a few other cities. Outside the United States, several locations in Europe, as well as in India, China, and Israel, are considered up-and-coming, according to technology expert Martin Kenney of the University of California–Davis.[10] But despite the relatively limited number of venture capital hot spots, venture capital firms often invoke the "twenty-minute rule." Only companies within a twenty-minute commute of the venture capital firm's office are considered worthy of a high-risk investment. Not even high-tech companies whose products and services are based in long-distance communication are considered worth the risk if their physical location is too far away. Firms do make exceptions, but given the hands-on demands of venture capitalism, proximity to clients, investors, and colleagues is highly prioritized. The twenty-minute rule in part explains why so many start-up companies eventually find themselves moving to Silicon Valley, even if they were founded elsewhere. And just three cities worldwide dominated the global market in initial public offerings (IPOs) as of summer 2007: London ($51 billion), New York ($46 billion), and Hong Kong ($41 billion).[11]

Star Scientists

Scientific discovery—the source of much technological innovation—is also concentrated and spiky. Most significant discover-
ies occur in a handful of locations, primarily in the United States
and Europe.

The fourth map (see Figure 2.4) shows the residence of the
1,200 most heavily cited scientists in leading fields. It is based
on data originally compiled by geographer and urban planner
Michael Batty of University College London.[12] A 2006 National
Bureau of Economic Research study by Lynne Zucker and
Michael Darby identified a similar pattern. Tracking the location of more than five thousand star scientists and engineers between 1981 and 2004, across 179 U.S. regions and twenty-five
countries, Zucker and Darby find major concentrations on the
East (Boston, New York, Washington-Baltimore) and West
coasts (San Francisco, Los Angeles, and Seattle), around
Chicago and several other North American regions, as well as
major European (London, Amsterdam, Paris) and Japanese
cities, as well as in several other locations.[13]

Note the similarities between the third and fourth maps.
Commercial innovation and scientific advance are both highly
concentrated, and there are places that enjoy both and do very
well in the global economy. But not all regions do both well.
Several cities in East Asia—particularly in Japan—are home to
significant commercial innovation but depend on scientific
breakthroughs made elsewhere. Similarly, other locations excel
in scientific research but not in commercial adaptation.

When you look at the four maps together, an intriguing pattern appears. With each layer that is added—population density,
economic activity, and innovation—the map becomes increasingly concentrated. At the base, population is already highly
concentrated: most of the world's people live in a relatively

FIGURE 2.4. STAR SCIENTISTS IN A SPIKY WORLD

MAP BY TIM GULDEN

SOURCE: MICHAEL BATTY, CENTRE FOR ADVANCED SPATIAL ANALYSIS, UNIVERSITY COLLEGE LONDON

small number of big cities. The distribution of economic activity is even more skewed. Many locations, despite large populations, barely register. Innovation and star scientists come from fewer places still.

The world gets spikier and spikier the farther you climb up the ladder of economic development, from producing basic goods to undertaking significant new innovations.

Geographic concentration is particularly important for innovation, as we'll see in Chapter 4. Ideas flow more freely, are honed more sharply, and can be put into practice more quickly when innovators, implementers, and financial backers are in constant contact with one another, in and outside of work. Creative people cluster not simply because they like to be around each other, or because they all happen to prefer cosmopolitan centers with lots of amenities, though both of those things tend to be true. Creative people and companies cluster because of the powerful productivity advantages, economies of scale, and knowledge spillovers such density brings.

So although it may not be necessary to emigrate to innovate, geographic concentration remains a prerequisite for cutting-edge innovation. Innovation, economic growth, and prosperity continue to occur in places that attract a critical mass of top creative talent. Because globalization increases the returns on innovation—by allowing for fast rollouts of innovative products and services to consumers worldwide—it increases the lure of innovation centers for our planet's best and brightest. All this only reinforces the spikiness of economic activity across the globe.

Peaks and Valleys

In the past, cities of one country or region competed for investment and for talent with other cities in that same country or region. Now locations across the globe compete with one another. Increasingly, the most competitive global contests are for bright, innovative, and entrepreneurial people.

The landscape of the spiky world can be characterized by four kinds of places.

- The first group comprises the relatively small number of locations that generate innovations. Those are the tallest spikes. They have the capacity to attract global talent, generate new knowledge, and produce the lion's share of global innovation. Thanks to the ever-increasing efficiency of long-distance communication and transportation, ideas circulate among these places easily and constantly.

- The second group includes regions that use established innovation and creativity—often imported from other places—to produce goods and services. Those are the world's emerging peaks. Some of them, such as Dublin, Seoul, and perhaps Singapore and Taipei, are transitioning into places that not only use knowledge but generate it. Most of them, though, function primarily as the manufacturing and service centers of the twenty-first-century global economy. From Guadalajara and Tijuana to Shanghai and the Philippines, they produce the world's goods, take its calls, and support its innovation engines.

- The third group is composed of the megacities of the developing world—with large population concentrations but insufficient economic activity to support their people. Many of these megacities are ravaged by large-scale "global slums" with dense concentrations of homelessness, poverty, and deprivation, high levels of social and political unrest, and little meaningful economic activity.[14] These places, increasingly disconnected from the global economy, make it difficult to celebrate what appears to be a level world for a fortunate few.

- Finally, there are the huge valleys of the spiky world— rural areas and far-flung places that have little concentration of population or economic activity, and little connection to the global economy.

The main difference between now and even a couple of decades ago is not that the whole world has become flatter but that the world's spikes have become more dispersed, and that the world's hills or emerging peaks—the industrial and service centers—have proliferated and shifted. For the better part of the twentieth century, the United States claimed the lion's share of the world's economic and innovative peaks, with a few outposts in Europe and Japan. But the United States has since lost many of those peaks, as industrial-age powerhouses such as Pittsburgh, St. Louis, and Cleveland have fallen back from the global front lines. At the same time, regions in Europe, Scandinavia, Canada, and the Pacific Rim have stepped up.

For some, the world today looks flat because the economic and social distances between the peaks have gotten smaller. People in spiky places are often more connected to each other, even from half a world away, than they are to people and places in their own backyards. This peak-to-peak connectivity is accelerated by the highly mobile creative class of about 150 million people worldwide. They participate in a global technology system and a global labor market, both of which allow them to migrate more freely among the world's leading cities. While the world itself is far from flat, the dense network of interconnections among its peaks can make it appear that way to a privileged minority.

A Brookings Institution study by demographer Robert Lang and world cities researcher Peter Taylor documents the connective fibers linking the world's peaks, as well as the growing economic and social distance separating them from the world's valleys.[15] Lang and Taylor identify a relatively small group of leading interconnected locations—places like London, New York, Paris, Tokyo, Hong Kong, Singapore, Chicago, Los Angeles, and Milan. They also identify a much larger group of city-regions that enjoy far less connectivity to the world economy.

A 2007 *Economist* report on global finance markets reached similar conclusions. While technology has made cross-border financial dealings a snap, the world's major financial centers are spikier and more clustered than ever. "Why would financiers want to live and work in pricey, jam-packed urban jungles?" the article asks. "Armed with broadband, mobile phones and Black-Berries, they could work from almost anywhere." But London, New York, and Tokyo, as well as rising hubs like Hong Kong and Singapore, are consolidating their hold on global finance. The article adds, "Unlike the walled medieval city-states, today's financial centers are increasingly dependent on their connections to one another. Technology, the mobility of capital and the spread of deregulation around the globe have created a vibrant and growing network. When one city is asleep, another is wide awake, so trading goes on round the clock. The number of transactions between financial centers has surged recently as investors have diversified across regions and asset types."[16] It's just more evidence of peak-to-peak connectivity among the world's spikiest places, the flip side being the growing economic and social distance between them and the rest of the globe.

Conceiving of the world as spiky has very different geopolitical and economic implications than seeing it as essentially flat. The flat world theory says that emerging areas can easily plug in to the rest of the world. Emerging economies like India and

China combine cost advantages, high-tech skills, and entrepreneurial energy, which allow them to compete effectively for
manufacturing and standardized service industries. In the flat
world view, the tensions set in motion by the increasingly leveled playing field afflict mainly the advanced countries, which
see not only manufacturing work but also higher-end jobs, in
fields like software development and financial services, moving
offshore.

That theory blinds us to far more insidious problems building
in the world economy and, worse yet, leaves policymakers with
little leverage over them. It's no longer sufficient to think of the
world in traditional binaries: rich and poor, advanced and developing. For the foreseeable future, global politics will hinge on
the tensions brewing among the world's growing peaks, sinking
valleys, and shifting hills. Through that lens, we can see divides
and tensions developing on several overlapping fronts: between
the innovative, talent-attracting "have" regions and the talent-
exporting "have-not" regions; in the escalating and potentially
devastating competition among second-tier cities from Detroit
to Nagoya to Bangalore for jobs, people, and investment; and in
rapidly worsening inequality across the world and even within
its most successful and innovative regional centers.

This is a noxious brew, far more harrowing than the flat world
Friedman describes and a good deal more treacherous than the
old rich-poor divide. Contrary to Samuel Huntington's famous
thesis, which pits so-called modern Judeo-Christian values
against Muslim ones, what we face is not a clash of civilizations
but a deepening economic divide among the world's spikes and
valleys. Most of the world's conflicts—even those seemingly un-
related to economics—stem from the underlying forces of a
spiky world.

More than a decade ago, the political theorist Benjamin Barber presciently wrote that the rise of the global economy, which

he called "McWorld," was so powerful and all-encompassing that it was reinforcing an enormous backlash.[17] That tendency—what he dubbed "jihad"—has its roots in the anxiety and fear felt by millions upon millions of people in regions whose factions or "tribes" are being threatened by the impersonal force of globalization. Lacking the education, skill, or mobility to connect to the global economy, these people are stuck in places that are falling further and further behind.

Not surprisingly, spiky globalization is wreaking havoc on transitional and emerging economies. China's rapid growth in the past decade has brought it to the front lines of the global economy. It is increasingly seen as the "world's factory," the manufacturing center and outsourcing destination for the world's leading companies. Experts note that China is quickly moving up the creative ladder by expanding its science workforce, improving its universities, and attracting the world's top technological workers.

China's remarkable growth is the result of a handful of propulsive regions that are attracting the majority of its talented people, generating the great bulk of its innovations, and producing most of its impressive wealth. Talent is concentrated in a few spiky centers such as Shanghai, Shenzhen, and Beijing, each of which is a virtual world apart from its vast impoverished rural areas. The top ten Chinese regions account for just 16 percent of the nation's population, yet they house nearly 45 percent of its talent-producing universities and 60 percent of its technological innovations.[18]

China exemplifies the growing class divide affecting rapidly developing economies. Its major cities are home to some 560 million people who reside in increasingly innovative, energetic, and cosmopolitan places. Left in their wake are their countrymen—750 million Chinese who inhabit the rest of the mostly rural country. According to detailed polling by the Gallup Organization in

2006, average household incomes in urban China were two and a half times those in rural areas, and have nearly doubled since 1999. According to our own calculations, residents of China's leading megaregions are three and half times wealthier than those in the rest of the country. A Chinese student of mine summed it up succinctly: "In Shanghai, regular middle-class people live better than those in the United States, while in the countryside, just outside the city, people live in what can only be described as precivilized conditions." His impressions are borne out in statistics: 17 percent of China's population lives on less than a dollar a day, almost half lives on less than two dollars a day, and 800 million farmers cannot afford to see a doctor.

The spiky and uneven nature of China's economy is rearing its head in the country's politics. In 2005 the Chinese countryside was the scene of an estimated 87,000 riots and demonstrations, up 50 percent from 2003.[19] In response, the national government began implementing new mechanisms—such as rural development projects in business, education, and health care—to cope with the widening socioeconomic rift.[20] Still, the prospects for bridging the gap are bleak. As China's internationally connected peaks grow closer to their global counterparts, rural areas and their populations are sure to be left behind.

But all that pales in comparison with the growing pains felt by India's poor. India's growing economic spikes—city-regions such as Bangalore, Hyderabad, Mumbai, and parts of New Delhi—are also pulling away from the rest of that crowded country. As Stanford University's Rafiq Dossani has noted, India's technology and business services—industries that are quickly growing—lack the broad employment base enjoyed by China's manufacturing industry.[21] Until India figures out how to provide jobs to its low-skill workers, globalization will only deepen the country's internal economic, political, and social divisions.

The backlash to the spiky world extends beyond emerging economies. In 2005 France and the Netherlands rejected the European Union constitution, fueled by concerns among lower-skilled suburban and rural workers who understandably fear globalization and integration. They may live in the advanced world, but they are also being left behind.

Spiky globalization is also behind political and cultural polarization in the United States, where economic and social rifts between innovative and globally connected metropolitan regions and the rest of the country are ever increasing. As my own calculations show, the spikiest, most innovative centers in the United States—Silicon Valley, Boston, and North Carolina's Research Triangle, for example—also boast the nation's highest levels of inequality.

This spikiness also plays a key role in the divergence of the two ends of an increasingly split housing market (more on this in Chapter 8). As homes in cities like London, New York, San Francisco, and Hong Kong have appreciated over the past two decades, home values in the hinterlands of those countries stagnate or decline.

Left unaddressed, the festering anxiety caused by spiky globalization has already spurred a potentially devastating political backlash against the global engines of innovation. Across the world, fear, insecurity, anger, and resentment are emanating from those falling farther and farther below the world's peaks. On top of that, countries are witnessing the departure (or intended departure) of their best and brightest. And there is no shortage of narcissistic political zealots out there—whether in rural Pennsylvania, the French countryside, Eastern Europe, or the Middle East—willing to stoke these mounting fears for political gain.

If this resembles a Hobbesian world, it's because globalization, poverty, and affluence have all given rise to a new sorting process that geographically separates economic and social classes both domestically and globally. In today's spiky world, social cohesion is eroding within countries and across them. Little wonder we find ourselves living in an increasingly fractured global society, in which growing numbers are ready to vote—or tear—down what they perceive to be the economic elite of the world.

The flat-world theory is not completely misguided. The world is becoming increasingly interconnected, more goods are being produced than ever before, and wealth is growing in the aggregate. Overall, people around the world have more opportunity to participate in the global economy. But most people, justifiably, care less about aggregate effects than they do about their own well-being. While emerging economies stand to gain the most from spiky globalization, they will not be immune to its negative effects. And because modern communication makes the world smaller at the same time that globalization makes it spikier, those trapped in the valleys are looking directly up at the peaks, the growing disparities in wealth, opportunity, and lifestyle staring them right in the face.

We are thus confronted with the greatest dilemma of our time. Economic progress requires that the peaks grow stronger and taller. But such growth simply exacerbates economic and social disparity, fomenting political reactions that further threaten innovation and economic progress. By maintaining that the world is flat, that the playing field is level, and that anyone and everyone has a shot, we make it impossible to confront the problems of globalization that afflict so much of the world. Only when we understand that the spiky nature of our world's economy leads to growing disparities and tensions can we begin to address them. Managing the disparities between peaks and valleys worldwide—raising the valleys without sacrificing the peaks—is surely the greatest political challenge of our time.

3
RISE OF THE MEGAREGION

THE WORLD-FAMOUS ROLLING STONES HAVE TRAVELED the globe countless times. But their 2006 world tour included a new, first-ever stop—Shanghai. "We all know that Shanghai is a big important city," Mick Jagger told the press, "so we wanted to make sure it's on our itinerary." The Stones recognized what international investors, global manufacturing firms, and investment bankers have known for years: Shanghai looks and feels nothing like the rest of China. Not only is it attracting talent and investment, it is determined to transform itself into a global creative center by supporting the arts, fostering a bustling nightclub district, and forging connections with cosmopolitan centers around the world.

The growing divergence between Shanghai and the rest of China is not an isolated case. It reflects a much broader and more powerful process—the rise of the megaregion as the fundamental economic unit of our time. Today, megaregions range in size from 5 to 100 million people, and they produce hundreds of billions—sometimes trillions—in economic output. They harness human creativity on a massive scale and generate most of the world's scientific achievement and technological innovations.

Cities have always been the natural economic units of the world. But over the past several decades, what we once thought of as cities—central cores surrounded by rural villages and later by suburbs—have grown into megaregions composed of two or more city-regions. A megaregion is an economic unit that results from city-regions growing upward, becoming denser, and growing outward and into one another.

The megaregions of today mass together talent, productive capability, innovation, and markets on a far larger scale than cities ever did. While cities in the past were part of national systems, globalization has exposed today's cities to worldwide competition. As the distribution of economic activity has gone global, the city system has also gone global, meaning that cities now compete on a global terrain. That means that bigger and more competitive economic units—megaregions—have superseded cities as the real engines of the global economy.

The Only Economic Unit That Matters

We usually think about economic growth and development in terms of nation-states. The classical economists Adam Smith and David Ricardo both argued that nation-states are the geographic engines behind economic growth. As Ricardo famously theorized, discretely defined countries have incentive to specialize in different kinds of industries, which would allow them to gain and maintain "comparative advantage" over others.[1]

The first person to see this was the great urbanist Jane Jacobs, who is best known for her scathing critique of urban planning, *The Death and Life of Great American Cities,* and two other very important books, *The Economy of Cities* and *Cities and the*

Wealth of Nations.[2] In *The Economy of Cities* (1969) Jacobs refutes the long-standing theory that cities emerged only after agriculture had become sufficiently productive to create a surplus beyond what was needed to survive. In fact, the earliest cities, according to Jacobs, formed around rudimentary trade in wild animals and grains, which led their inhabitants to discover agriculture and the economic benefits of product exportation. Even activities typically considered "rural" originated in cities before proliferating into outlying regions. Productivity improvements in agriculture, Jacobs points out, always originated in cities before they were adopted in farming areas. The mechanical reaper, for instance, was originally invented, perfected, and used in cities before the technology reached and revolutionized rural agricultural areas.

A dynamic city, according to Jacobs, integrates its hinterland and becomes a full-blown "city-region." As nearby farmland is revolutionized by city-created technology and innovation, rural dwellers move closer to town to assume jobs in urban industry. As the city generates more output, more money becomes available for civic and infrastructure improvement as well as for new technology and innovation to aid the city's outlying areas.

The comparative advantage that economist David Ricardo first identified in the eighteenth century still matters today, but national borders no longer define economies. Instead, the megaregion has emerged as the new natural economic unit. It is not an artifact of artificial political boundaries, like the nation-state or its provinces, but the product of concentrations of centers of innovation, production, and consumer markets. Today's megaregions, which are essentially agglomerations of contiguous cities and their suburbs, extend far beyond individual cities and their hinterlands.

In 1957 the economic geographer Jean Gottman first used the term "megalopolis" to describe the emerging economic hub that was the Boston to Washington corridor.[3] Derived from the Greek and meaning "very large city," the term was later applied to other regions: the great swath of California stretching from San Francisco to San Diego, the vast midwestern megalopolis running from Chicago through Detroit and Cleveland and extending to Pittsburgh, and the bustling Tokyo-Osaka region of Japan.

In 1993 the Japanese management expert Kenichi Ohmae wrote an influential *Foreign Affairs* article arguing that the globe's natural economic zones, or "region states," had replaced nation-states as the organizing economic units of what he famously dubbed the "borderless world."[4] Ohmae said, "Region states may lie entirely within or across the borders of a nation-state. This does not matter. It is the irrelevant result of historical accident. What defines them is not the location of their political borders but the fact that they are the right size and scale to be the true, natural business units in today's global economy. Theirs are the borders—and connections—that matter in a borderless world."

But not all large urban areas qualify as economic megaregions. Many cities in the developing nations are immense but lack the economic clout of megaregions. As Ohmae writes, they "either do not or cannot look to the global economy for solutions to their problems or for the resources to make those solutions work."

Ohmae's point is important. Population is not tantamount to economic growth. These megacities differ substantially from true megaregions that have large markets, significant economic capacity, substantial innovative activity, and highly skilled talent, on top of large populations.

Looking at economic growth and the creation of wealth solely through nation-state data is hugely misleading because national borders are less relevant to where economic activity is located. Money and capital flow to where the returns are greatest, and people move where opportunity lies. To be sure, this results in a more fully integrated global economy. But it also means that both capital and talent concentrate where opportunities for productivity and returns are highest.

National borders also have less to do with defining cultural identity. We all know how different two cities can be despite being in the same state or province, much less the same country. Those valley-bound places are experiencing more than just lagging economies; they're becoming culturally distinct from their megaregion neighbors as well. These growing pains, on top of glaring economic disparities, are exacerbating the divide between the haves and the have-nots—the urban "sophisticates" and rural people—of the world.

At the same time that cities within national borders are diverging, megaregions whose geographic locations could not be farther apart are growing closer. The more that two megaregions—regardless of their physical distance or historical relationship—have in common financially, the more likely they are to develop similar social mores, cultural tastes, and even political leanings. That isn't true just for the biggest cities like New York, London, and Hong Kong, which one report referred to as comprising the city-state of "Ny-Lon-Kong." Amsterdam, Sydney, and San Francisco have more in common than they do with smaller cities in their own countries.[5]

Mega Mapping

So let's dig beneath the surface of the nations of the world and look at a more realistic portrait of the global economy. A number of experts have updated Gottman's and Ohmae's work with empirical data, charting the scope and extent of megaregions in the United States and elsewhere. In a 2005 study, Robert Lang and Dawn Dhavale of the Metropolitan Institute at Virginia

Tech found that the ten megaregions which power the U.S. economy are home to nearly 200 million Americans, more than two-thirds of the national population, and are growing at considerably faster rates than the nation as a whole.[6]

Yet to this day, we still compare the size and growth of the U.S. economy with those of established competitors such as Germany and Japan, or emerging ones such as India and China. National borders dictate how we measure economic output and productivity, count population, tally innovation, and account for growth. All parties—from international organizations and media outlets to global financial firms—are limited to the same data. But that's not what we should really be comparing. We ought to compare the megaregions that drive the economy.

Fortunately Tim Gulden came up with a clever solution. He used satellite images of the world at night (described in Chapter 2) to identify megaregions as contiguous lighted areas. Based on that, he was able to distinguish the large areas of economic activity from smaller centers. And by combining the light data with other economic measures and finely calibrating against existing estimates of national and regional output, he was able to derive estimates of economic activity—the light-based regional product—for every megaregion in the world.[7] Gulden likes to say a megaregion is somewhere you can walk all the way across, from one side to the other, carrying nothing but some money without ever getting thirsty or hungry.

I realized the power of these world-at-night images on a plane trip from South Carolina to Toronto late one evening in fall 2007. When we left South Carolina in the heart of the great Char-Lanta mega, we could see brilliant lights for at least forty-five minutes. Then the ground went dark for about an hour, until we approached Buffalo at the outskirts of the Tor-Buff-Chester mega. The light in the clouds on the horizon ahead looked like daybreak, even though we were traveling in the dead of night.

Technically, a megaregion must meet two key criteria. First, it must be a contiguous lighted area with more than one major city or metropolitan region. Second, it must produce more than $100 billion in LRP. By that definition, there are exactly forty megaregions in the world (see Appendix A). Here are some key statistics.

If we take the largest megas in terms of population:

- The ten biggest are home to 666 million people, or 10 percent of world population.
- The top twenty comprise 1.1 billion people, 17 percent of the world total.
- The top forty are home to 1.5 billion people, 23 percent of global population.

When we look at economic activity, the figures are even more striking:

- The world's ten largest megaregions in terms of economic activity (or LRP), which house approximately 416 million people or 6.5 percent of the world's population, account for 43 percent of economic activity ($13.4 trillion), 57 percent of patented innovations, and 53 percent of the most cited scientists.
- The top twenty megaregions in terms of economic activity account for 10 percent of population, 57 percent of economic activity, 76 percent of patented innovations, and 76 percent of the most cited scientists.
- The top forty megaregions in economic activity, which make up about 18 percent of the world's population, produce 66 percent of economic activity, 86 percent of patented innovations, and house 83 percent of the most cited scientists.

Let's now take a look at some detailed maps of the world's most important megaregions.

The United Megas of North America

The first map shows the megaregions that compose the North American economy, demonstrating, among other things, what a mistake it is to conceive of the U.S. economy as composed of fifty states (Figure 3.1). In reality, the core of the U.S. and North American economy is made up of roughly a dozen megaregions that stretch into Canada and in some cases Mexico, and generate the great bulk of the country's economic output.

As the map shows, the largest megaregions are concentrated on the coasts. The Bos-Wash corridor stretching some five hundred miles down the East Coast from Boston through New York to Washington is the world's second largest in terms of economic output; only greater Tokyo is bigger. When originally identified by Gottman in 1957, it was home to about 32 million people. Today it is home to some 54 million, more than 18 percent of all Americans. Generating $2.2 trillion in output, it would rank among the biggest national economies in the world. Though broadly based, its economy has considerable specialization and strengths. New York is highly specialized in finance and business services, as well as arts and culture. Boston is known for its biotech industries and educational resources. Media, strategic intelligence, and biotech cluster in and around Washington, D.C.

Farther south, the Char-Lanta megaregion is home to 22 million people and produces $730 billion in LRP. Included in this mega is the regional headquarters center and talent magnet of Atlanta, a regional financial center in Charlotte, and a regional tech center in the North Carolina research triangle.

FIGURE 3.1. MEGAREGIONS OF NORTH AMERICA

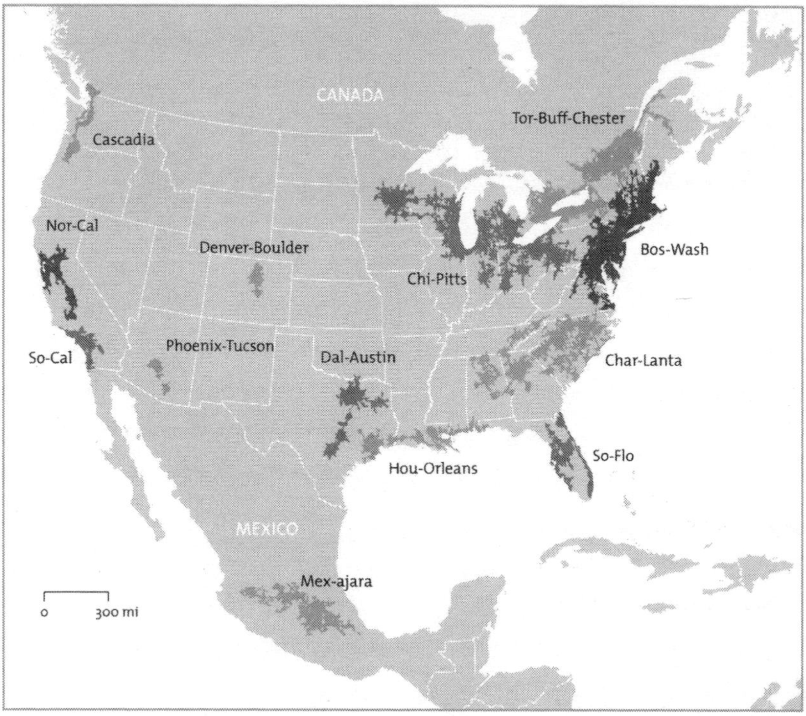

MAP BY TIM GULDEN AND RYAN MORRIS

Even farther south is a substantial megaregion covering southern Florida that includes Miami, Orlando, and Tampa—housing 15 million people and producing $430 billion. Its strengths include Miami's role as a center for Latin American banking and investment as well as entertainment and design; there is also considerable capability in arts and entertainment technology in Orlando, which is home, of course, to Disney World—a major incubator for pop culture.

On the West Coast, we also have three substantial megaregions. The largest, home to 21 million people and the source of $710 billion in cross-national LRP, runs from Los Angeles through San Diego and into Tijuana, Mexico. L.A. boasts pre-eminence in film, entertainment, and popular culture. It is also a major port and a key destination for finance, banking, and technology firms. San Diego adds world-class information technology, telecommunications, and biotechnology. And Tijuana brings one of the world's largest manufacturing centers—specializing in television, electronics, and high-tech production. This is a powerful combination. The region is one of very few in the world that combines cutting-edge creativity and innovation with the ability to manufacture products in a relatively low-cost environment.

A second megaregion surrounds the San Francisco Bay Area. Claiming 13 million people and more than $470 billion in output, it is a leading center of technology industry and venture capital and is home to a cluster of world-class universities, each boasting its own specialty: Stanford and UC-Berkeley in science and engineering, UC-San Francisco in biotechnology, and UC-Davis in agriculture and wine making. The region has established substantial capabilities in entertainment technology, housing companies such as Pixar, Electronic Arts, and Industrial Light & Magic. Of course, its core is Silicon Valley with its remarkable concentration of technology producers and innovators.

The West Coast also claims the Cascadia megaregion, which stretches up from Medford and Portland, Oregon, through Seattle and into Vancouver, Canada, and is home to nearly 9 million people generating $260 billion in LRP. On top of its historical strength in aerospace manufacturing, it is also a global center of software and Internet-based industries home to companies like as Microsoft, Amazon, and Real Networks, as well as leading lifestyle and consumer companies such as Starbucks, Nike, REI, and Costco. Two additional megaregions, Denver-Boulder and Phoenix-Tucson, each generate about $140 billion in LRP.

The southern coast of the United States does its part too. The great energy-producing belt that runs from Houston to New Orleans is home to nearly 10 million people and the source of $330 billion in LRP. Also in Texas is the region encompassing Dallas, San Antonio, and Austin, also housing nearly 10 million people while producing $370 billion in regional output. These megas may well combine to form a gargantuan "Texas Triangle," according to a 2004 report by the Federal Reserve Bank of Dallas. The successful discount carrier Southwest Airlines got its start shuttling passengers across these Texas cities. "Combining Houston's port, Dallas's inland distribution function, San Antonio's reach into deep South Texas and northern Mexico, and even the state's political capital into one place could have produced a Third Coast megalopolis to rival New York, Los Angeles and Chicago," the study finds.[8]

But the so-called fly-over states need not worry: a series of megaregions dot North America's heartland as well. Running from Pittsburgh and Cleveland through Detroit, Chicago, and Minneapolis, the great Chi-Pitts megaregion covers more than 100,000 square miles and is home to 46 million people. Churning out $1.6 trillion in LRP, it is the third largest megaregion in the world.

Nearby is another great binational megaregion. I actually named this megaregion while speaking at a conference on the future of Buffalo in 2002. When asked about the economic future of the Buffalo region and what recommendations I had for revitalizing the region, I blurted out, "Tor-Buff-Chester" in an effort to promote the integration of Toronto, Buffalo, and Rochester. But now with the benefit of our megaregion maps, I can see that it stretches much farther than that—from Waterloo and London, Ontario, through Toronto eastward to Ottawa, Montreal, and Quebec City and down to Syracuse, Ithaca, and Utica in the United States. Given that geography, perhaps a more appropriate name might be "Tor-Buff-Loo-Mon-Tawa." Whatever its name, this binational mega is home to a population of more than 22 million people and an economy of more than $530 billion, making it the fifth largest megaregion in North America and the twelfth largest in the world. Toronto is a significant economic center with superb universities, leading arts, entertainment, design, and culture industries; it also has what is arguably the most diverse population in the world. Like London, but unlike most major U.S. cities, Toronto offers schools that work, low crime, and safe streets. Unlike London, New York, Los Angeles, or San Francisco, it also remains reasonably affordable, which allows it to retain a wide mix of social and economic classes. Nearby Waterloo, Ontario, provides a major technology center, housing Research in Motion, the BlackBerry company. Montreal is home to Cirque du Soleil and a world-class music scene that produced the Arcade Fire, one of the leading and most successful bands of the early 2000s.[9] On the U.S. side of the border, Rochester, though losing residents, remains one of the world's leading centers for optoelectronic and research-intensive companies such as Xerox, Kodak, and many of their key suppliers.

Euro-Megas

Like the fifty states of America, the countries of Europe are also historical artifacts defined by political boundaries. The real economies of Europe are a dozen or so megaregions that house the bulk of the Continent's innovation and production (Figure 3.2).

Europe's largest megaregion is the enormous economic composite I call Am-Brus-Twerp. Housing nearly 60 million people and producing nearly $1.5 trillion in economic output, it is the fourth largest megaregion in the world.

FIGURE 3.2. MEGAREGIONS OF EUROPE

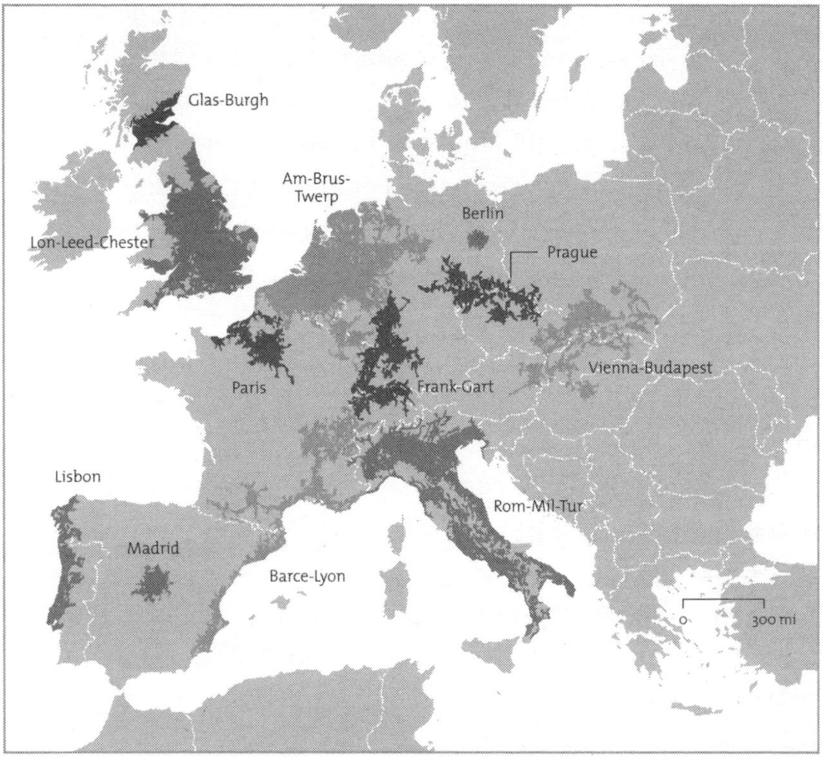

Glas-Burgh

Am-Brus-Twerp

Berlin

Lon-Leed-Chester

Prague

Paris

Frank-Gart

Vienna-Budapest

Lisbon

Rom-Mil-Tur

Madrid

Barce-Lyon

0   300 mi

MAP BY TIM GULDEN AND RYAN MORRIS

Next in size is the British megaregion stretching from London through Leeds, Manchester, Liverpool, and into Birmingham. Home to a huge global creative class, including a significant number of U.S. expatriates, London is emerging as the world's leading financial and creative center, rivaled only by New York City. Specializing in cultural creativity that includes film, theater, and music (some of the world's best bands originated in this area, including the Beatles, Rolling Stones, Led Zeppelin, and the Sex Pistols), this mega is home to 50 million people and responsible for $1.2 trillion in economic output, making it the sixth largest regional economy in the world.

The great Italian megaregion stretching from Milan through Rome to Turin is a leading center for fashion and industrial design. Some 48 million people produce roughly $1 trillion in output, making it the third largest economic conglomerate in Europe and the seventh largest in the world.

In Germany, the megaregion encompassing Stuttgart, Frankfurt, and Mannheim is home to 23 million people, many of whom work in finance and manufacturing, producing $630 billion in LRP.

To the west is greater Paris, a megaregion of nearly 15 million people accountable for $380 billion in output and the leading authority in fashion and haute-culture.

The binational megaregion Barce-Lyon claims some 25 million people who churn out $610 billion in LRP. While northern Europeans have long vacationed in this region, job seekers are increasingly relocating there as well. A high-ranking minister of trade from the Netherlands confided privately to me that she is nervous about losing northern European companies to the sunbelt's climate, physical beauty, and talent pools.

Vienna-Budapest ($180 billion in LRP), Prague ($150 billion LRP), Lisbon ($110 billion LRP), Scotland's Glas-burgh ($110 billion LRP), Madrid ($100 billion LRP), and Berlin ($100 billion LRP) complete the list of Europe's megaregions.

Mega-Tigers

Asia's economy too is defined by its megaregions (Figure 3.3). Japan is home to four of them, including two of the world's largest. Greater Tokyo, home to more than 55 million people and responsible for nearly $2.5 trillion in economic output, is the world's biggest mega, with world-class strengths in finance, design, and high technology.

FIGURE 3.3. MEGAREGIONS OF ASIA

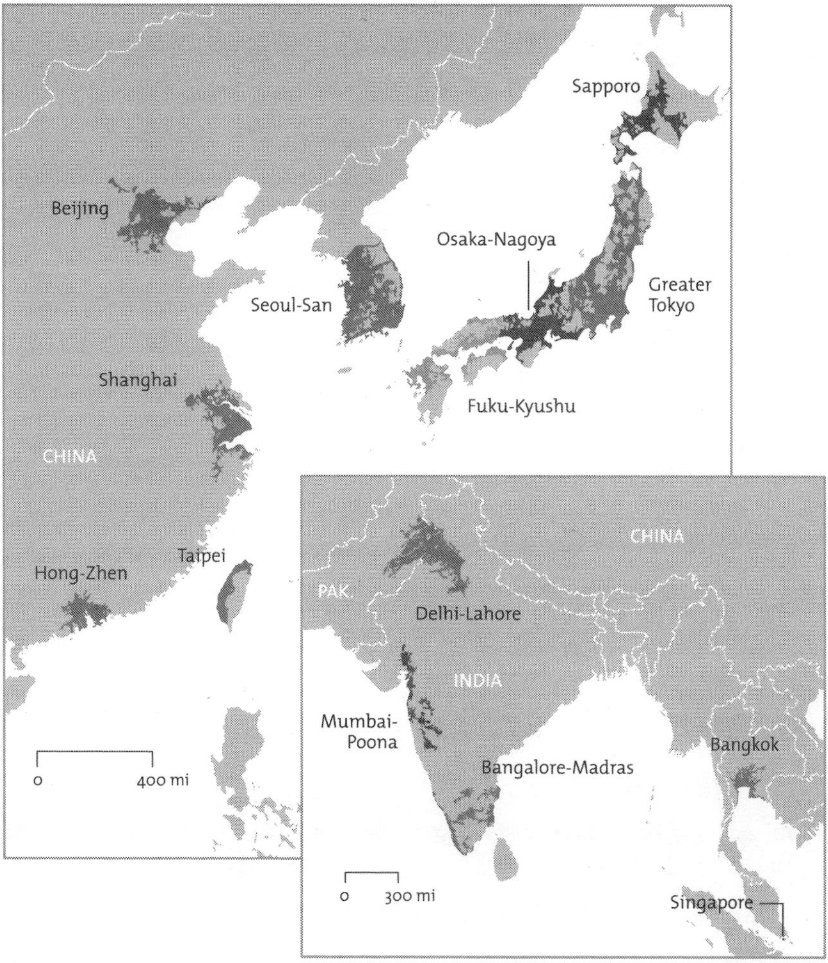

MAP BY TIM GULDEN AND RYAN MORRIS

A second Japanese megaregion, stretching from Osaka to Nagasaki, is home to 36 million people who generate $1.4 trillion in output. Its niche specialties include high-tech innovation and manufacturing—from automobiles to cutting-edge electronics. Fuku-Kyushu houses 18 million people and produces $430 billion in LRP, while greater Sapporo is home to more than 4 million people, producing $200 billion in LRP. The boundaries of Japan's great megaregions are already blurring. Much of Japan may be well on its way to becoming the world's first integrated super-megaregion—a single, gargantuan, and geographically overlapping economic entity of more than 100 million people producing $4.5 trillion in LRP.

The megaregion that runs from Seoul to Busan houses 46 million people and produced $500 billion in LRP, housing a growing number of highly innovative companies whose portfolios include everything from electronics and telecommunications to semiconductors and flat panel displays.

Taipei is the nucleus of a megaregion of more than 20 million people whose $130 billion LRP includes products similar to those of its northern neighbor, housing some of the world's leading semiconductor production facilities.

Greater Singapore is a classic city-state, whose population of 6 million generates LRP of $100 billion. It has "willingly and explicitly given up the trappings of nation-states," Ohmae writes, "in return for the relatively unfettered ability to tap into . . . the global economy." A major center for global disk drive production, Singapore boasts strong niche industries in science and technology and, as a result, has succeeded in luring top Western universities to establish branches there. Its long-term strategy to be a creative center has paid off: considerable investments in the arts, both high culture and street culture, have made Singapore a top destination for innovative people of all lifestyles and interests. In Thailand, the Bangkok megaregion is home to 19 million people, producing $100 billion in economic output.

Megas in the Emerging Economies

Megaregions play an even larger role in the economic development of the so-called emerging economies. Some years ago,

Goldman Sachs researchers coined the acronym "BRIC" to identify the rapidly growing emerging economies of Brazil, Russia, India, and China.[10] But growth and development in the BRIC nations and other emerging economies from Mexico to Malaysia are far from uniform, geographically speaking.

Powering the growth of these emerging economies are large megaregions. Some of these megas are experiencing rapid economic growth, while others are growing more slowly if at all, attracting large population influxes from rural areas and giving rise to destitute global slums. Most of these emerging economy megas are sources of significant economic and geographic inequality because their economies are doing much better than surrounding rural areas and because there is a significant economic divide that separates the haves and have-nots inside their borders.

China's economy, for example, is dominated by just three megaregions along its eastern coast. The largest in terms of population is the Shanghai-Nanking-Hangzhou triangle (Shan-Nan-Han), home to more than 66 million people and $130 billion in LRP. To the north, greater Beijing houses 43 million people, generating $110 billion in LRP. To the south, the Hong-Zhen corridor encompasses about 45 million people and produces $220 billion in LRP. These three megas account for $460 billion in LRP, 43 percent of the country's total economic activity measured as LRP. And when we add up all of China's megaregions, they produce $735 billion in LRP, 68 percent of the country's total.

Boasting massive investment in new universities, increasing flows of global research and development, and a seemingly unlimited talent pool, these three megaregions are likely to transform quickly from their current status as the world's factory into an emerging center for innovation and creativity. What remains to be seen is whether China's megaregions can generate the necessary openness, tolerance, and independence required of such a world center.

India's economy too is defined by megaregions. Delhi-Lahore is home to more than 120 million people, generating $110 billion in LRP. Two other great population centers in India are on track to become full-fledged megaregions. To the north, 62 million people inhabit a megaregion stretching from Mumbai to Poona that generates $60 billion in LRP. This region is home to the Bollywood film industry, the largest single producer of films in the world with more than nine hundred releases each year.

The technology corridor of Bangalore through Madras in southern India is home to 72 million people producing $50 billion in LRP. Both of these regions are growing explosively, about 10 percent per year or more. Since our estimates are from 2000, it is reasonable to think that both have already crossed the $100 billion threshold to become full-fledged megaregions. Possessing both Bollywood film and Bangalore technology, India is not just a low-cost offshore production center. Its prestigious Indian Institutes of Technology is one of the preeminent engineering and technology schools in the world. Its fashion and product designers are on the rise, and the music scenes of London, Toronto, and New York are infused with Bhangra beats. Little known to most, its video game industry is projected to grow tenfold by the end of the decade, and its animation industry is expected to nearly triple its current size.

Megaregions play an increasingly significant role in other emerging economies around the world. In Latin America, greater Mex-ajara is home to more than 45 million people and generates $290 billion in LRP, more than half of Mexico's total.

In Brazil, the megaregion of Rio-Paolo generates $230 billion, more than 40 percent of the country's total, and is home to 43 million people. Greater Buenos Aires is home to roughly 14 million and generates $150 billion in LRP, more than half of that country's total.

In the Middle East, the giant megaregion stretching across Tel Aviv to Amman, Damascus, and Beirut is home to more than 30 million people and pumps out $160 billion in LRP.

It's worth emphasizing that many of these emerging economy megaregions, while home to huge populations and a significant level of economic activity, also suffer from tremendous economic and social inequality, and in some cases are home to millions upon millions of destitute people in the world's worst slums and shantytowns—a fact you have to bear in mind as you start to narrow down your choice of where to live.

* * *

Chapters 2 and 3 have provided empirical and visual proof that the world is not flat. It's spiky, powered by megaregions—substantial conurbations of multiple cities and suburbs—which at times span national borders and form vast swaths of trade, transport, innovation, and talent.

What explains such concentrations of economic activity and growth? Why is place still such a critical factor in the global economy? How can it be that economic activity is not pulled apart by the powerful forces of globe-stretching trade and world-shrinking technology? How do cities and regions stay physically connected in the face of such forces? And what exactly enables them to beat the odds stacked so considerably against them?

4
THE CLUSTERING FORCE

I F WE POSTULATE ONLY THE USUAL LIST OF ECONOMIC forces," the Nobel Prize–winning economist Robert Lucas wrote in 1988, "cities should fly apart."[1] After all, Lucas reminds us, land "is always far cheaper outside cities than inside." Why, then, don't businesses and people move en masse out to where costs are substantially lower? Lucas answers his question with another, equally simple observation: "What can people be paying Manhattan or downtown Chicago rents for, if not to be around other people?"

With that one sentence, Lucas brings place front and center into the debate over the forces behind economic growth. He identifies the underlying economic power of the clustering force—the clustering of people and productivity, creative skills and talents that powers economic growth.

That's why cities and megaregions are the true economic units that drive the world forward. These organized geographic production systems and markets, where human beings and talents cluster, Lucas argues, offer social and economic advantages that other places simply can't. Their benefits in terms of innovation and productivity far outweigh the higher costs of living and doing business there.

Jane Said

The study of economic growth is an arcane field that until recently has paid little attention to the importance of location. In 1776 Adam Smith published *The Wealth of Nations*, which argued that specialization, efficiency, and division of labor are the cornerstones of modern economic growth.[2] Later, David Ricardo's theory of comparative advantage argued that not just firms but countries gain advantage by specializing in certain kinds of economic activity.[3]

The far-seeing urbanist Jane Jacobs agrees that specialization has its uses, but she focuses on an even more fundamental source of economic growth—what she terms expansion. Like the great economist Joseph Schumpeter, she emphasizes the critical importance of innovation and entrepreneurship. In her eyes, the prospect of new types of work and new ways of doing things drives large-scale economic expansion. But where most economists locate momentum in great companies, entrepreneurs, and nation-states, Jacobs presciently identifies great cities as the prime motor force. Companies come under extraordinary pressure to specialize—to do things more cheaply, efficiently, and uniformly. But cities are host to a wide variety of talents and specialties, the broad diversity of which is a vital spur to creating things that are truly new.[4]

In *The Economy of Cities*, Jacobs writes, "The diversity, of whatever kind, that is generated by cities rests on the fact that in cities so many people are so close together, and among them contain so many different tastes, skills, needs, supplies, and bees in their bonnets."

Ever since Alfred Marshall's seminal writings, economists have thought of cities as clusters, or "agglomerations," of firms, factories, and industries. Jacobs has added substantially to our understanding of the forces of agglomeration, arguing that the true power of cities comes from the clustering of people, rather than the clustering of firms. Subsequent economics research has shown that companies perceive less benefit from being around other companies than from gaining access to a common pool of talent. This human clustering makes all who reside in it more productive, which in turn makes the place they inhabit more productive. Our collective creativity and economic wealth grow accordingly.

Mainstream economists continued to focus mainly on the nation-state as the engine of economic growth and development until Lucas brought cities and place squarely back into the picture. To do so, he went back to Jacobs's earlier writings. He realized the enormous debt that he, along with the entire field of economic growth, owed Jacobs and predicted that her insights would ultimately become the focus of growth economics: "I will be following very closely the lead of Jane Jacobs, whose remarkable book, *The Economy of Cities*, seems to me mainly and convincingly concerned (although she does not use this terminology) with the external effects of human capital." He later added in a widely circulated email that these insights are so fundamental that Jacobs—who was neither a trained economist nor a college graduate—deserves the Nobel Prize.

Building on Jacobs's fundamental contribution, Lucas declares that the "multiplier effects" which stem from talent clustering are the primary determinant of economic growth. Cities are more than the sum of their parts because the parts can interact and become more productive, and create new things. Labor, capital, and technical knowledge are all well and good, he concedes, but would not amount to anything significant if people could not combine their talents, ideas, and energy in real places.

When people—especially talented and creative ones—come together, ideas flow more freely, and as a result individual and aggregate talents increase exponentially; the end result amounts to much more than the sum of the parts. This clustering makes each of us more productive, which in turn makes the place we inhabit even more so—and our collective creativity and economic wealth grow accordingly. This in a nutshell is the clustering force. One consequence of it is that regions are sorted into an economic hierarchy. As Chapters 6 and 7 will show, as talented and highly educated people cluster together in certain regions, the location of work becomes more concentrated and specialized as well. According to the theory, when people cluster together in cities, they will produce more and thus the cost of living in those places will inexorably rise, generating those "Chicago rents" Lucas mentions. Eventually communities and people will sort themselves into an economic pecking order.

Lucas picked up on what I consider to be Jacobs's most fundamental contribution to the field—the central role that the clustering of people and their creativity plays on economic growth. Jacobs saw it that way too. When asked in 2001 what she hoped to be remembered for, she responded:

> If I were to be remembered as a really important thinker of the century, the most important thing I've contributed is, "What makes economic expansion happen?" This is something that has puzzled people always. I think I've figured out what it is, and expansion and development are two different things. Development is differentiation—new differ-

entiation of what already existed. Practically every new thing that happens is a differentiation of a previous thing. Just about everything—from a new shoe sole to changes in legal codes—all of those things are differentiations. Expansion is an actual growth in size or volume of activity. That is a different thing.[5]

By expansion, Jacobs means the more ordinary side of economic growth—increasing the volume of economic output, for example, revving up the production of an assembly line. Looked at this way, a city is just a bigger version of a town, a megaregion just a bigger version of a city.

But there is a second, more explosive kind of economic growth—innovation—which according to Jacobs comes from the diversity contained in cities. While companies tend to specialize, places give rise to a wide variety of talents and specialties, the broad diversity of which is a vital spur to innovation. This is an epigenetic process. Cities don't just get bigger in size; they become multifaceted and differentiated. And in doing so, they—and not firms—are the wellspring of new innovations that generate new work and new branches of industry. The city, Jacobs argued, is a complex, self-organizing ecology whose form cannot be predetermined or controlled from the outside. Its diversity is the true source of innovation and economic growth.[6]

Faster, Faster

Jacobs's insights illustrate how place affects productivity and innovation. But what about the inevitable drawbacks and obstacles to city growth? Traffic congestion, rising crime rates, and unaffordable housing are all predictable by-products of city life that pose significant barriers to a city's future development.

Although seemingly such diseconomies could kill a city, compelling research suggests otherwise. According to a multidisciplinary team of researchers led by Geoffrey West of the Santa Fe Institute, large cities and megaregions possess a basic mechanism by which they transcend such limitations.[7]

Any scientist will tell you that the metabolic rate of biological organisms—the rate at which living things convert food into energy—slows as organisms increase in size. The Santa Fe team wondered whether cities and megaregions might function in a similar way. Do their "metabolisms" increase as their population and therefore their productivity and innovation grow? To test this idea, the researchers collected data from the United States, Europe, and China at a variety of times, and looked at a wide range of characteristics, such as crime rate, disease transmission, demographics, infrastructure energy consumption, economic activity, and innovation. Sure enough: "Social organizations, like biological organisms, consume energy and resources, depend on networks for the flow of information and materials, and produce artifacts and waste. . . . Cities manifest power-law scaling similar to the economy-of-scale relationships observed in biology: a doubling of population requires less than a doubling of certain resources. The material infrastructure that is analogous to biological transport networks—gas stations, lengths of electrical cable, miles of road surface—consistently exhibits sublinear [less than one] scaling with population."

This might have been expected. But researchers did not expect to find that the correlation between population growth and characteristics with little analogy to biology—such as innovation, patent activity, number of supercreative people, wages, and GDP—is greater than one. In other words, a doubling of population results in more than two times the creative and economic output. Unlike biological organisms, which slow down as they grow larger, cities become wealthier and more creative the bigger they get. They called this phenomenon "superlinear" scaling: "By almost any measure, the larger a city's population, the greater the innovation and wealth per person." This increased speed is itself a product of the clustering force, a key component of the productivity improvements generated by the concentration of talented people.

How Big Will They Grow?

Thanks to thinkers like Jacobs and Lucas, we now have a handle on how cities and regions stimulate innovation and drive economic development. We know that the clustering of human talent and labor leads to increased productivity and creativity, and we have seen that city development is spurred from within. And we know that the world is composed of many cities and megaregions of various sizes—large ones like Tokyo, New York, and London, fast-growing ones like Shanghai and Bangalore, highly innovative ones like the Silicon Valley, smaller and medium-size ones, and declining ones. How does this broader system of cities form and evolve?

To get at this, I partnered with Robert Axtell, a brilliant computer modeler at George Mason University who researches everything from how societies evolve to how firms are established to how economies grow.[8] Together, we endeavored to build a basic model that simulates the growth and development of the cities and regions that compose the world economy. We wanted our model to address how these cities initially emerged, why some grew while others failed, and how they evolved into a global system.

We structured our model around three basic assumptions:

- People can choose how hard they want to work. Some work hard, others less so. We prefer to spend our time in different ways. Not everyone chooses to develop the same skills or work at the same intensity.

- As in the real world, we established that the hardest-working and most able people would cluster together, at least initially. These firms would be most likely to grow, while those that employed less productive people would languish and ultimately fail.

- We presumed that productive firms would be drawn to similarly productive locations. Places that housed dynamic firms would grow, while places that didn't would decline.

Economic growth in our model takes place through a basic law of "preferential attachment": skilled and productive people attract other skilled and productive people. As they team up into firms, these creative organizational units begin to develop new ideas and products. And as those units grow, they attract other hardworking and productive agents.

It's a dynamic model built to emulate the real world. Hard-working, adventurous, and creative people come together to form new firms that migrate to certain places. Some of these destinations, so long as they can retain their talent, grow and prosper. Others dissolve when their residents decide to migrate elsewhere. Places in the former group experience their first wave of economic growth during the early phases of firm forma-tion, when relatively high-skilled individuals populate small to midsize companies. Over time, these cities attract more like-minded people and more businesses, and eventually they grow into regions. These regions attract an even more diverse range of people who begin to cluster around the original population. As new firms continue to form and old ones dissolve, the new-comers are absorbed into the mix. Certain cities expand and grow.

Then something very interesting starts to happen. Rather than simply growing upward, these city regions expand outward until they are forced to combine with other city regions. Through this process of nucleation, these city regions merge together as a megaregion. The largest megaregions have the longest staying power. Smaller megaregions, or individual large cities, rise and fall at a much faster clip. But no city or regional formation is invincible. While they tend to last longer, even the largest megaregions can eventually decline.

This model is a near perfect simulation of our world today. Creative people and their firms cluster tightly to form the top of a hierarchy of city regions in a way that strikingly reflects George Zipf's famous power law.[9] In the middle of the distribution, individual cities and regions constantly vie for prime spots, while at the top there is far less moving around. This is more than a hierarchy of places. It is a hierarchy of productivity rates, metabolic rates, and costs. Places at the top are more productive, operate at faster speed, and are more expensive than those further down the hierarchy. The people who can afford to be in the top places are increasingly required to work in a highly productive way in specialized industries (think investment funds in London or New York, or movie production in Los Angeles). Consequently, there is less and less economic space for, say, the struggling artist or even the average person at the top of the hierarchy. The sorting of places due to the clustering force is inevitably a sorting of people.

Our model also forecasts a world increasingly dominated by massive megaregions. By 2025, our world will be considerably more concentrated around megaregions than it is today. By then, something as sci-fi sounding as a megaregion with several hundred million people may exist. It may sound far-fetched, but given historical precedents and current rates, such a world may be far from a fantasy. Think of it this way: just two hundred years ago, the largest cities held fewer than 100,000 people; back then, a city of a million people was unimaginable. By 1900, the population of New York—the largest city in the United States—had reached roughly 3.5 million. Do you think a city of 10 million was unfathomable then? Yet fifty years later, the populations of metropolitan areas like New York and London hovered just under 10 million. Today, there are already megaregions of 25, 50, 100 million people and more.

Given these growth patterns, is a megaregion of several hundred million beyond the pale? Hardly. When Axtell calculated how big the largest megaregion would be in a world with megaregions that were perfectly Zipf-distributed, with the smallest one housing 10 million people, he came up with a super-megaregion of 400 million people. What kind of place could hold that many people? This is how Axtell explains it: "Assume every person needs 5,000 square feet of space for living, parking, office space, schools, roads, and green space. So that's 25,000 square feet for a family of five. People in Tokyo use 1,900 square feet each, so Tokyo is two and a half times denser than my assumption. Then 400 million people need 2 trillion square feet of space, which equals 45 million acres or 72,000 square miles—a square 270 miles on a side, or alternatively 100 miles wide by 700 miles long. That could be BosWash from the New Hampshire border to Norfolk, Virginia, 100 miles wide from the Atlantic coast, or Sacramento to Tijuana, 100 miles from the Pacific inland."

As our models show, it's less likely that an existing megaregion will simply grow upward by adding taller buildings or more people. More likely, such expansion will occur as two or more come together to form a super-megaregion. Already, the light-emission patterns that span Japan suggest that a super-megaregion running from north of Tokyo all the way to Fukuoka could emerge. For the foreseeable future, megaregions will be the economic units that structure and orient the world economy.

Of course, super-megaregions will bring all sorts of new challenges. As rates of innovation and migration accelerate, we can expect more key functions to concentrate in the world's leading megaregions. And the social and economic distance between leading megaregions and lagging cities and regions will grow larger. Megaregions will become more congested and pricier, causing greater social and economic segregation. Major new advances in transportation and environmental technology will surely be required. For the leading megaregions, retaining rates of innovation will be their primary challenge. Without it, as West and his colleagues caution, they "will stop growing and may even contract, leading to either stagnation or ultimate collapse."

The challenges facing second- and third-tier regions worldwide will be even greater. While some will thrive and grow, many more will struggle under the weight of ferocious global competition. The global system of cities and regions is going through the same kind of consolidation and restructuring that reshaped global industries like steel and autos and electronics around a smaller number of larger and more efficient players worldwide. The many second- and third-tier city regions may be hit particularly hard, as both global and domestic megaregions up the ante, accelerating their rates of innovation while drawing in more top talent. These cities will find themselves increasingly squeezed between twin pincers as top business functions gravitate to larger regions like Chicago, New York, London, Seoul, or Frankfurt while production shifts to centers like Shanghai. Smaller technology centers will face increasing competition not only from the Silicon Valley but also from up-and-comers like Bangalore, Dublin, and Tel Aviv. The world economy of the future is likely to take shape around an even smaller number of megaregions and specialized centers, while a much larger number of places will see their fates worsen as they find themselves struggling just to stay in the game.

PART II

THE WEALTH OF PLACE

5
THE MOBILE AND THE ROOTED

E VER SINCE MARX, CLASS HAS BEEN SEEN AS A DIVISIVE force in all societies. Much has been written on the widening gulf between the highest paid and the average worker and the growing share of economic output pocketed by society's top 1 percent.[1] But there is another angle to our diverging economic fortunes that few have looked into—the role of location.

I think of this geographic dimension of socioeconomic class in terms of the mobile and the rooted. The mobile possess the means, resources, and inclination to seek out and move to locations where they can leverage their talents. They are not necessarily born mobile, nor are they invariably rich. The mobile understand that the pursuit of economic opportunity often requires them to move.

Roughly three-quarters of the residents of global cities said that they "chose" their city, according to a 2008 survey of some 8,500 residents across fourteen large global cities. The precise figures amount to almost 70 percent of those in Tokyo; 70 percent of

residents in London, Berlin, New York, and Chicago; 80 percent
in Paris, Sydney, and Los Angeles; and more than 90 percent of
the residents of Shanghai and Beijing.

The Hungarian-born investor George Soros has said many
times that had he stayed in his home country he would have
amounted to little because there was no infrastructure through
which he could leverage his talents. But once he moved to the
United States—well, the rest, as they say, is history.

Today approximately 200 million people—1 in every 35
people worldwide—live outside their country of birth. And
many, many more are the first- and second-generation descen-
dants of those international migrants. The late *New York Times*
writer Herbert Muschamp dubbed the growing ranks of the internationally mobile as a new class of "global nomads."[2] Regardless of what they are called, in some city regions in the United
States, Canada, Europe, and Australia, the ranks of the foreign
born run upward of 40 percent. My own classroom is a perfect
microcosm of our highly mobile society: I have students who hail
from Europe, Japan, China, India, South America, and Africa—
not to mention Canada and, of course, the United States.

A far greater number constitute the rooted—people who are
tied to place. Some, of course, have the good fortune to be
rooted in places with thriving economies and optimistic futures.
But many others find themselves trapped in areas with limited
resources, moribund economies, and declining financial opportunities. Of course, many are born poor and do not possess the
resources to move.

But not all of those who are rooted are stuck because of economic circumstance. Many people with the means to move
choose to stay rooted. Some are satisfied with their lives, even
though they know they could potentially do better elsewhere.
This isn't always a bad thing; research indicates that being near

family and friends and seeing them regularly can increase well-being and happiness.

Should I Stay or Should I Go Now?

When social scientists talk about mobility, they are typically referring to socioeconomic mobility—the ease with which people move up or down the ladder of social and economic status. But my research and personal experience have convinced me that socioeconomic mobility and geographic mobility are interdependent and far from mutually exclusive.

Mobility and class increasingly track together. A detailed study of mobility among Canadian regions by Tara Vinodrai, a professor at the University of Waterloo, and Greg Spencer, a doctoral student at the University of Toronto, found creative class members to be the most mobile group of Canadians—nearly 25 percent of all movers in 2001, compared to 20 percent for service workers (who are far more numerous) and 19 percent for manufacturing workers. Aside from managers and workers in "protective service" and oil and gas drillers, creative class members dominated the ranks of the most mobile job categories—engineers, computer and information systems professionals, professors, life scientists, and physical scientists.[3]

A 2007 study by researchers at Sheffield University shows the powerful role that location plays in people's class position, health status, education options, and economic mobility. The study found that people born in disadvantaged locations tend to carry that initial disadvantage across subsequent life stages. "Every step of the way your chances are much more constrained," says Bethan Thomas, one of the study's authors. "This is not deterministic; obviously there are people from disadvantaged areas who do make the leap and people from the most advantaged who can't be bothered, but those cases are much less common." The researchers found that while the number of neighborhoods that rank above and below average once resembled a bell curve (with rich and poor areas at each end but most in between), today we're split into just two distinct categories, with one set of locations for the disadvantaged and another for the advantaged. The researchers conclude that this new geography of class reveals "ever more clearly that where you live can limit or assist your life chances from cradle to grave."[4] Today location constitutes an additional divisive line that separates the haves from the have-nots, alongside race, education, occupation, and income. In the past, a person's status was largely determined by place of birth. In today's highly mobile and interconnected society, one's life chances are significantly affected by the ability to move and relocate as well.

Economists and demographers have shed some light on the mobile and the rooted. Those who move tend to be highly educated people whose careers require them to do so. They also include young people, who, as attached as they may be to family and friends, stand to make significant gains from relocating.

For most of human history migration has been involuntary. People moved out of necessity—to avoid war, escape political or religious persecution, or find work. Even as recently as the 1950s and 1960s most people—white-collar and blue-collar workers alike—moved to find jobs. Nobody had much choice, actually. Blue-collar work was heavily concentrated in cites that had grown up around natural resources and transportation hubs. White-collar workers were company men who went where their superiors told them to go. In the 1970s, IBM workers joked that their company name stood for "I've Been Moved." There was much truth to that sentiment, and it applied to companies other than the computer giant.

Today, however, more moves are voluntary. And in the advanced nations only a minority are tied to work. The leading reason people in the United States move is for housing. According to the 2000 census, over half (51.6 percent) of all people who move do so for that reason. They are renters wanting to own, young couples wanting to upgrade, and retirees looking to downsize. Another quarter (26.3 percent) of people say that they move for family-related reasons—getting married, getting divorced, having children, combining families, death of a spouse, and that sort of thing.

Moving on account of work actually comes in third. Fewer than 1 in 6 U.S. residents says that the main reason for moving is work related. Not surprisingly, highly educated people are most likely to move because of work. But even among those with bachelor's degrees, only 1 in 4 moves for work-related reasons.

The reasons people move are many and varied, but why do so many stay put? Economic circumstance plays the key role: the decision is seemingly not much of a choice. Many of the rooted have relatively little education or money and relatively low professional aspirations or personal expectations.

My own family history reflects the tension between the rooted and the mobile. My grandparents, who hail from the Campania region of southern Italy, immigrated to the United States in the early part of the twentieth century. Knowing not a word of English, they made the nearly five-thousand-mile trip from their peasant village in southern Italy to New York—then the largest and most dynamic city in the world. In the span of one generation, they made their way from Ellis Island to New York's Little Italy and then to Newark to take up simple factory work and raise a family. And in doing so, they improved their economic position from rural peasant class to urban working class, creating even greater potential for upward economic

mobility for their children and grandchildren. But upon settling in Newark, my family became rooted. Only one of my
dozens of aunts or uncles ever moved more than twenty miles
from where they grew up. That made it possible for my mother
and her five sisters, her brothers, and all their children to
gather routinely on Sundays for supper at my grandmother's
home in Newark.

Fortunately my parents stressed the importance of going to
college. For them, a college degree was tantamount to social
mobility—a way to a better life. Unfortunately, they preferred
that we stay close by—attend a local college, live at home, and
commute by car. But I wanted desperately to go away to school,
enticed by the freedom that being away promised—the ability
to come and go as I pleased, to stay out late and have fun with
my friends without parents and relatives looking over my shoul-
der. But my intuition also told me that I would benefit even
more from leaving the working-class, tough-guy peer group of
my youth. Many of my friends were already well into drugs and
petty crime. Few who stayed behind had ambitions to go to college, let alone pursue careers. I knew on some level even then
that going off to college would do more than help me achieve
my dreams—it would be my way out.

A Garden State scholarship allowed me to do just that. With
financial aid that covered not only tuition but room and board as
well, I was able to convince my parents to let me enroll at Rutgers College, just thirty or so miles south of home on the New
Jersey Turnpike in New Brunswick. It was hard for me to believe that Rutgers—which felt so far away—had been so close
by all along. Still, my family behaved as if I were moving a world
away. From the looks of their Chevy Impala, in which they
made a monthly pilgrimage to bring me food, beer, and other
necessities—you'd think I had.

College was just the first of many moves, and with each one my parents treated me as if I were embarking on a great journey. Even when I was a graduate student at Columbia University in New York City, just a commuter train ride away, they made the trek to the city a total of two times over a period of five or so years. By the time they passed away, they had visited maybe three states—and not once did they fly on a plane or take a proper vacation. Travel was expensive; taking trips would have required taking funds away from more important things. But it also meant leaving home and family, which is the primary place my parents wanted to be.

My parents were happy, but they were rooted. I was mobile. Through hard work and by purchasing a small home in a suburb of Newark, they upgraded their economic position from urban working class to lower middle class. But had it not been for my geographic mobility, I would never have been able to attend graduate school, and ultimately become a professor and author. Still, without ever taking a course in economics, my parents were quite aware of the respective trade-offs involved in staying rooted or going mobile.

A 2007 study by economist Nattavudh Powdthavee of the University of London used survey data to estimate the monetary value of frequent visits with friends and relatives.[5] The study found that seeing friends or relatives in person almost every day is worth more than six figures in additional income. For example, Powdthavee found that if you relocate from a city where you regularly see your family and friends to one where you do not, you would need to earn $133,000 just to make up for the lack of happiness incurred by the distance. Powdthavee drives home the importance of making a conscious choice about your time when he writes, "Since it normally requires both time and effort to achieve either higher income or a stable social relationship with someone, the weight attached to each individual's investment decision thus depends upon the type of possession—money or friendship—that he or she believes will yield a larger impact on happiness than the other."

Putting an accurate price tag on our personal relationships is impossible. Still, by Powdthavee's accounting I owe my wife, Rana—who left behind five siblings, two parents, a host of nieces and nephews, and countless close relatives and friends when we got married—a very big pile of money.

Many people elect to stay rooted even when it's economically feasible to move elsewhere. Perhaps they are intuitively aware of the economic value of close social relationships. And many who have moved ultimately decide to return home someday. The draw of home is incredibly powerful—the pull of family ties, the need to take care of aging parents or help with children, the desire to be close to lifelong friends. Strikingly, out of the roughly two hundred detailed locational histories I collected for this book, many of those who had moved around chose to return home later in life.

Roger Thompson explains how the trade-off between going mobile and staying rooted is playing out in his life.

> I currently work at the corporate office based in Toronto of a large company that mainly operates in the United States. Work is going so well that they want to transport me into one of the operating companies as an executive in Florida, Maryland, or New Jersey. From a career perspective, it's the right move. I'm thirty years old, and if all goes well I will be in a position to retire early because of the equity and compensation upside that would be involved in the deal. The problem, my social and family network is in Toronto. My only sister just had a baby. My wife always says, "I don't care how much we make, I want to be there

for the birth of all my friends/families babies and share the excitement of starting a family with all of them." To help us navigate through my dilemma, we ask ourselves the question, How much do I have to earn to make us pick up and leave? We always say that work gets in the way of life and it is the *place* decision that drives our decision making every single day.

Jane Apor lived in New York and London before deciding to return to Toronto after 9/11.

It was 1995 and I had just completed an MBA. The thought of staying in Toronto was not appealing. It felt slow, boring, and provincial. I craved to meet new people, experience a faster-paced environment. I moved to NYC. I found a great, secure, and conveniently located apartment seven blocks from work. NYC life was exactly what I had been looking for. I was meeting people from all over the world, had more entertainment options than I knew what to do with, and was barely sleeping in the city that never sleeps. I felt comfortable from the moment I arrived. I transferred to the UK and actually advanced a level in the corporation by doing so.

But then September 11 happened. Suddenly London felt very far from all that was important to me. Eight months later, I made the decision to move home to Toronto. Seven years earlier I had said "good-bye and good riddance" to Toronto: I was bored, uninspired, and itching to move. In coming home I established myself as my own person within a city that held my "roots," my security, and all that meant the most to me, especially my family. People often ask me how I can be happy/content living in Toronto after NYC and London and my response is consistent.

Those cities were fabulous for me at that time in my life.
But nothing can replace where you are from, where your
roots are, your family, and all that is important.

Linda Maguire did the reverse, sort of. A talented opera
singer, she left a successful career in Toronto to return to her
home state of Virginia. "I have had the unbelievable luxury of
living an artistic, creative, and academic life, thanks to a govern-
ment-supported career and via having sung as a top-level professional singer," she wrote. "I just got to the point where I
could not deny who I really was—an American from Virginia
soil. It is unbelievable and most wonderful to be home again."

The social scientist Albert O. Hirschman provides a framework that can help us think about our own choice of whether to
go mobile or stay rooted. Born in Berlin in 1915, Hirschman immigrated to the United States from Germany during the Nazi
years and later served in the U.S. Army during World War II,
before taking up professorships at Yale, Columbia, Harvard, and
the Institute for Advanced Study at Princeton. In his 1970 classic *Exit, Voice, and Loyalty*, Hirschman argued that when faced
with an unsatisfactory situation we can either "exit" the situation
or "voice" our discontent. The more "loyalty" we feel, the more
likely we are to use the latter option. As far as location is concerned, our decision to move turns on our loyalty to the place
we live in and our social relationships there.[6]

But today's economy may be tipping the balance between
these two poles. As the benefits to clustering increase and the
world becomes spikier, more people may feel compelled to join
the ranks of the mobile in order to prosper economically.
There's another tipping point too: the more people who move to
new areas to take advantage of economic opportunity, the more
others will feel free to move too as the bonds of family and

friends are broken. This does not mean that we are all doomed to be global nomads forever. It does mean that to reach our potential and find happiness, we must recognize the importance of place, know how best to weigh our options, and be willing to move when necessary.

6

WHERE THE BRAINS ARE

———

HUMAN BEINGS HAVE ALWAYS MIGRATED — TO FIND food, to escape military conflict, to avoid religious or political persecution, or to gain economic opportunity. For most of history, however, human settlements remained relatively small. A 2007 story in *The Economist* summed up the long sweep of human migration this way:

> Whether you think the human story begins in a garden in Mesopotamia known as Eden, or more prosaically on the savannahs of present-day east Africa, it is clear that Homo sapiens did not start life as an urban creature. Man's habitat at the outset was dominated by the need to find food, and hunting and foraging were rural pursuits. Not until the end of the last ice age, around 11,000 years ago, did he start building anything that might be called a village, and by that time man had been around for about 120,000 years. It took another six millennia, to the days of classical antiquity, for

cities of more than 100,000 people to develop. Even in
1800 only 3% of the world's population lived in cities.
Sometime in the next few months, though, that proportion
will pass the 50% mark, if it has not done so already. Wisely
or not, Homo sapiens has become Homo urbanus.[1]

And this trend is far from finished. According to U.N. predictions, by the year 2030, more than two-thirds of the world's population (4.4 *billion* people) will be urbanites.[2]

Some contend that since the 1960s, migration patterns have
shifted away from cities and urban centers and toward the suburbs. This outward movement of millions to the suburbs, they
argue, has reversed the great rural-to-urban trend. Indeed, tens
of millions of people have moved from urban centers to suburbs
that offer newer housing, newer infrastructure, and a perceived
better quality of life.[3] That has undoubtedly given rise to new
divisions of class and race, a heightened dependence on the
automobile, ever growing mass consumption, and wholly new
living patterns.

Populations have also shifted from the older, colder, urban
centers to warmer, sunnier regions. And finally, there is the continued outward movement to the exurbs and edge cities, which
are organized around highway interchanges, business parks, and
shopping malls.[4]

But confounding this trend is the worldwide urban shift as
well as a significant back-to-the-city movement. A powerful
wave of gentrification has swept urban areas, bringing loft housing, condo conversions, historic preservation, new restaurants,
retail outlets, and nightlife back to city neighborhoods. Some
even predict that this trend may soon recede, as housing becomes less affordable for the very groups that powered the gentrification in the first place. Alan Ehrenhalt dubs this "the
demographic inversion."[5]

One of the many upshots of these two competing movements, according to leading demographers and political sociologists, is a new "sorting" of population by values, culture, and politics. This tension is perhaps best captured by David Brooks's two iconic American characters, the cappuccino-drinking urban "bourgeois-bohemian" ("bobo" for short) and suburbia's "patio man."[6]

The Means Migration

In 2006 I argued in *The Atlantic* that an even more significant demographic realignment is currently at work: the mass relocation of highly skilled, highly educated, and highly paid people to a relatively small number of metropolitan regions, and a corresponding exodus of traditional lower and middle classes from those same places. Such geographic sorting of people by economic potential on this scale is unprecedented. I dubbed it the "means migration" and referred to the regions capturing this demographic group as "means metros."

The means migration can be seen most clearly in the increasing geographic concentration of college graduates (Figure 6.1). While our detailed data profiles the United States, our own research and other studies document the same trend in the Scandinavian countries and China. According to research by Edward Glaeser of Harvard and Christopher Berry of the University of Chicago, in 1970 human capital was distributed relatively evenly across the United States.[7] Nationally, 11 percent of the population over twenty-five years of age had a college degree; in fully half of America's 318 metropolitan regions the figure ranged between 9 percent and 13 percent. Over the past three decades, the percentage of Americans holding a college degree has more than doubled, reaching 27 percent by 2004. But as the map shows, those gains have not been evenly spread. For instance, more than half of all residents in the San Francisco region now

FIGURE 6.1. THE HUMAN CAPITAL MAP

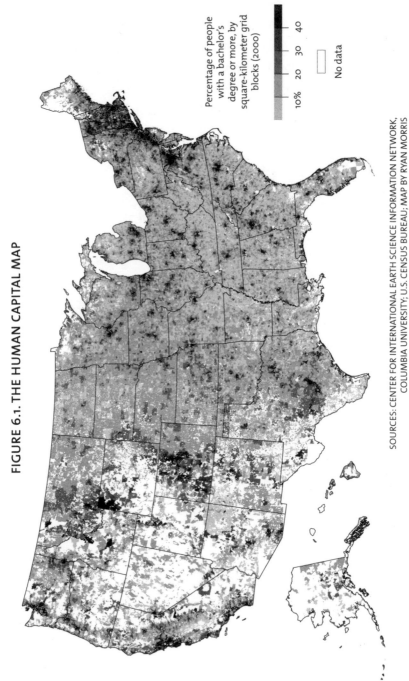

Percentage of people with a bachelor's degree or more, by square-kilometer grid blocks (2000)

10%   20   30   40

☐ No data

SOURCES: CENTER FOR INTERNATIONAL EARTH SCIENCE INFORMATION NETWORK, COLUMBIA UNIVERSITY; U.S. CENSUS BUREAU; MAP BY RYAN MORRIS

have college degrees. In 2004 there remained twelve metropolitan regions nationwide where less than 20 percent of the adult population had graduated from college, and in several of those, fewer than one in ten residents had a bachelor's degree. In the downtown neighborhoods of high-powered cities, the concentration of well-educated people is even greater. In 2000 more than two-thirds of the residents of downtown Chicago and Midtown Manhattan held college degrees—levels that are more typically seen in advantaged suburbs.[8] The trends are even more pronounced in other countries.

Many older industrial cities, suburbs, and outlying rural areas are being left behind. Significantly, as Chapter 12 will show, young, single populations are flocking in ever greater numbers to these means metros (those with high concentrations of educated and higher-income people), where they often live in penury until either making it or being forced out by the high cost of living.

The means migration can also be seen in regional differences in income. The past decade or two has seen a dramatic concentration of high-income households in the means metros. In 2006 the median household income in San Jose, California, was $80,638. By comparison, median household income was $28,660 in McAllen, Texas, and $27,672 in Brownsville (Figure 6.2).

What's behind this phenomenon? It's not just that people prefer to live in means metros. To be sure, many of them are aesthetically pleasing—beautiful, energizing, and fun to live in—but others are cramped, dense, and expensive.

But there is a deeper, more fundamental reason that is rooted in economics. Increasingly, the most talented and ambitious people need to live in the means metros in order to realize their full economic potential. The proximity of talented, highly educated people has a powerful effect on innovation and

FIGURE 6.2. THE INCOME MAP

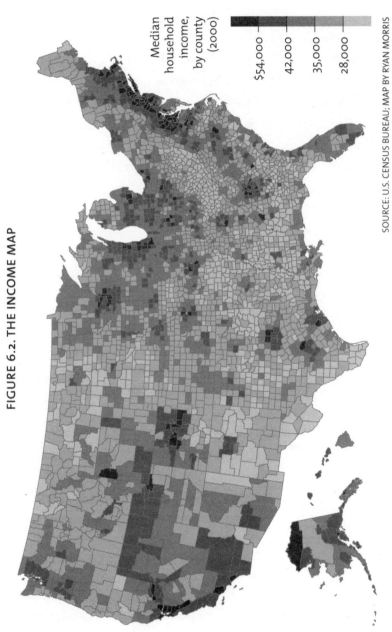

Median household income, by county (2000)

$54,000
42,000
35,000
28,000

SOURCE: U.S. CENSUS BUREAU; MAP BY RYAN MORRIS

economic growth, as shown in Chapter 4. Places that bring to-gether diverse talent accelerate the local rate of economic evo-lution. When large numbers of entrepreneurs, financiers, engineers, designers, and other smart, creative people are con-stantly bumping into one another inside and outside of work, business ideas are formed, sharpened, executed, and—if successful—expanded. As the number of smart people in-creases and the connections among them grow more dense, the faster it all goes. It is the multiplier effect of the clustering force at work.

In addition to the benefits of living near smart people and their creative ideas, the means metros have a larger and simpler advantage over other regions: a head start. For a variety of his-torical reasons (the presence of great universities is usually one) the means metros started off with a relatively high concentra-tion of relatively talented people. As more and more such people are added, the multiplier effect on growth keeps increas-ing. That's true not only for growth in the aggregate but for indi-vidual incomes and opportunities as well.

Opportunities do not exist equally for everyone. For most of human history, population growth has meant economic growth. In agricultural economies population growth meant more people to work the farms, or in industrial economies more people to work in the factories. In both cases, overall population growth was key to economic growth, and economic growth meant more opportunities across the board.

The means migration severs the long held connection be-tween population growth and economic development. Chang-ing technology, increased trade, and the ability to outsource routine functions have made highly skilled people less reliant on the location of the unskilled and moderately skilled in the same place.

Today what matters most isn't where most people settle, but where the greatest number of the most skilled people locate. Because the returns from colocation among the ablest is so high, and because high-end incomes are rising so fast, it makes sense for these workers to continue to bid up the price of real estate (as I'll explain in Chapter 8) and accept other costs that traditional middle-class workers and families cannot afford. As traditional middle-class families are displaced by smaller, higher-income households, population can decline even as economic growth continues. The most successful cities and regions in the United States and around the world may increasingly be inhabited by a core of wealthy and highly mobile workers leading highly privileged lives, catered to by an underclass of service workers living farther and farther away.

Consequently the means migration is dividing the world into two kinds of regions with very different economic prospects. A small number of means metros attract the lion's share of the mobile and the skilled, who see their incomes and real estate values climb, while the great majority witness the exact opposite. Some of today's means metros could eventually fall back as housing prices and living costs rise. But there are powerful reasons to believe that the economic disparity between some city regions and others will continue to grow and perhaps even accelerate, thanks to the snowball effect of talent attraction.

"This spatial sorting," says Wharton economist Joseph Gyourko, "will affect the nature of America as much as the rural-urban migration of the late nineteenth century did."[9] He asks us to imagine a future society in which people interact only with those who share the same educational, financial, and psychological backgrounds. "We already have fairly intense segregation by income within metropolitan areas," he writes. "But how different will things be if almost every community within the metro region is roughly as rich and skilled as mine?"

To Gyourko's question, I add my own: How will the growing division between the mobile and the rooted affect the fabric of society? Will other nations and regions follow the United States down this road to class and geographic polarization? My travels around the world lead me to suspect they already are. And what does this mean for you as you think about where you really do want to live?

7
JOB SHIFT

L ET'S LOOK AT THINGS ON A FINER SCALE. JUST AS THE
clustering force concentrates talent within regions, it also
sorts people by work and career. What we earn is influenced by
where we are; so is what we do and how well we are able to
do it.

Regions are becoming more distinct in the kinds of jobs they
offer. The work we do is growing more and more specialized,
not just by field but also by location. The concentration of high-
end finance in London and New York or high-tech entrepreneurship in Silicon Valley are the most obvious examples. While
this is not happening in every career—doctors, lawyers, nurses,
and teachers are in demand just about everywhere, and their
pay is fairly consistent—its effects can be seen in a growing
number of jobs and careers.

Most of us put a lot of thought into what we do for a living.
We study hard, go to college, and in many cases continue on to
graduate school. After we graduate, we spend time identifying

companies we'd like to work for. We conduct job searches, send out résumés, and go to interviews. Once employed, we try to impress our boss. We work our way up and earn raises and promotions. We spend time and money to upgrade our talents and acquire new skills. We network with others in our field to broaden our prospects. Some of us decide to be our own bosses and become free agents, which requires finding work and clients.[1] We do all of this to make a living and support our families. Few people appreciate how much it matters where we work. I'm not talking about people who decide where to live before they search for work. In this chapter, I'll show how the job market itself is geographically concentrated, that is, how employment opportunities and salaries differ by location.

Geeks and Grunts

The advanced economies today are going through an epochal transformation that in scale and magnitude dwarfs the shift from farm to factory a century or two ago. As a consequence, they are shedding manufacturing jobs and generating jobs in two other economic sectors: (1) low-paid service work in everything from retail sales to personal service and (2) high-paid professional, innovative, and design work in what I call the creative sector of the economy. This transformation is painful and disruptive for many. It is especially tragic for the scores of people who have lost good, high-paying jobs in manufacturing over the past several decades.

I know firsthand how much those jobs mean to the families that depend on them. My father worked for more than fifty years at Victory Optical in Newark's Ironbound neighborhood. That job provided the means by which my parents bought our small house outside Newark, sent my brother and me to private Catholic school, and ultimately put us through college.

My years in Pittsburgh, at a time when the region was losing more than 150,000 blue-collar jobs and steel mills were being shuttered and torn down, afforded me a close view of how painful economic dislocation is for people and entire regions. More recently, I have seen what the decline of automotive manufacturing has meant to Detroit, my wife's hometown.

In the advanced nations, manufacturing, which supplied roughly half of all employment in the 1950s, declined to just 20–25 percent of jobs and continues to decline. Meanwhile, the United States and other advanced nations are generating new kinds of jobs. The workforce is splitting into two distinct labor groups, which UCLA economist Edward Leamer has dubbed the "geeks" and the "grunts." The geeks enjoy higher-paying, higher-skilled work in the creative sector; the grunts are laborers in the service sector, who have fewer skills and receive less pay.

We've effectively become the "postindustrial society" that Harvard sociologist Daniel Bell predicted in the 1970s, hinging our prosperity on the growth of a knowledge class, relying on science to bring forth innovation and social change, and depending more on services than goods.

The future of the service sector matters a great deal to both the U.S. and global economies. Not everyone wants to be a doctor, lawyer, engineer, or professional. Given that the bulk of manufacturing jobs have been lost forever, the millions of new service sector work opportunities our economy is generating must be transformed into secure, respectable, high-paying jobs. When I asked a group of my students whether they would prefer to work in a reliable, high-paying job in a factory or a lower-paying, temporary job as a hair stylist, they overwhelmingly chose the latter; it was more creative and therefore seemed more rewarding. The market appears to reflect this psychology. Vocational training programs for machinists are in dire need of students, while cosmetology classes are routinely overenrolled.

This hit home to me in late summer 2007, my first month in Toronto, when I got my hair cut by a stylish young man in his late twenties or early thirties, who, it turned out, once resided in Birmingham, an upscale suburb of Detroit where my wife was living when we met. Without thinking, I said, "My wife used to get her hair done in Birmingham; what salon did you work in?"

"I wasn't a hairstylist then, man. I worked for General Motors," he said.

"Really?" I said, trying to dig myself out of a hole. "What plant did you work at?"

"Plant?" came his reply. "I didn't work in a factory. I'm a mechanical engineer and I worked on new product development."

My jaw dropped. This man had quit a high-paying job in a good company so he could cut people's hair. He had left the creative class because it wasn't creative enough for him and had gone into a service industry to express his creativity.

It wasn't the first time. In spring of 2005, when I visited a local health spa in Washington, D.C., I asked the attendant where she was from.

"Connecticut," she replied.

"How did you end up in D.C.?"

"For college."

"Where did you go to school?"

"The University of Maryland."

That's a very good school, I thought. What had she studied there?

"Economics."

Hold on, how had economics led her to taking a job in a spa?

"Well, after college I went to work for the Bureau of Labor Statistics."

"The BLS?" I asked in surprise. The government source of nearly all my best data? The basis for the arguments of my previous books?

"Yep."

So I asked her why she'd switched jobs. I remarked that moving from the BLS to a spa didn't sound like a shrewd career move for someone in her twenties with her educational background. She didn't care about that, she said.

"I was bored. I sat in a cubicle all day and looked at spreadsheets. It was tolerable only because I could go out with my friends every night, since I didn't have to think too hard during the day. But after a while I just couldn't take it. It was just so boring." A career change was in order. "I wanted a purpose."

She enrolled in cosmetology school. She took a job in a plastic surgeon's office and got to know the work better. Now she works in the Four Seasons Hotel in Georgetown and another spa in the Virginia suburbs.

I asked her whether her salary was steady, did she get good benefits, things that we're all supposed to want. "None of that matters," she said, without a moment's hesitation.

She makes great money—based on commission—and can work as much or as little as she wants. She loves her job. She's excited every day. She likes the freedom; she's mobile. She wasn't looking for job security—at least not yet. Still, I had to imagine that at some point she would want—and need—the assurance that she could continue to do what she loved without risking her financial well-being.

In her old life, this woman had been what the late Peter Drucker called a "knowledge worker." She'd gotten a good education and scored a job in high-level information with a reputable agency of the federal government.[2] And she ended up hating it. The key to her professional happiness, she realized, was not in applying the knowledge she had learned in school but in using her innate creative abilities. My point is not that her current line of work is objectively better than her old one—or the factory job my father held for so many years, for that matter—but that our society has an interest in making sure that these creative service jobs are stable and well paying because, among other things, they are the ones least likely to be outsourced.

Why these jobs don't pay well is a controversial question. Some contend that market forces conspire to keep wages for this kind of work low. Others say the sector needs substantial productivity upgrades before higher pay will be granted. But while economists and politicians bicker, companies around the world—from Starbucks to Ikea—are devising strategies aimed at upgrading service work. They are bumping up pay and benefits, and enabling employees to use their creative talents to serve customers better, all on the assumption that such efforts will add to their bottom line.

Best Buy is a good example. The world's largest specialty retailer of consumer electronics, it employs some 140,000 people and boasts annual sales of $36 billion. Taking a page from Toyota's much lauded management system, Best Buy CEO Brad Anderson has made it his company's stated mission to provide an "inclusive, innovative work environment designed to unleash the power of all of our people as they have fun while being the best." In its effort to increase sales and profits while making the workplace more productive and enjoyable, Best Buy encourages its employees to improve on the company's work processes and techniques and to design new ways to better serve customers. In many cases, small ideas devised on the salesroom floor—a teenage sales rep redesigning a Vonage display, or an immigrant salesperson acting on an idea to increase outreach and service to non-English-speaking communities—have been implemented in stores nationwide, generating hundreds of millions in added revenue. Anderson understands that succeeding in a service industry like retail means more than implementing new technology and designing attractive new products. He likes to say that the great promise of the creative era is that, for the first time in our history, our nation's economic competitiveness hinges on the development of human creative capabilities.

Or as I would put it, our future economic success depends on our ability to harness the creative talents of each and every member of the workforce—regardless of sex, age, race, ethnicity, or sexual orientation.

Working Smarter

A second group of jobs, those held by the creative class, is growing even more quickly and is even more important to our nation's economic growth. This sector includes jobs in science and technology, arts and design, entertainment and media, law, finance, management, health care, and education.

The creative sector has experienced tremendous growth over the past century. Constituting just 5 percent of all employment in 1900, the creative class rose to roughly 10 percent in 1950, 15 percent in 1980, and more than 30 percent by 2005.[3]

The creative class is more than just a group of highly educated people. When economists measure human capital, the total knowledge and skill of the workforce, they typically focus on formal education—the percentage of the population with at least a bachelor's degree. But education is only one indicator of creative potential.

Our society is rife with remarkably creative and successful people who never graduated from college. Like Microsoft's Bill Gates, many of the world's most important entrepreneurs actually dropped out of college. In fact, of the twenty-six self-made people on the *Forbes* 2007 list of the world's fifty richest people, eleven did not graduate from college.[4]

This is not to say that any college dropout can become a wildly successful entrepreneur like Steve Jobs. For most people a college education pays significant economic dividends. But skill is made up of more than a college degree. On-the-job experience, wisdom and savvy, creativity, ambition, and entrepreneurial talent are among the many qualities that can't be formally taught but are requisite for success in the creative economy.

How many people working in the creative economy have university degrees? Charlotta Mellander used microdata on Sweden's working population to determine (1) how many university graduates have a creative occupation and (2) how many people in creative occupations have a university degree. Her answers are illuminating. Nearly nine in ten (88 percent) Swedes with a university degree work in a creative occupation. Seems reasonable enough. But of Swedes working creative occupations, just a quarter held a university degree of three years or more; three-quarters of all those working in creative jobs did not have a university degree.

Indeed, these two factors—university education and creative occupations—play very different roles in economic growth. Research I undertook with Charlotta Mellander and Kevin Stolarick found that the creative sector and the general college-educated populace affect regional economic development through different channels.[5] Compared with members of the creative class, people with college degrees enjoy higher incomes—defined as money from all sources, including work earnings, investments, capital gains, benefits, and so on. But members of the creative class earn higher wages—money paid for a specified quantity of labor. Because wages reflect work that is done in a particular place, they are better indicators of a region's productivity.

Our research uncovered another important way in which occupations affect regional growth. When we looked at the correlations between occupations and regional income, we found that certain kinds of jobs mean more to regional economies than others. Business and financial operations and computer and mathematical occupations had the largest correlation to regional income, followed by sales occupations and then arts, design, media, and entertainment. Next in line were management and engineering occupations, followed by law and science.[6] The finding for artistic and entertainment occupations is particularly interesting. Many people presume that wealth generates and sustains arts and entertainment, not the other way around. But what if arts and entertainment occupations actually contribute to regional wealth as well?

Many regions that have lost manufacturing jobs have rebuilt their economies around education and health care. In many deindustrialized cities around the world, the largest employers are colleges, universities, and hospitals.

This is seemingly good news—at least residents of these cities can find work. But according to my team's analysis, high concentrations of these sectors ultimately do not bode well for cities' economies. Although they may employ many people and provide important services, education and health care add relatively little to regional income.[7] And as the share of education and health care jobs rises, regional earnings fall. As more creative class members take jobs in education and health care, the region's wages tend to fall.

What explains this? Education and health care sectors tend to monopolize a region's workforce. Because the demand for employees is so great, it leaves other sectors with smaller hiring pools. Education and health care—like police and fire departments—are basic necessities. Every region must devote some of its workforce to them. They also bring in relatively little money from outside the region. Aside from out-of-state tuition and government research grants, most of their income comes from within the region. Contrast that with an innovative and creative company or cluster of companies that brings in money from clients worldwide. Growing regions tend to have relatively higher concentrations of other key occupational groups, and it's those other jobs that are concentrating geographically.

Come Together

Jobs and industries have always clustered to some extent. The great concentration of steel factories and automobile manufacturing complexes are just two historical examples of this industrial concentration.

The classical theorists on location, Johann-Heinrich von Thünen and Alfred Weber (brother of the famous sociologist Max Weber), wrote extensively on processes of industrial location as a trade-off between raw materials and transportation costs.[8] Firms in heavy industries would seek out locations with abundant raw materials as well as major waterways and transportation routes that could minimize transportation costs.

The regions of the industrial era were organized around a single core industry or, in some cases, several core industries. They grew upward and then outward in concentric zones around the center.[9] Manufacturing sections developed around ports, and over time these cities saw the rise of specialized downtown business districts that offered a mix of business and financial services. Houses and apartments, which originally surrounded ports and factory complexes, gradually developed along streetcar lines, giving rise to the early suburbs. Most of these regions were served by farms and agricultural producers located relatively close by.

The rise of the creative economy changed this calculus by dramatically reducing dependence on natural resources. The expectation was that jobs and industries would decentralize, and many did, as basic manufacturing industries relocated from the advanced nations to developing ones. But not all industries decentralized. A good example is Italy in the 1980s. Economists and sociologists were struck by the resilience of the nation's garment and fashion industries. How were these traditional sectors continuing to thrive in Italy when they were being driven out of business elsewhere (or at least to offshore locations) by lower-cost competitors in India and China?

The answer can be found in the great economist Alfred Marshall's concept of "agglomeration."[10] Some firms take advantage of economies of scale by integrating their activities and growing larger. But companies can also benefit by the agglomeration economies that come from locating close to one another. More recently, social scientists have dubbed this the power of the "industrial district." Whatever it is called, companies like Armani, Prada, and Gucci benefited from high levels of productivity and innovation, but even more so from being part of a tight cluster of suppliers, users, and customers. The economic power and efficiency of these clusters was more than enough to offset mounting pressures to relocate abroad.

By the early 1990s, the resilience of certain industrial clusters had captured the attention of leading economists and social scientists, like Harvard Business School professor Michael Porter.[11] Considered one of the most important management thinkers in the world, by the mid-1990s Porter was devoting almost all of his research and resources to the study of the world's leading industrial clusters.

Porter's research generated a new economic map of the world that took shape around clusters. According to Porter, these clusters managed to survive because of their proximity to sophisticated users and customers, their ability to draw from highly skilled pools of local talent, and their access to supportive regional institutions such as universities and vocational training programs. Many believed that off-shoring and globalization would undercut these clusters, but Porter argued the opposite: "Now that globalization continues to power forward," he said in a 2006 online interview with *Business Week*, "what has happened is that clusters must become more specialized in individual locations. The global economy is speeding up the process by which clusters get more focused."

Most of us recognize that the films we go to see are produced in Hollywood, that global finance is clustered in New York, London, and Hong Kong, and that Silicon Valley is the world technology leader. But other economic activity is clustered across the globe—watches in Switzerland, disk drives in Singapore, flat panel displays in South Korea, semiconductors in Taipei, and so on. You can fill in your own examples, and that's the point: this kind of clustering is ubiquitous. Figure 7.1 maps some leading economic clusters worldwide.

What's even more interesting is that high-tech industries like software and biotechnology—which have few if any industrial inputs—exhibit even greater clustering. In a detailed study of the biotech industry published in 2001, Joseph Cortright and Heike Mayer found that three-quarters of all biotech firms founded in the 1990s were located in just nine regions.[12] Compared with others, those nine regions boasted eight times as much biotech research, ten times as many biotech companies, and thirty times more biotech venture capital.

Venture capital is another useful indicator of how high-tech industries cluster, and it's one reason for the success of Silicon Valley. "There's a unique set of resources in Silicon Valley that don't exist in other places," VideoEgg founder, Matt Sanchez, told the *Wall Street Journal*. "So if you're going to build a tech company, this is the place to do it."[13]

It's not just high-tech industries that cluster. Many other industries also benefit from being located near one another. To start, let's look at the trends in the two main sectors of the economy: the service sector and the creative sector.

105

FIGURE 7.1. GLOBAL INDUSTRY CLUSTERS

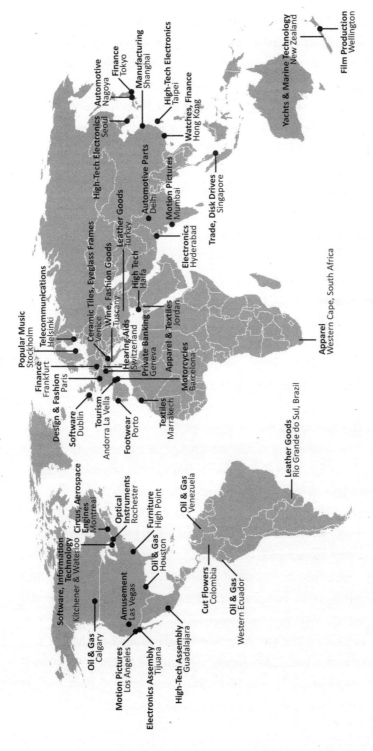

SOURCE: CLAAS VAN LINDE, "CLUSTER META-STUDY: LIST OF CLUSTERS AND BIBLIOGRAPHY." INSTITUTE FOR STRATEGY AND COMPETITIVENESS, HARVARD BUSINESS SCHOOL, OCTOBER 2002. HTTP://DATA.ISC.HBS.EDU/CP/INDEX.JSP. MAP BY PAULO RAPOSO

Many places that top standard lists of those with the fastest
growing job markets generate large numbers of service jobs. On
the other hand, regions such as London, Stockholm, Copenhagen, Amsterdam, Toronto, Sydney, and Silicon Valley are far
more popular when it comes to creative sector jobs. In these regions and others, 40 percent or more of the workforce is employed in creative sector work.

A number of urban economists and regional scientists have
charted the increasing geographic specialization of work. Ann
Markusen, a regional economist and pioneer in the field of occupational analysis, calls this the rise of the "distinctive city,"
where work and economic life have become more specialized.[14]

Roger Martin, my dean and colleague at the Rotman School
of Management, says that while firms can do a lot internally to
bolster their competitive advantage, location plays an additional
role in business success. He calls it jurisdictional advantage, the
fact that every location has unique assets which are not easily
replicated.[15] Or, as he explains:

> The means by which a jurisdiction—whether a city, a re-
> gion, a province or a country—gains advantage over other
> jurisdictions in attracting certain types of human capital
> and certain types of business enterprises by being the opti-
> mal place for them to locate to carry on their appointed
> tasks. We refer only to certain types of people and busi-
> nesses because we believe that no jurisdiction on the planet
> is or will be the optimal jurisdiction for all types of people
> and businesses. Some varieties of highly skilled people and
> some great businesses may think Boston, Massachusetts, is
> the best place on the planet, while others may think that
> Grand Rapids, Michigan, is—and for each, they are un-
> doubtedly right. For this reason, numerous jurisdictions in

the modern economy will enjoy jurisdictional advantage in their areas of specialization.

My team and I used detailed occupational data from the U.S. Bureau of Labor Statistics to estimate the clustering of jobs and work by region. We estimated employment "location quotients" (LQ)—a statistical ratio that compares a region's share of a particular activity with that of the nation—for all major occupations and all major regions across the United States. An LQ of 1.25 is considered reasonably high by most experts, indicating a regional cluster of work. There are nine U.S. regions across the country with LQs over 100. Thirty-seven regions have LQs over 50, and there are more than five hundred with LQs over 10, still a very high concentration.

- Three-quarters of the nation's entertainers and performers work in Los Angeles, as do a quarter of agents.
- Washington, D.C., is home to 78 percent of all political scientists, as well as a huge share of economists, mathematicians, and astronomers.
- More than half of all fashion designers work in New York. The New York region is also home to a quarter of all jobs for brokerage clerks. More than a third of petroleum engineering jobs are in Houston.
- More than 30 percent of all gaming supervisors work in Las Vegas, along with 20 percent of the nation's booth cashiers and 16 percent of all slot key and costume attendants.

Some people would endure very long commutes rather than leave these clusters. An August 2005 article in the *Pittsburgh*

Post-Gazette caused quite the brouhaha when it reported that several top executives were making commutes from New York and Charlotte to Pittsburgh because they did not want to damage their long-run careers by leaving those financial centers.[16] They felt they had to be part of the core cluster—to keep their contacts and networks up—to move ahead in their professions.

This regional concentration and specialization of jobs is a direct consequence of the clustering force examined in Chapter 4. Recall Lucas's answer to his now infamous question, "What would people be paying sky-high rents for?"—to leverage the productivity of others. What makes it advantageous for people who do the same type of work to live near each other—software engineers in Silicon Valley, investment bankers and fashion designers in New York and London, entertainment moguls, actors, and directors in L.A.—is not just that the industries and the companies are there. The companies are there because people can plug into the existing cluster, increase their overall productivity, and make good money. Or as the Santa Fe Institute researchers have found, these larger cities and larger clusters have to generate faster and faster rates of urban metabolism to keep up. The productivity gains brought on by clustering of work is creating a new and more specialized geography of work in the United States and around the world, as jobs and employment opportunities sort into a regional hierarchy by city and location.

Making the Scene

The physical proximity inherent in clustering provides ample face-to-face communication, information sharing, and teaming required to innovate and improve productivity. In contrast to highly standardized work of the industrial age, in which knowledge could be codified in and taught through standardized procedures and engineering diagrams, creative work relies heavily on innate knowledge—the kind that can be found only in (and, as I like to say, "in between") people's heads.

Networks are the human connections that make it possible for people and firms to share this vital information, described in detail by Harvard political scientist Robert Putnam in his best-selling book *Bowling Alone*. Putnam's ideas on the decline of tightly formed networks (the sort represented by 1950s bowling leagues) and the rise of a less caring society, more isolated individuals, and the decline of civic life have become incredibly popular.[17] These networks are formed by two kinds of social capital: bonding and bridging. Bonding represents the close ties that exist within extended families or ethnic communities and is the phenomenon whose decline Putnam lamented.

Bridging reflects looser ties that extend across and connect different groups. For clustering, the second type is what matters. It "puts people in the flow of the many different thoughts and actions that reside in any one world," writes Andrew Hargadon, director of technology management programs at the University of California–Davis.[18] At its heart, bridging "changes the way people look at not just those different ideas they find in other worlds, it also changes the way they look at thoughts and actions that dominate their own. Bridging activities provide the conditions for creativity, for the Eureka moment when new possibilities suddenly become apparent."

In her study of the high-tech industry in Silicon Valley and on Route 128 outside Boston, Berkeley's AnnaLee Saxenian found that the resilience and superior performance of Silicon Valley companies during the 1990s turned on the adaptive capabilities of the region's decentralized but cooperative networks of entrepreneurs, venture capitalists, technologists, and newly minted university talent.[19]

No matter what form it takes, networking reflects what Stanford University sociologist Mark Granovetter calls "the strength of weak ties," a remarkable phrase that captures the essence of what's going on.[20] In a widely influential study that examined how people find jobs, Granovetter concluded that it is our numerous weak ties, rather than our fewer strong ones, that really matter. The idea that proximity to total strangers is more important than connections to lifelong friends may seem strange, until you think about how networks function. The beauty of weak ties is that they bring us new information. Chances are, you and your friends travel in mostly the same circles. You know the same people, frequent the same places, and hear about the same opportunities. Weak ties are more numerous and take less effort to maintain. They introduce a bit of chaos into the equation, which more often than not is the key to identifying new opportunities and ideas.

While the venues in which we network differ depending on our occupation, the role and function of these activities are the same. In traditional office jobs, they may take the form of conversations around the water cooler or weekend games of golf. For investment bankers, it's power lunches. In high-tech fields, it's breakfast meetings, beer bashes, or bicycle rides. One venture capitalist drove this last point home when he said, "If you're not part of the peloton [the main pack of bicycles in a road race], you're not part of the deal." He wasn't being metaphorical.

Or consider the scenes that grow up around artistically creative work like music, writing, and art. These provide a useful lens through which to better understand why jobs and work cluster. Creative work requires little, if anything, in the way of physical inputs (like iron ore or coal) to succeed and doesn't generate economies of scale. Artistic endeavors are textbook cases of individual production. They require little more than small groups to make their final products, which are unique and different.

What's behind a scene? When most people think of an art or music scene, they think of a concentration of people who make art or music—what economists call producers. Scenes have long enabled talented people to collaborate and compete with one another—to seek inspiration, look over, and learn from each other's work. In the world of music, the term "scene" is used in relation to a distinct style of an area's musical taste—such as New Orleans jazz, Nashville country, or Chicago blues. But scenes cannot survive without social and economic infrastructure.

As Harvard economist Richard Caves explains in his book *Creative Industries,* the success of the music industry is contingent on a system in which artists, writers, and musicians do the work, and agents and managers sell that work. And as Elizabeth Currid's book *The Warhol Economy* shows, these scenes also draw from a social environment of clubs, restaurants, and performance venues where networking takes place.[21]

Scenes are vehicles for producing, consuming, and improving products—and they're responsible for creating experiences too. They represent "modes of organizing cultural production and consumption," according to Daniel Silver, Terry Clark, and Lawrence Rothfield, leading students of the subject at the University of Chicago.[22] But, they ask, "What makes these scenes 'scenes'?" What makes a collection of theaters in London or New York City different from theaters anywhere else?

A scene is defined, the authors note, by the opportunities it gives you to "look at other people and be looked at by them." It is "total entertainment culture that pushes work out of mind." The key, they argue, lies in the way "collections of amenities and people serve to foster certain shared values and tastes, certain ways of relating to one another and legitimating what one is doing or not doing." Scenes provide a key lens into why work continues to cluster today.

Jack White Goes to Nashville

One would think that as individual artists, musicians should be able to live anywhere they want. The arts are needed everywhere—these places have every reason to "fly apart." But they don't, and the numbers prove it.

Scott Jackson, a doctoral student at George Mason University, and I tracked the locations of musicians and musical groups between 1970 and 2004 using data from a wide range of sources.[23] Our analysis documents the clear trend toward increasing concentration and specialization in the music industry. The proportion of musicians across the thirty-one metro regions increased from 52 percent in 1970 to 63 percent in 2004. But one region rose head and shoulders above the rest. In 1970 Nashville was a minor center for country music. By 2004 only New York and Los Angeles, both huge cities, housed a greater number of musicians.

Nashville's rise is even more impressive when you look at its location quotient. In 1970 Nashville was not even among the top five regions as ranked by their music industry location quotient. By 2004 it was the national leader, with a location quotient nearly four times the national average. The extent of its growth was so significant, Jackson found, that when he charted the growth in location quotients between 1970 and 2004, Nashville was the only one that registered positive growth. It had, in effect, sucked up all the growth in the industry by expanding its reach from country to all musical genres, particularly rock and pop. Today it is home to much of the world's best studio talent and has eclipsed even New York and Los Angeles as the place for music writing, recording, and publishing.

Just as high-tech companies trek to Silicon Valley, top musical talent usually ends up in Nashville's orbit. In 2005 one of the most significant rock musicians of the past decade, Jack White, founder of the legendary White Stripes, relocated his newest band and recording project, the Raconteurs, from Detroit's legendary music scene (the home of innovative and highly influential rock bands the MC5 and Iggy Pop and the Stooges as well as Motown and other musical styles) to Nashville.[24] Earlier, White had produced and performed on Loretta Lynn's highly regarded album *Van Lear Rose,* which was recorded in Nashville. Impressed by what he saw, he left Detroit and bought a house in Nashville. None of the musicians in the Raconteurs is originally from Nashville. White and Brendan Benson are from Detroit; the drummer, Patrick Keeler, and bass player, Jack Lawrence, had been members of a Cincinnati band, the Greenhornes. When asked why he relocated, White said that Detroit's scene had become too negative and confining. People who were once his friends and associates reportedly got jealous of the White Stripes' success. Nashville was different, he said: more professional, less confrontational, less melodramatic. Like Silicon Valley, it was a place where the best and the brightest in their field could collaborate with other top talent and draw from a world-class economic infrastructure. In a more recent interview he said Nashville is a place that allowed him to write hits.

The kind of work we do is a critical part of our economic wealth and well-being. But how we use the money we make is a different matter. For most of us, the biggest investment we will make is in our home. And if the place we choose to live has a big effect on how much we pay for our house, it has an even bigger impact on how fast and how much our biggest investment will grow over time.

8
SUPERSTAR CITIES

T**HE BIGGEST INVESTMENT MOST PEOPLE EVER MAKE IS** their house. But housing prices in Vancouver, London, Moscow, Tokyo, New York, and San Francisco far exceed real estate prices in other regions of those countries. And the gap is getting wider.

Why such a wide divergence? It all boils down to that old real estate adage: location, location, location. Many people say they want to stretch their money in order to get a big house at an affordable price. In my travels around the globe, I've often heard people boast, "You can buy a mansion here for less than the price of a studio apartment in London or Manhattan." Nobody ever questions why those mansions are less valuable than four hundred square feet overlooking an airshaft.

Buying real estate is not a single purchase. The cost of the structure is usually the less valuable part. It's the cost of the land—the value of location—that really matters. That's where that old real estate adage originates. Where demand is high, and especially where it exceeds supply, the location itself can cost a fortune.

Location plays a role in determining what you pay to begin with, as well as how much your investment will grow over time. In real estate, as with any other investment, the test is not how much it costs to get in but how much your purchase will gain in value. When buying a house, it's crucial for you to realize how big an effect the rate of appreciation can have on our personal wealth in the long run.

As this chapter will show, location is becoming a bigger and bigger factor in real estate; housing prices increasingly vary by location. Leading real estate economists have charted the rise of so-called superstar cities, where prices have appreciated in excess of the national average. And the most dynamic of these real estate superstars are located in the leading megaregions of the world.

Everything Has Its Price

Economists say that the price of real estate is the best reflection of the effective demand for a location. There is a large gap between the most affordable and the most expensive communities, according to data from the American Community Survey of the U.S. Census Bureau (Figure 8.1).[1] The most expensive metro area in 2006 was San Jose, California, where the median housing value was more than $740,000; the least expensive was Odessa, Texas, where the median house was valued at a mere fraction of that, $54,000.

The discrepancies are even greater when you look at finer geographic detail—zip codes, for example. According to a 2007 *Business Week* report, there were five zip codes in the United States in which the median price of a home was more than $2 million. There were twenty-four in which the median price was

FIGURE 8.1. THE REAL ESTATE MAP
Median housing value, by metro area (2006)

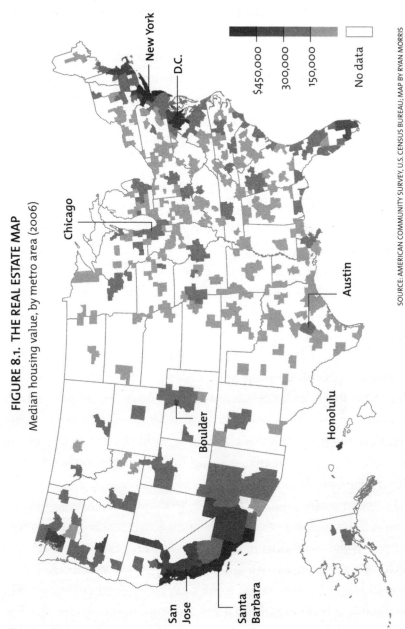

$450,000

300,000

150,000

No data

New York

D.C.

Chicago

Austin

Boulder

Honolulu

San Jose

Santa Barbara

SOURCE: AMERICAN COMMUNITY SURVEY, U.S. CENSUS BUREAU; MAP BY RYAN MORRIS

between $1.5 and $2 million. In another sixty-six zip codes, the median price was between $1 and $1.5 million.[2] And these are median prices. Fully half the homes in these areas were more expensive.

Nonetheless, these places pale in comparison to the world's most expensive cities. While these data are for the most expensive cities overall, housing prices presumably account for the bulk of their costs. Moscow ranks first, with Tokyo in second and London coming in third. Oslo, Seoul, Hong Kong, Copenhagen, Geneva, Zurich, and Milan round out the top ten. Osaka, Paris, Singapore, Tel Aviv, Sydney, Dublin, Rome, St. Petersburg, Vienna, and Beijing complete the top twenty. New York is the only U.S. city to make the top fifty, coming in at twenty-second place.

Several years ago, *New York Times* economic columnist David Leonhardt called me with some questions on this subject. Why weren't firms and people moving to Buffalo or Cleveland? Basic economics would suggest that at least some cost-sensitive businesses and people would want to take advantage of inexpensive real estate. But most don't, and for a very basic reason. Housing costs reflect what people are willing to pay to live in a particular location. Prices rise in places that are hotly desired, and stagnate or fall where demand is lower. Low prices mean that fewer people, relatively speaking, want to live in any given location, which would make hiring more complicated and difficult if a firm were to relocate.

Location matters more than ever in the era of spiky globalization. A 2008 report by real estate giant Knight Frank asked high net worth individuals to name the most important factors in the location of a primary residence or second home. Accessibility topped the list, with 76 percent naming it for a primary residence and 71 percent citing it for a second home. When the list was narrowed to even more specific factors, access to work came in first, crime and security second, and access to airports third, well ahead of social networks, taxes, educational institutions, and leisure activities.[3]

Star Struck

Using long-term trends in housing prices as their gauge, Wharton real estate expert Joseph Gyourko and his colleagues Todd Sinai and Chris Mayer of Columbia University identified the rise of what they call "superstar cities" (comprising central cities and their suburbs) across North America.[4]

According to Gyourko and his collaborators, the dramatic real estate appreciation in superstar cities is a long-term trend. In the short run, real estate prices in superstar cities experience significant ups and downs, but over time they will consistently appreciate in value. But some may ask, What about a place like Las Vegas, which has witnessed dramatic population growth—at or near 50 percent—in four of the past five decades? Most people would think that makes Las Vegas a major growth center. It's a mistake to equate population growth with superstar status, Gyourko says, unless it's accompanied by a significant rise in housing prices. As for Las Vegas, he adds, given its relatively low price appreciation and falling housing prices, most anyone who would like to live there can.

The price many people are willing to pay to live in this small set of superstar cities says something powerful about their economic importance. Of course, housing markets fluctuate and bubbles burst, but superstar cities possess a remarkable staying power that dates back at least half a century. They are, Gyourko says, "by their nature exclusionary—and due to the prices they command, residents have to pay a significant financial premium to live there." They maintain their status by consistently attracting more of the same—increasingly skilled and wealthy households. In Darwinian fashion, richer households move in over

time, and lower-income households are forced out. Because demand for space in superstar cities is so great and because there
is a limited supply of it, Gyourko and his collaborators argue, all
it takes is an increase in national income for these cities to appreciate faster than the rest of the nation.

Adding fuel to the fire is the globalization of real estate markets in the United States and around the world. This dawned on
me when my wife and I were looking for a house in Toronto last
spring. Noting the high prices in Toronto's inner-ring residential
neighborhoods (significantly higher than northwest Washington,
D.C., where we were coming from), I asked our real estate
agent what was driving this. She replied without missing a beat:
"Foreign buyers, not Americans, mainly Russians, are taking virtually all the properties at the high end of the market."

With globalizing markets and a weak dollar, real estate in
Manhattan or Beverly Hills can look like a bargain compared to
London, Tokyo, Hong Kong, Moscow, or other global centers.
This causes an affordability dilemma in these superstar markets.
In the past buyers competed for real estate with others in a rela-
tively local market; now demand extends literally around the
world.

With the rise of a spiky world organized around a relatively
small number of global megaregions, we may be entering a new
phase in real estate in which the housing market splits into globally oriented centers where prices rise considerably over time
and local ones where prices are stable or, in some cases, decline.

However, not all economists think that high real estate prices
in superstar cities are here to stay. Among those who see this
trend ending is Yale economist Robert Shiller, author of the best-
selling *Irrational Exuberance,* which predicted the collapse of
tech stocks in the early 2000s. In a May 2007 op-ed, Shiller
asked, "Why should home values in glamour cities increase forever?"[5] To be sure, there is no way to increase the size of super-

star cities like New York or London. But "in every case," Shiller writes, "there are vast amounts of land where a new city could be started," as has been done time and time again in the past. Private developers, Shiller points out, "tend to be ingenious at developing glamorous new areas from little towns within an hour's commute from major cities. It happens in so many places and so regularly that we take it for granted and rarely even notice it."

Shiller's analysis suggests that during the housing boom of the early 2000s, overall housing values appreciated to such a degree that by 2007 they had become completely misaligned with income.[6] He predicted that housing prices would fall anywhere from 30 to 50 percent by the end of the decade. Maybe. But housing is different from other investments, and for a very simple reason. The primary purpose of investing in a home is not to make money but to put a roof over one's head.

"This is the problem I have with the real-estate-equals-dotcom argument," Roger Lowenstein, the economic journalist, writes. "Most homeowners buy to have a place to live. If prices fall, they react precisely unlike stock traders; rather than bail out, they stay put longer. Every share of Cisco may be for sale every day, but every house is not."[7]

When times are bad, many homeowners sit tight. Housing markets seldom adjust through an instantaneous pop. Rather, they stagnate for many years until incomes catch up and demand grows so great that the cycle of rapid price appreciation starts over.

Karl Case, an economist at Wellesley College and Shiller's research partner, tracked more than six hundred real estate listings in Boston during 2006 as prices began to decline. After four months, most of the houses had not sold, yet the sellers only lowered their prices by 4 percent at most. Case concluded that real estate is "stickier" than other financial assets. Shiller disagreed and called owners naive for thinking that real estate only goes up.

Cities are not interchangeable, as the blogger Ryan Avent points out.[8] Living and working in New York, London, Toronto, or Hong Kong is nothing like living and working in smaller places. Superstar cities have advantages in production and consumption other cities can't replicate. Moreover, newcomers to these places are likely to increase those advantages, not reduce them.

Additionally, Avent reminds us, it makes sense that a superstar city would act as a natural filter for residents who expect to see high returns for their education and skills. After all, individuals who expect to achieve smaller returns for their skill sets will not find it advantageous to locate in New York or London, especially if housing costs are high. They'll go elsewhere, and the gap between New York and London's advantages and those in other cities will continue to widen. The clustering force and the superstar city work together to sort people geographically.

"Bohemian Today, High Rent Tomorrow"

As with any investment, the key to getting a great return on real estate is figuring out how to identify the hot spots in advance. Real estate developers and investors have been interested in my indexes of city and regional performance—like the bohemian index and the gay index—for years. Albert Ratner, cochairman of the board at Forest City Enterprises, one of the biggest real estate companies in the world, likes to remind me that he alone has promoted *The Rise of the Creative Class* enough to secure its spot on the best-seller list. Another real estate investor once said of my work, "You have provided a map of where to invest." That was hardly what I had intended, but it is nonetheless true: by their very nature, my regional indicators identified real estate hot spots.

Intrigued by the correlation, I decided to take a closer look. In winter 2007, Charlotta Mellander and I examined how various regional factors—amenities and population, among others—might shape housing prices.[9] According to economic theory, these prices are set at the intersection of supply (the availability of housing units) and demand (determined by wages and income). In places where new homes can be built relatively easily, supply will increase to meet demand, and prices will stay more or less stable. But if highly desirable areas or places with complex or strict zoning rules experience a rise in residents' incomes, prices will increase and values will appreciate.

Superstar cities command a premium because of their limited supply of housing. There is no single national real estate market, and there are many reasons why certain places are more expensive than others. Regions that attract highly educated and high-earning households tend to experience high demand for housing, especially from people willing to pay extra to live there. Regions with concentrations of high-tech, high-growth industries are also likely to see housing prices exceed income gains, as a 2002 study of Silicon Valley revealed.[10]

Areas with more amenities and attractions, such as coastal locations, typically command higher real estate prices—a correlation pinpointed in 1982 by economist Jennifer Roback Morse, who found that amenities carry as much weight in determining housing prices as do land costs and wages.[11]

Other studies confirm this. In their research on the "Consumer City," Edward Glaeser and his colleagues found that in cities, housing prices tend to rise faster than wages, suggesting that urban amenities, not high incomes, explain higher housing values.[12] Glaeser and his collaborators stated this in a simple formula: urban productivity premium + urban amenity premium = urban rent premium.

But beautiful beaches, sidewalk cafés, and bicycle trails aren't the only indicators of a real estate hot spot. "Want to know where a great place to invest in real estate will be five or ten years from now?" asked a 2007 issue of *Business Week*.[13] "Look at where artists are living now." The article notes that sociologists and policy makers have long thought of artists, designers, musicians, and writers as urban pioneers—economic cure-alls who stimulate local economies and drive up neighborhood real estate values with their presence.

Regional economist Ann Markusen and her colleagues call this phenomenon the artistic dividend.[14] Similarly, sociologists have shown how gentrification, frequently set in motion by artists, creatives, and gays, pushes up urban housing prices.

Mellander and I probed all of these factors and more in our study. We looked closely at the effects of high-tech industry, human capital, high-paid workers and occupations, wages and incomes, and artist, bohemian, and gay populations. We used statistical techniques to isolate the correlations between each of these factors on housing values as well as on each other across more than three hundred U.S. metropolitan regions. The results were striking.

We found that two factors combine to shape housing values. The first is pretty obvious: income; the wealthier the residents, the pricier the housing. But the correlation was to wealth, not salaries. Wages alone, in the absence of capital gains and other earnings, had little relation to housing values. For that matter, neither did levels of education, human capital, the presence of a creative class, or the mix of occupations.

The second and much larger factor is reflected by our Bohemian-Gay Index, which combines the concentration of artists, musicians, and designers with the concentration of gays and lesbians in a region. Regardless of which variables we applied, what version of the model we used, or which regions we looked at, the concentration of bohemians and gays consistently had a substantial correlation with housing values.

Many people believe that gays and lesbians do not cause growth but are merely drawn to certain types of places. By using path models (advanced statistical tools that relate independent, intermediary, and dependent variables), we were able to isolate the relationships between the bohemian and gay populations and other factors on housing values and on each other.

Our initial findings were on target. We found that the presence of these populations had a direct relation to housing values as well as other locational variables (such as income and human capital), making these places more attractive to other populations and demographics. In other words, the presence of these groups was related not only to higher housing values but to higher incomes as well.

Why would this be? Our theory is that bohemian and gay populations capitalize on two distinct factors of high-value housing.

The first is an aesthetic-amenity premium. Artists and bohemians not only produce amenities but are attracted to places that have them. As selective buyers with eyes for amenity, authenticity, and aesthetics, they tend to concentrate where those things abound.

The second is a tolerance or open culture premium. Regions with large bohemian and gay populations possess low cultural barriers to entry, allowing them to attract talent and human capital across racial, ethnic, and other lines. Artistic and gay populations also cluster in communities that value open-mindedness and self-expression.

And their status as historically marginalized groups means that artistic and gay populations tend to be highly self-reliant and receptive to newcomers. They've had to build networks from scratch, mobilize resources independently, and create their own organizations and firms.

Consequently regions in which artists and gays have migrated and settled are more likely than others to place high premiums on innovation, entrepreneurship, and new firm formation. It's not that gays and bohemians drive up housing simply by paying more; their effect on housing prices is far less direct. Bohemian and gay residents drive up housing value because they make areas that were already ripe for growth even more desirable, and to a greater number of people.

When a Place Gets Boring . . .

As usual, not everyone benefits from this kind of growth. Housing in superstar cities has become prohibitively expensive for all but the truly wealthy.

My research with Mellander highlights the factors behind the affordability problem. Housing has become disconnected from local wealth building, local productivity, and local economic development. According to our findings, the key determinants of housing prices are income, human capital, and concentrations of bohemian or gay populations, rather than local wages or local occupations. Income, unlike wages, follows the person who owns it.

Escalating real estate prices can inhibit innovation. Many forms of innovative and creative activity—whether high-tech businesses, art galleries, or musical groups—require the same thing: cheap space. That's what Jane Jacobs was getting at when she famously wrote, "New ideas require old buildings." These spaces, formerly abundant in places like Silicon Valley and downtown New York City, are where everyone from Steve Jobs to Bob Dylan got their start. Cheap space in these towns is now hard to come by. Several Silicon Valley garages that witnessed high-tech start-ups in the 1990s have been turned into museums. When housing prices rise and buildings are converted into expensive condos or high-end retail shops, venues for fostering creativity disappear.

Extreme real estate prices also hinder the ability of places to attract and amass new talent. Thirty years ago, a young researcher at MIT, Stanford University, or the University of California–San Diego could find affordable housing near campus. Today, it is hard to imagine how a young scientist could afford to buy a house within a ten-mile radius of any of those schools. I know professors—midcareer people in their forties with families—who cannot buy in. They're forced to move from apartment to apartment as their rentals turn into condos. When creative, productive regions become the province of affluent people who have already made their money (usually elsewhere), the cycle of local wealth building falls apart. At that point, Jacobs once presciently told me, "When a place gets boring, even the rich people leave."

And yet these places survive. That is partly due to the efforts some universities have made to provide housing for their own. Other people are simply willing to devote a disproportionate share of their income to live where they want or to double and triple up with roommates in order to cut costs. There are the regional productivity gains that come from the collocation of talented and creative people. And of course certain industries, such as finance and high-tech, promise compensation so great that their workers can afford to live in places like London or Silicon Valley.

When I asked a high-ranking official at a leading investment bank if rising Manhattan real estate prices were affecting his firm's ability to attract talent, he said simply, "We're the cause, not the effect, of the real estate market." This doesn't mean that such places aren't paying a price. While Manhattan remains a place of creative markets, the actual production of creative and innovative work is moving beyond city limits to the

outer boroughs, nearby cities in New Jersey, and even downtown Philadelphia.

An even bigger danger lies in the ways housing markets can
thwart mobility. Tim Harford, author of *The Undercover Economist*, asked in *Slate*: Why do some people "still live in Detroit,
which has suffered so much? Why not move to Chicago or New
York?"[15] He cites a study by British economist Andrew Oswald
which found that home ownership can trap people, especially
those who are not well off.[16] Across both the United States and
Europe, Oswald found, high levels of home ownership are correlated with high levels of unemployment, and more so than
with other factors such as unionization or welfare benefits.
Other research, Harford points out, indicates that while homeowners and nonhomeowners are able to find work in the same
period of time, nonhomeowners are far less resistant to commuting longer distances.

Real estate limits mobility. As one economist puts it, "Houses
do not walk." The availability of housing simply does not corre-
late with economic opportunity. "No matter how bad things get
in Detroit or Treorchy [Wales], the houses will still be there,
and if they are cheap enough, people will want to live in them,"
Harford writes. "The likely result is a gloomy sort of segregation: those who feel that they can find a good job in the boom
cities will move there and pay the higher rents. Those who are
less confident of that would rather have no job in a cheap house
than no job in an expensive house." This simple fact ensures
that declining cities "will have residents for a long time to
come."

In this respect, the way we house people today seems a bit
out of sync with other demands of our highly mobile and flexible
economy.

I can't help but wonder whether this dream doesn't belong to
a bygone industrial era. A central element of the creative econ-

omy is flexibility. People change jobs often. Companies out-source tasks. Technology enables us to work from places we couldn't before. An increasing number of individuals and businesses find their mobility a necessity for taking advantage of new opportunities. Strangely, our system of home ownership dramatically limits mobility, and in a country where nearly two-thirds of residents are tied to their houses, this means that the economy will suffer.

The creative age may well require alternative forms of housing—something between ownership and renting. In many markets today, it makes more financial sense to rent rather than own. But rental options can be limited, and renovating a rental apartment to suit your taste can be pricey. One option might be to follow the lead of commercial real estate developers and managers who build out office space to owner specifications in exchange for a long-term commitment. As we've seen, there are many reasons to live in a superstar or hot spot city, but wanting to own a home should not necessarily be among them.

PART III

THE GEOGRAPHY
OF HAPPINESS

9
SHINY, HAPPY PLACES

WE MEASURE HUMAN PROGRESS IN MATERIAL TERMS. Success is registered in wealth. A family's social status is defined by its house and its cars. A country's development is gauged by its gross domestic product, a city's by the economic opportunities it provides for its residents. This doesn't make us shallow people. Material wealth has been crucial to our survival and growth as a species since time immemorial.

In his captivating best-seller *Stumbling on Happiness*, Harvard psychologist Daniel Gilbert writes that "most of us make at least three important decisions in our lives: where to live, what to do, and with whom to do it."[1] He happens to list the "where" question first. But like most who study happiness, his book mostly focuses on the "what" and the "who."

Gilbert and other happiness researchers have mainly ignored the "where." But it's clear that many elements of a happy life— how much we make, how much we learn, how healthy we are, how stressed we feel, the job opportunities we find, and the people we meet—are in large part determined by where we live. Place plays a fundamental role in our endeavors to be happy. In many ways, it is the precursor to everything else.

This chapter and the next show how where we live affects our ability to lead happy and fulfilled lives. Drawing from a large-scale Place and Happiness Survey I conducted with the Gallup Organization, this chapter shows how much the place we live matters to our overall happiness, while the next one outlines the things that we truly value—and that make us truly happy—in the place we live.

Finding Happiness

There's one thing happiness researchers agree on: money does not buy happiness. In wealthier countries, where many citizens already enjoy a relatively high quality of life, individuals tend to seek satisfaction through less tangible things such as personal fulfillment, self-actualization, pleasure, and positive emotions. Martin Seligman and Edward Diener explain this in their comprehensive review of hundreds of studies in the field. "Because goods and services are plentiful and because simple needs are largely satisfied in modern societies," they write, "people today have the luxury of refocusing their attention on the 'good life'—a life that is enjoyable, meaningful, engaging and fulfilling."[2] They note that "people rank happiness and satisfaction ahead of money as a life goal" and go on to suggest that advanced countries should account for well-being in the way they account for income and economic output. If there is GDP for gross domestic product, why not a GNH for "gross national happiness"?

Happiness is associated with income—but only to a point. People in wealthier countries are generally happier than those in the poorest ones. A recent comprehensive review of the field, as well as new data on GDP and happiness by economists Justin Wolfers and Betsy Stevenson, suggests that happiness remains connected to income. And the happiest nations tend to be affluent ones—Denmark, Switzerland, Austria, Finland, Sweden, Canada, Norway, Iceland, and New Zealand, as well as the United States, rank atop various lists.[3] But after a certain threshold of income is crossed, the effect of money and material goods on happiness levels out. Higher levels of income or economic growth do not necessarily translate into higher levels of happiness.

Psychological studies suggest that while the correlation between money and happiness is real, conventional wisdom has it backward. It is not that people with more money are happier; it's that happier people may be better earners: "Part of the typical correlation between income and well-being," write Diener and Seligman, "is due to well-being causing higher incomes, rather than the other way around. Happy people go on to earn higher incomes than unhappy people." Unhappy people tend to channel their time and effort into the pursuit of material goods. They become materialistic, missing out on the relationships and experiences that researchers believe have the greatest effect on personal fulfillment. A new car, a new set of golf clubs, a new handbag, or even a new house produce only temporary happiness. The car gets scratched, the handbag goes out of style, the basement develops a leak. Experiences and relationships, even with their ups and downs, tend to bring longer lasting returns than any one material thing.

If not money, what does genuinely make us happy?

According to research, a vibrant social life is one source of happiness. People who do things they enjoy with people they like are happier than others. Good physical and mental health is another. Not surprisingly, people who suffer from depression and other mental illnesses report far lower levels of well-being.

To a large extent happiness hinges on personal bonds. Loving relationships with a spouse or significant other and with children, as well as a high frequency of meaningful interactions with family members and friends, are essential to happiness. Studies find that on balance, married people are happier than single people. Religion and faith can also have a highly positive effect. Happiness is related to employment, though again, it's the substance of the work, not the pay, that appears to matter.

The Place Connection

Place is the missing link in happiness studies. That is surprising, since so many people take great joy and fulfillment from where they live. The closest most studies get to the "where" factor is to examine the negative effects of commuting. Generally speaking, commuting is a source of unhappiness.

But even researchers who look at commuting often miss a key connection: in spite of its negative effects, people do it anyway. According to a 2007 report, about one in six American workers commutes more than forty-five minutes to and from work, and extreme commuters—those who travel at least ninety minutes each way—are the fastest growing category.[4] Why would people do this to themselves? The obvious answer is that they aren't able or willing to move their home closer to work, and at the same time they aren't able or willing to work where they live. Either way, the choice or the need to commute is grounded in place. Something—keeping a good job, sleeping somewhere (or close to someone) you love, working in a stimulating environment, staying close to aging parents—makes all that driving worth it. But no studies I'm aware of have systematically probed why place remains a decisive factor in our subjective well-being.

In partnership with the Gallup Organization, I undertook a major study of place and happiness. We divided happiness into four basic categories, three of which we took from leading happiness studies—happiness in personal life, happiness on the job, and financial happiness. To these three categories we added a fourth: happiness with one's place. The survey asked people direct questions about their level of satisfaction with their communities; about their experiences and expectations in those communities; about their intentions to move or stay; and whether they would recommend their community to a friend or relative.

Then we zeroed in on the elements of place that might affect community satisfaction and overall well-being, asking questions about the job market, schools, health care, arts and culture, parks and open space, and many other factors. (More on this in Chapter 11.) We ended up posing more than one hundred questions on every aspect of happiness and community satisfaction we could imagine. We pretested the survey and did a detailed statistical analysis to ensure that we would elicit answers that accurately reflected the concepts and theories we wanted to examine. The first survey, conducted in the summer of 2005, raked in 2,300 responses from people in twenty-two U.S. cities. A follow-up survey done a year later covered a much larger group—more than 27,000 people across some 8,000 communities nationwide. That diverse sample reflected a full range of incomes, occupations, ages, races and ethnicities, household types, sexual orientations, and educational levels. I will also be drawing from a related European version of the survey conducted by Robert Manchin of Gallup Europe.[5]

The findings show the overwhelming importance of place to happiness. Place forms the third leg in the triangle of our well-being, alongside our personal relationships and our work. When asked to rate happiness in relation to things like work, finances, personal life, and place on a 1 to 5 scale, place scored 3.63, behind personal life (4.08) and work (3.98) but ahead of finances (3.46).

To more accurately gauge how these factors interact, Irene
Tinagli of Carnegie Mellon and I conducted a multivariate statistical analysis that included measures of place satisfaction, job
satisfaction, financial satisfaction, and a sense of safety and
stress, as well as control variables for demographic factors such
as age, race, gender, and income.

Together, according to Tinagli's analysis, place, financial, and
job satisfaction accounted for a quarter of the total variance in
overall life satisfaction—a substantial amount statistically speaking. This becomes even clearer when we consider that all of the
demographic factors taken together, including income, account
for only 1.2 percent of the variance in overall life satisfaction.[6]
The place we live is more important to our happiness than education or earnings.

All of this was further confirmed when we examined happiness from the other end of the telescope. High levels of depression or stress reflect low levels of well-being or satisfaction.
More than two-thirds (67 percent) of survey respondents reported at least moderate stress. Eleven percent described their
stress as "extreme." But place barely registers as a source of
stress. When asked to name what stressed them out, more than
30 percent of respondents said their jobs, 20 percent said finances, 13 percent said family, 10 percent said health, and 8
percent said crime. Only 3 percent identified their location
alone as a source of stress in their lives. Out of all the possible
factors, place ranked dead last.

Manchin's survey of happiness in European cities found that
levels of community happiness vary quite a bit by city. Roughly
three-quarters of residents of Stockholm (77 percent) and
Dublin (74 percent) reported being very satisfied, compared
with two-thirds of those in Helsinki (67 percent) and about half
in Berlin (56 percent), Madrid (54 percent), Barcelona (54 percent), Paris (49 percent), and London (46 percent).

Tinagli and I also looked at how factors such as income, education, age, and gender affect how happy we are with where we live. A close parsing of the survey data shows several clear trends.

- *Income:* In general, income has a relatively small effect on how happy people are with their community.[7] But when we looked at specific income groups, we found that community satisfaction rises with income at least to a point. Only 43 percent of those making less than $20,000 reported being either satisfied or very satisfied with their community. This rose to 56 percent for those making $20,000–40,000; 65 percent for those in the $40,000–60,000 range, 72 percent for those making $60,00–100,000, and peaking at 77 percent for those making $100,000–150,000 before falling off for the next higher bracket.
- *Homeownership:* Interestingly, while most people believe that homeownership is the core of the so-called American dream, renters, according to the survey results, are actually slightly more satisfied with their communities than homeowners are.
- *Education:* Most studies find that education is closely correlated with professional and financial satisfaction. The more education people have, the more likely they are to feel professionally and financially satisfied. Tinagli also found a significant positive correlation between education and place satisfaction. Seventy-three percent of respondents with a graduate-level education and 68 percent of college graduates reported being satisfied or very satisfied with their communities, compared with 57 percent of those without a high school diploma and 63 percent of those who had completed only high school.

Conversely, those who lack a high school education were more than twice as likely than those with graduate degrees to report being very unsatisfied or not satisfied with where they live (7 percent and 16 percent, respectively). People with higher levels of education have greater levels of mobility and choice in where they live.

- *Marital status:* Married people are happier with the place they live. Sixty-nine percent of married people reported being either satisfied or very satisfied with their place of residence, compared to 53 percent of those who are separated and 60 percent of those who are divorced.

- *Age:* Older people on balance are happier with their communities: 71 percent of those over sixty-five years of age reporting being satisfied or very satisfied with their communities, compared to 65 percent of those twenty-five to forty-five and 56 percent of those under twenty-five.

Town and Country

With the correlation between place and happiness firmly under our belts, my team and I then looked into how various types of communities affect residents' well-being.

Various downtown, suburban, and ex-urban neighborhoods house residents who derive an especially great proportion of their happiness from their personal lives. It is widely assumed that people in suburbs or rural areas are happier than those in dense city centers, and a 2006 survey by the Pew Center found that, over all, this is only slightly true. But people can find happiness in all kinds of places. Some of us may find peace in the quiet pace of small town life, while others need the hustle and bustle of the big city to feel at home.

According to the Place and Happiness Survey, urban dwellers derive satisfaction from features that rural people may not value. While people who live in rural communities derive great satisfaction from clean air and natural beauty, urbanites tend to put a premium on schools, job opportunities, and safety. They value their ability to meet new colleagues and make new friends; they prize their access to diverse cultural resources such as theaters, museums, art galleries, live music, and vibrant nightlife filled with bars, clubs, and restaurants. They appreciate the availability of public transit; many city residents tell me they would rather not use, or even own, cars. They also derive satisfaction from living in communities that are open to a range of groups—racial and ethnic minorities, immigrants, young people, and gays and lesbians. And there are other incentives for living in cities too. Some people trade their big suburban house for an urban condo when the kids move away, or they decide to live closer to the city center. Or maybe their lifelong dream was to live near all the action.

But here's the really interesting point: the Place and Happiness Survey showed that the majority of us are quite happy with where we have chosen to live. On the question of whether they were merely "satisfied" or "very satisfied" with their communities overall, 68 percent of suburbanites, 67 percent of rural dwellers, and 64 percent of city residents responded affirmatively. Fifty-six percent of all city residents and 57 percent of both suburbanites and rural residents ranked their communities as the "best" or "near-best" places to live.

When asked whether they would recommend their communities to their friends, 61 percent of suburbanites and 57 percent of city residents and rural residents, respectively, said they would.

While many people make the trek from the country to the big city, others do the reverse. I received a number of locational histories from people who traded the hustle and bustle of the big city for a slower paced, more sylvan rural life. Liva Sansom moved from Toronto to Paris and then back to a small university town in Canada.

> We started our married life in Toronto, Ontario, where my husband was completing his PhD and I was completing my MBA. My husband got a post doc working in Ottawa at the National Research Council. We really enjoyed living in Ottawa—easy access to the outdoors, close to my husband's family, wonderfully charming neighborhoods and a safe downtown, where we rented our townhouse. The second year of my husband's post doc was in Paris, France. Coincidentally, we rented an apartment in the 14th *arondissement* and made the most of our time in Paris, traveling, sightseeing, and taking the *métro* everywhere.
>
> Eventually we ended up returning to Ottawa. My husband's passion, however, was academia and he set about applying to university faculty positions. When a position was posted at Queen's University in Kingston, Ontario, we had high hopes. We knew Kingston and thought it was a good place to raise a family—picturesque and friendly. It was an easy traveling distance to our favorite urban locations of Toronto, Ottawa, and Montreal, and it provided easy access to the country for hikes and agricultural experiences, like berry picking and visiting farms. The cost of living was attractive as well.
>
> We moved from a two-bedroom rental in downtown Ottawa to a split-level home in "suburban" Kingston. I have no desire to move again. Our neighbors are wonderful, and we have largely found both our groove as parents and

adults, as well as age-appropriate activities for our two children. Our children have many friends, we live in a great
neighborhood, my husband is enjoying his job and we can
easily travel to where we want—what else could we ask for?

The majority of respondents to the Place and Happiness Survey reported that they were satisfied enough to continue to live
in their current location: 71 percent of city dwellers, 73 percent
of suburbanites, and 78 percent of rural residents—the group
most traditionally tied to their land.

A 2008 survey of 8,500 residents in fourteen global cities
found that more than two-thirds expressed substantial confi-
dence in their city's future, including more than 8 in 10 residents of Shanghai and Beijing; three-quarters in Chicago, Paris,
and Prague; more than two-thirds in Los Angeles, Mexico City,
and Sydney; and more than half of those in New York, London,
Tokyo, and Berlin.[8]

When she analyzed the Place and Happiness Survey, Tinagli
discovered that what people value about their communities is
remarkably similar across the board, whether city center, suburb, or rural area. To be sure, city residents and country
dwellers experience their communities differently, but the psychological mechanisms that influence place happiness are pretty
much the same. There seem to be three basic reasons for this.

First, place is a major source of excitement and creative stimulation, an essential component of our psychological well-being.
The leading psychologist of creativity, Mihaly Csikszentmihalyi,
has long argued that creative activities such as writing, playing
music, computer programming, mountain climbing, and chess
playing are major sources of enjoyment and productivity. Such
activities, he says, put us in a state of "flow," or intense, unfet-
tered focus and concentration.[9] The beauty of this state is that
we can have fun and be productive. The most creative people

tend to fluctuate between intense interaction and intense concentration. They also tend to be the happiest when engaging in a state of flow.

Csikszentmihalyi told me that the great physicist Freeman Dyson would often just sit in his office with his door open. To the casual observer, he appeared to be doing nothing. But in fact Dyson was searching for the stimulation of interesting hallway conversation. After a week or two of absorbing the buzz, he would retreat behind closed doors to work alone on a new discovery. Creative places work in similar ways. They are filled with stimulating cultural offerings, great people to work with and watch, and invigorating outdoor scenes. There is abundant external stimulation to plug into and absorb, but there's also plenty of room for privacy and retreat.

My earlier research, along with Ronald Inglehart's, has documented the connection between creativity, self-expression, and economic development. But creativity and self-expression also go hand in hand with happiness and well-being. In her research on workplace performance, Teresa Amabile of Harvard Business School discovered that happiness leads to creativity, not vice versa.[10] Controlling for a wide variety of factors, Amabile and her team found that a positive mood can predict creative thinking and workplace innovation; they also found evidence that innovation leads to positive mood.

Finding a place that makes us happy has a powerful effect on our "activation." Such places encourage people to do more than they otherwise would, such as engage in more creative activities, invent new things, or start new companies—all of which are both personally fulfilling and economically productive. This kind of activation, Tinagli found, stems in large part from the visual and cultural stimulation that places can provide—parks and open space, cultural offerings, things she calls "symbolic amenities." This creates a regenerative cycle: the stimulation unleashes creative energy, which in turn attracts more high-energy people from other places, resulting in higher rates of innovation, greater economic prosperity, higher living standards, and more stimulation.

The second has to do with a sense of self. Generally speaking, people derive happiness from being themselves—cultivating their individuality. Sociologists and psychologists have long pointed out that self-expression is a major source of happiness. A place is a means to that end. It gives us an environment we can adopt and make our own. An undeniable advantage of today's mobile society is that we are not forever tied to the identity of our birthplace—the handed-down norms and customs of our families, religions, and hometowns. We can, if we choose, re-create our identities based on the things that matter to us: work, lifestyle, personal interests, or activities. We seek out (perhaps not consciously) places that fit our psychological needs in order to establish ownership over our lives.

The third reason is the flip side of the coin. Place gives us something to which we can belong, providing a sense of pride and attachment. Place offers us characteristics by which to define ourselves and a physical and figurative space in which to live. Some of us root for local sports teams; others are energized by a stunning natural environment; still others by neighbors. The connection between place and identity is all around us.

Now that we have a handle on how place affects happiness in general, what is it about our places that we like and dislike? What are the big ticket, and small ticket, items that make us happy with communities—or not?

10

BEYOND MASLOW'S CITY

IN 1943 PSYCHOLOGIST ABRAHAM MASLOW SET FORTH THE concept of a hierarchy of needs.[1] Maslow's theory, often illustrated in the shape of a pyramid, posits that humans require more than just food, water, air, and sex in order to be fulfilled. These rudimentary physiological needs constitute the base layer of the pyramid. Moving up the hierarchy we find the need for security, the need for love and belonging, the need for self-esteem, and finally the need for self-actualization. Only by fulfilling each of the first four layers—what Maslow calls the "deficiency needs," meaning the needs that arise because of deprivation—can we reach the top of the pyramid and fulfill our true potential.

By the time he died in 1970, Maslow had concluded that his original theory of self-actualization—the method by which humans come to "be all they can be"—was not complete. He broadened the area of self-actualization to include our constant quest for knowledge and perpetual desire for aesthetics and beauty, and created an even higher level called "transcendence," on which people—having satisfied all the other needs—feel compelled to help others in order to reach fulfillment. These higher-level needs have seemingly little to do with our physiological survival, but in a modern and affluent society, they inevitably shape our psychological development. They motivate us in all ways. They signify the key to a happy and fulfilled life.

The interesting thing is this: everyone seems to want the things promised by the top of the pyramid, whether or not the "prerequisite" needs have been satisfied. Maslow's theory implies that fulfilling the needs on each level is contingent on having satisfied the preceding ones. In other words, before people can fulfill the need for self-esteem, they must have already satisfied their basic physiological needs and their need for security. But in a society in which the haves live next to the have-nots, no one sees the top of the pyramid as a luxury. Part of this has to do with the American dream, which in addition to life and liberty promises the pursuit of happiness for all. In this way, the process of self-actualization is viewed as a right, not something to be earned.

But somehow the conversation about place remains stuck in an either-or debate. Even in the face of our affluent, self-expressive society, some urban experts and community leaders remain convinced that only basic needs matter. The key to a great community, they contend, lies in good schools, safe streets, and up-to-date infrastructure. Anything else—parks, trails, museums, or other amenities—is a luxury, aimed at the yuppies and the privileged classes. Or they say it's something that comes only when a community is already rich. Jobs and basic services are what's needed to generate wealth and income. The rest is what we pay for with the resources so generated. As this chapter will show, they're wrong. The places that make us truly happy don't get trapped in any such trade-off. They do it all, providing great schools, safe streets, and nice parks to boot.

This chapter looks at what really matters to people in the places they live. To get beyond the posturing and sloganeering that has dominated the debate to this point, it uses the more than 27,000 responses from the Place and Happiness Survey to identify the key factors that underpin our happiness with place. It also draws from the results of a survey of happiness and community satisfaction in European cities by Robert Manchin of Gallup Europe, and another survey of quality of life in fourteen global cities conducted by the Veolia Urban Observatory.[2]

The Place and Happiness Survey covered dozens and dozens of specific community attributes, which we then clustered into five major categories.

1. *Physical and economic security:* perceptions of crime and safety, the overall direction of the economy, and availability of jobs
2. *Basic services:* schools, health care, affordable housing, roads, and public transportation
3. *Leadership:* the quality and efficacy of elected and unelected (business and civic) leadership and the opportunity for public and local engagement
4. *Openness:* the level of tolerance for and acceptance of diverse demographic groups including families with children, ethnic and racial minorities, senior citizens, immigrants, and gays and lesbians
5. *Aesthetics:* physical beauty, amenities, and cultural offerings

Since the survey collected a wide range of demographic data, we also looked at how what people value in their places is affected by factors such as income, education, occupation, age, race, and ethnicity.

What, then, are the things that matter most to people about their communities? While all five factors play important roles, two top the list: aesthetics and basic services, with openness coming in a reasonably close third. (For those who are so inclined, Appendix B summarizes the key statistical findings from the survey.) As we will see, there's no trade-off here, at least in the minds of the 27,000 respondents to the Place and Happiness Survey. It goes without saying that each category matters a great deal.

The Beauty Premium

While our findings on the importance of aesthetic factors—physical beauty and outdoor space—may at first seem controversial, it actually makes a great deal of sense. Most people expect their communities to provide basic services, and most communities do. And as our survey shows, they value basic services highly. But aesthetics also matter a great deal. The higher people rate the beauty of their community, its physical environment, and recreational offerings, the higher their overall level of community satisfaction.

Consultant Simon Anholt's City Brands Index named Paris, Rome, Sydney, London, Barcelona, Madrid, St. Petersburg, Amsterdam, Prague, and San Francisco as the world's most beautiful cities; Geneva, Oslo, Stockholm, Helsinki, Reykjavik, Sydney, Vancouver, Montreal, and Melbourne were named the cleanest (Figure 10.1).

A comprehensive data-driven study of global cities named Vancouver, Dusseldorf, San Francisco, Frankfurt, Vienna, Munich, Zurich, Tokyo, Copenhagen, and Paris as the world's top ten "most livable" cities (Figure 10.2).[3] On a separate ranking of

FIGURE 10.1. PERCEIVED CLEANLINESS OF GLOBAL CITIES

Geneva	1	New York	51
Oslo	2	Rio de Janeiro	52
Stockholm	3	Nairobi	53
Helsinki	4	Beijing	54
Copenhagen	5	Shanghai	55
Reykjavik	6	Mumbai	56
Sydney	7	Manila	57
Vancouver	8	Cairo	58
Montreal	9	Bangkok	59
Melbourne	10	Mexico City	60

Note: Respondents were asked: "The environments of cities vary in terms of air, visual, and other types of pollution. How clean or dirty do you think the city is?"

Source: Anholt City Brands Index, 2nd ed., 2006.

quality of life in global cities developed by Tyler Brûlé that is based on a combination of quantitative factors and subjective assessments, the top ranked locations were Copenhagen, Munich, Tokyo, Zurich, Helsinki, Vienna, Stockholm, Vancouver, Melbourne, Paris, and Sydney.

The results of several other global surveys back up the findings of the Place and Happiness Survey. Robert Manchin's Gallup survey of community satisfaction in European cities found that the "beauty of the city" and being a "clean city" to be among the top five factors that make members of Europe's creative class satisfied with their city. The Veolia survey of global urban lifestyles asked 8,500 residents in fourteen global cities to name their top priority changes to keep future generations in the city: 24 percent responded "less polluted"; 20 percent said "more spacious"; 19 percent, "less densely populated"; 15 percent, greener; and

FIGURE 10.2. THE LIVABILITY FACTOR

City	Index Value
Vancouver	94.4
Dusseldorf	93.9
San Francisco	93.4
Frankfurt	93.4
Vienna	93.4
Munich	93.2
Zurich	92.8
Tokyo	92.7
Copenhagen	92.6
Paris	92.6

Source: MasterCard Worldwide Centers of Commerce Index, 2008.

13 percent, "cleaner." The flip side is also instructive. When the Veolia survey asked residents what they "dislike the most" about their city, pollution came in second (with 38 percent of respondents), followed by "noise" (28 percent) third and "dirtiness" (26 percent) fourth.

In her book *The Substance of Style* and other writings, Virginia Postrel provides powerful insight into the economic value of aesthetics.[4] "Given a modicum of stability and sustenance," Postrel writes, "people enrich the look and feel of their lives through ritual, personal adornment, and decorated objects." Even primitive people who scavenged for food and lived in caves found ways to adorn their bodies with jewelry and cosmetics and decorate their abodes with baskets and pottery. Postrel argues that the instinct to make something "special" is not only "emotionally and sensorially gratifying" but also part of a universal and innate desire that all human beings experience.

Beauty is so powerful that it can affect how we perceive places and what we value in them. One of our respondents, Zoe, was awestruck by the beauty of Paris and carries its lessons with her to new places.

> I still viscerally miss the place because it is so beautiful. More than the buildings and views, I miss the public parks. Each one is a unique jewel, landscaped for interest throughout the year, well-maintained, and safe during the day. The ugly parts of town are redeemed by their gardens, shoehorned anywhere they can find the space. There even is a garden on top of the train sheds at the Gare Montparnasse. I used the station half a dozen times before I realized that the garden was there. Landscaping fashions of half a dozen centuries are maintained in one place or another. Some parks are for children, others have sports facilities, others capitalize on a view or honor the history of the individual neighborhood. One has huge glass conservatories, another is a scent garden for the blind. One is built on top of an old railway viaduct. It's perhaps forty feet wide, several miles long, and passes through at least one modern building. I haven't seen them all.
>
> After returning home to a college town, I have become an advocate for public beauty, particularly for our small downtown. I argue that, when competing with big box stores in strip malls, we cannot afford *not* to make downtown beautiful. People will go out of their way to spend time in beauty, and once there they will linger. Visiting alumni don't buy artist's prints of the local Wal-Mart.

So what is it about aesthetics that makes us feel satisfied and happy with our communities? To get why aesthetic beauty resonated so deeply with these residents, the Place and Happiness Survey asked respondents to rank all aspects of their location's physical environment—its overall beauty; its outdoor parks, playgrounds, and trails; even its climate and air quality. We then compared these ratings with people's satisfaction with the community. The results are intriguing. The physical beauty of our communities is the one that matters the most. It's followed by outdoor parks, playgrounds, and trails. Climate and air also matter but are less important than the first two.

So did Maslow have it all wrong? Not entirely, argues Postrel. When his theory is portrayed as a simple pyramid, it can lead to a false conclusion: "That aesthetics is a luxury people only care about when they're wealthy." Postrel points out that there is no pyramid of needs in which moving up requires that one first completely satisfy the needs under it. "The next increment of what we consume changes depending on what we already have. . . . The marginal value of some characteristic, such as nutrition or shelter, is high initially—we don't want to starve or freeze to death in a snow storm—but that value drops off faster than the marginal value of other characteristics, including aesthetics." Human beings crave physical beauty. We look for it in the things that surround us, and especially in the places we live.

Economists call this the "beauty premium." People are drawn to and pay more for something that has aesthetic appeal. Consider how much attention home sellers—and home buyers— pay to a house's curb appeal. A 2007 study by economists in Britain and the Netherlands looked for patterns in the appearance of players eliminated from a Dutch TV game show.[5] It found that the beauty premium extends beyond objects. As much as there is a bias toward beautiful people, there is an even greater bias against unattractive people. Researchers found that attractive players were "substantially less likely to be eliminated" and that the least attractive player was "almost twice as likely to be eliminated at the end of the first round than any other player." Less attractive players, the study concluded, "are discriminated against, for reasons that are uncorrelated with their performance or behavior during the game." If it is human nature to distance ourselves from unattractive people, despite the psychological damage that such discrimination may inflict, it's hardly surprising that we would treat our communities and their physical surroundings any differently.

In this vein, some people say that the rust belt cities may as well pack it in. How can Pittsburgh, Manchester, or Rotterdam compete with places like San Francisco, Barcelona, or Sydney when it comes to beauty, ambience, natural scenery, and outdoor recreation? Thankfully for the Pittsburghs and Rotterdams of the world, there is more to aesthetics than pretty parks and mountain vistas. Many older communities have a wonderful mix of natural features and industrial age buildings. They are filled with old warehouses, historic homes, and terrific neighborhoods. Many have magnificent urban park systems handcrafted by great landscape designers of the nineteenth and early twentieth centuries.

Having lived in Pittsburgh for nearly two decades, I am a fan of the industrial aesthetic. I found the juxtaposition between the city's three beautiful rivers and its rugged, industrial landscape incredibly appealing. I used to ride my bike through the city's industrial corridors and up into its hilly suburbs and exurbs, where climbing skills are really put to the test. Pittsburgh may not be everybody's cup of tea, but my experience living there is a testament to the idea that every place holds appeal for somebody.

Chicago's lakefront renaissance—its incredible twentieth-century architecture and marvelous refurbished neighborhoods—illustrates how established cities can highlight their own brand of aesthetics. Much of this renewal is due to the efforts of Mayor Richard M. Daley, who has reached beyond landmarks like the new Millennium Park and the improved lakefront to bolster many of the city's neighborhoods by refurbishing smaller community parks and gardens, planting trees, installing public art, and adding hand-painted benches and flower beds.

I recall driving through one such neighborhood on my way to a seminar at the University of Chicago. When my host pointed out that we were driving through a lower-income community, I felt perplexed. The lush tree canopy, improved streetscape, and community parks had the visual characteristics I associate with more affluent communities. At that minute it dawned on me that what makes less advantaged communities look "poor" more often than not is their denuded streetscape—a complete lack of trees and green space.

And while many people prefer their place neat and manicured, what I love about Toronto is its "messy urbanism"—high-rise condos next to ramshackle Victorians, luxury boutiques next to mom-and-pop shops, sylvan streets than run smack into highly trafficked commercial routes, stunning ravines that cut through dense urban neighborhoods, bike commuters sharing the road with streetcars, buses, and luxury sedans.[6]

People Meeting People

Not surprisingly, it turns out that the ability to meet people and make friends is one of the most important factors in determining how happy we are with our communities. Nearly one in five

FIGURE 10.3. THE WELCOME FACTOR

Sydney	1	Cairo	51
Rio de Janeiro	2	Paris	52
Barcelona	3	Warsaw	53
Melbourne	4	Nairobi	54
Rome	5	Shanghai	55
Madrid	6	Johannesburg	56
Vancouver	7	Beijing	57
Las Vegas	8	Lagos	58
Toronto	9	Jerusalem	59
Amsterdam	10	Moscow	60

Note: Respondents were asked: "Think about how people in general would behave towards you . . . whether they might be warm and friendly, cold, or show prejudice. How welcome do you think people in general would make you feel in the city?"

Source: Anholt City Brands Index, 2nd ed., 2006.

residents in the Veolia survey of fourteen global cities said that the "possibility of meeting new people" was among the factors they liked the most about their city. Anholt's City Brand Index counts Sydney, Rio de Janeiro, Barcelona, Melbourne, Rome, Madrid, Vancouver, Las Vegas, Toronto, and Amsterdam as the world's most open and welcoming cities (Figure 10.3).

Unfortunately, a growing number of us lack this capability in our lives. A study conducted in 2006 by a team of sociologists from the University of Arizona and Duke University found that the share of Americans who feel socially isolated in their communities (defined by having no one to talk to about personal matters) increased from 10 percent in 1985 to more than 25 percent in 2004.[7] The study found that educated middle-class families have been hit hardest, possibly as a consequence of longer commutes and working hours. The authors note that people are spending more time "interacting with multiple computers in the home, instead of with each other." But the biggest change since 1985, the study reports, has been the decline of neighborly ties. An increasing number of people live alone, and many of them lack friends or family nearby.

That explains why so many people interviewed say they wish they lived in a community that made it easier for them to connect with others and form new relationships. Those who have friends where they live value what they've got. Just ask any group of young singles who live and act together in what author Ethan Watters has dubbed "urban tribes."[8]

It's ironic that a by-product of a globalized world is increased isolation. Little wonder that participants in the Place and Happiness Survey placed such a high value on meeting people and making friends.

Culture Vultures

There is a growing movement in cities around the world to invest in culture as a way of improving their reputation and spurring economic growth. The Place and Happiness Survey found that culture and nightlife do play a significant role in place satisfaction, although less than physical beauty and sociability. Anholt's City Brands Index ranked Paris, Rome, London, New York, Sydney, San Francisco, Madrid, Barcelona, Los Angeles, and Amsterdam as the world's most exciting and interesting cities. Thirty percent of respondents in the Veolia global cities survey reported that "cultural dynamism" was among the things they like the most in their city, and an additional 26 percent cited "possibilities for going out and having fun."

And that's exactly what Clara Venice, a young artist and musician, found in Berlin:

What I loved about Berlin (besides the opera, which was completely radical) was the general attitude of "why not?" like, an entire city of people who were genuinely open and up for anything, which I totally related to. From a musical perspective, I found the city very interesting in that it is like a living mash-up everywhere you go, with every style and era played alongside every other style and era, without any sense of judgment (of one genre being "better" or "cooler" than another) or playlist to curate the various scenes.

People today have a broader view of culture than what I've affectionately termed the SOB—symphony, opera, and ballet. While those cultural forms remain appealing to many, the most vibrant artistic and cultural communities combine traditional high-culture institutions with street-level art, music, and theater scenes.

In a society where many people have little control over their own schedules, time has become one of our scarcest resources. Previous generations seemingly had more time for regular extracurricular activities. Today it's virtually impossible to plan in advance. Still, even if people lack the flexibility or freedom to fill their schedules with fun events, they like knowing they could go out and do something if they wanted to. The fact that such opportunities are there for the taking—when inspiration strikes or when family and friends come for a visit—is sufficient for many.[9]

It All Comes Down to the Basics

Basic services also matter a great deal to people's happiness and sense of satisfaction with their communities. The higher people ranked their community's basic services, the higher their satisfaction with that community. As already noted, the Place and

FIGURE 10.4. HEALTH AND SANITATION IN GLOBAL CITIES

Rank 2007	City	Country	Index 2007
1	Calgary	Canada	131.7
2	Honolulu	United States	130.3
3	Helsinki	Finland	128.5
4	Ottawa	Canada	127.2
5	Minneapolis	United States	125.7
6	Oslo	Norway	125.0
6	Stockholm	Sweden	125.0
6	Zurich	Switzerland	125.0
9	Katsuyama	Japan	123.8
10	Bern	Switzerland	123.7
10	Boston	United States	123.7
10	Geneva	Switzerland	123.7
10	Lexington, KY	United States	123.7
10	Montreal	Canada	123.7
10	Nurnberg	Germany	123.7
10	Pittsburgh, PA	United States	123.7
10	Vancouver	Canada	123.7
18	Auckland	New Zealand	123.1
18	Wellington	New Zealand	123.1
20	Dublin	Ireland	122.9
21	Amsterdam	The Netherlands	122.4
21	Toronto	Canada	122.4
23	Lyon	France	122.3
24	Copenhagen	Denmark	122.2
25	Kobe	Japan	122.0
25	Omuta	Japan	122.0
27	Washington, DC	United States	121.0
28	Dusseldorf	Germany	120.9
28	Frankfurt	Germany	120.9
28	Luxembourg	Luxembourg	120.9
28	Munich	Germany	120.9
28	Vienna	Austria	120.9
33	Tsukuba	Japan	120.4
34	Portland, OR	United States	119.7
35	Adelaide	Australia	119.5
36	Brussels	Belgium	118.4
37	Cleveland, OH	United States	118.3
37	Hamburg	Germany	118.3
37	San Francisco,	United States	118.3
37	St. Louis, MO	United States	118.3
37	Winston Salem, NC	United States	118.3
42	Yokohama	Japan	118.1
43	Melbourne	Australia	117.4
43	Perth	Australia	117.4
45	Berlin	Germany	117.1
46	Yokkaichi	Japan	116.5
47	Brisbane	Australia	116.2
48	Glasgow	United Kingdom	115.7
49	Seattle	United States	115.1
50	Singapore	Singapore	114.0

Source: Mercer Human Resource Consulting, Worldwide Health and Sanitation Ranking, 2007.

Happiness Survey found no trade-off between aesthetics and basic services: both are important to how happy people are with where they live.

A global survey of health and sanitation ranked Calgary, Honolulu, Helsinki, Ottawa, Minneapolis, Oslo, Stockholm, Zurich, Katsuyama, Bern, Boston, Geneva, Lexington, Montreal, Nuremberg, Pittsburgh, Vancouver, Auckland, Wellington, Dublin, Amsterdam, and Toronto as atop the list of global cities (Figure 10.4).[10]

The Place and Happiness Survey asked people to evaluate several aspects of their community infrastructure—primary and secondary schools, colleges, and universities; job opportunities; traffic and public transportation options; and affordable housing.

Of all those factors, primary and secondary schools play the biggest role in community satisfaction. People in a community depend on accessibility to local primary and secondary schools for their children's education; college-age children travel greater distances for higher education. Anholt's City Brands Index ranked London, Paris, New York, Washington, D.C., Boston, Sydney, Geneva, San Francisco, Toronto, and Tokyo as the top global cities for higher education.

The Place and Happiness Survey found, surprisingly, that people who place the greatest value on proximity to colleges and universities are, interestingly enough, those with less education. Possibly they value the example or aspiration such institutions set for their children. Or maybe they view such institutions as possible options for their own continuing education. Or perhaps it is simply because they (and their children) are less mobile, requiring that access to all levels of education be close and thus more affordable.

Jobs matter a great deal as well: not just any job, but a job in one's chosen field. Yet most communities seem to be doing a poor job of meeting that need. According to the Place and Happiness Survey, just over 17 percent of respondents rated their satisfaction with job opportunities as "very good"; more than 30 percent rated their communities in this respect as "bad" or "very bad."

Manchin asked his survey respondents in Europe about how easy it is to find a job. The highest ranked community was Dublin, where more than 30 percent of respondents strongly agreed with the statement "it is easy to find a new job." Next in line was London with 18 percent; about 15 percent of respondents in Stockholm (15 percent) and Helsinki (13 percent) said so; less than 10 percent in Barcelona (9 percent), Madrid (6 percent), and Paris (6 percent); and just 2 percent in Rome, and 1 percent in Berlin.

That suggests a potential disconnect between places where people live—or want to be—and the kinds of work they do. To my mind, this is a key issue—and trade-off—all of us need to be aware of in choosing a place to live and work.

While the Place and Happiness Survey found that factors like housing affordability, traffic, and public transportation play a smaller role in community satisfaction in the United States, they play a significant role in global cities. Manchin's European survey found housing affordability to be a huge concern. He asked respondents if it is "easy to find good housing at a reasonable price." The answers ranged from a high of just 12 percent who "strongly agreed" in Berlin to a low of 1 percent in three cities—Rome, Helsinki, and Paris. In between were Madrid at 7 percent, London and Barcelona at 5 percent, Dublin at 3 percent, and Stockholm at 2 percent.

The Veolia survey asked residents in fourteen global cities what they most disliked about their city. Topping the list was "traffic jams," cited by nearly half of respondents. On the flip side, "ease of getting around" was the top-ranked factor, named by 36 percent of respondents, when asked what they like most about their city.

Open City

> Montreal is where I call home. If you are looking to live in a place where you can pretty much walk around naked with a cat as a loincloth and not have anyone give a crap, then it is here. Live and let live. You don't have to have cash, or status or title, just live your life how you see fit. I think the poorer economy and loss of the more traditional finance and business sectors in the quiet revolution set up a less ambitious and less traditional value system—the conditions and values for a very laissez-faire and by Canadian standards chaotic lifestyle. For anyone who has ever spent any significant time here, there is no argument, this is a very distinct thing. I feel lucky to be a part of it.

That's what a reader of my blog wrote to me when I asked for explanations of why we pick the places we do.

Gwenn Seemel was born in France and traveled widely before finally settling in Portland. "I dress colorfully," says Seemel, "and by that I mean both brightly and strangely. I wear plastic clogs in lime or teal. My sweaters are ordered from old lady catalogs because I can't find that particular shade of ultramarine anywhere else. My scarves and hats are mostly knitted by my failing grandmother, so that a would-be pointy Peruvian hat becomes a crocheted head condom with dog ears. My denim pants aren't blue, but instead paint-dyed to go from yellow at my hips to magenta at the cuffs."

When she's in Paris, Seemel says, "people stare at those pants, sneer, and make some snide comment to their companions—

and they do so audibly because someone dressed like me couldn't possibly be French. Except that I am French. My cousins there refuse to take me clubbing unless they've approved my wardrobe beforehand." New Yorkers are more polite, but hardly encouraging of her eccentric wardrobe. One of her New York friends told her that he'd only ever seen such a combination of colors once before—on a homeless man.

But in Portland, Seemel feels totally at ease with her unique style. "People look at my pants and their gaze travels up the rest of my body to my face, where they make eye contact with me. They smile at me and then laugh with me. Some even say 'nice pants.'"

This kind of openness has been a powerful draw for Portland, putting it on the map as an indie-rock Mecca, according to Taylor Clark.[11] "Sonically," Clark writes, "there's not a whole lot that the twisty pop of the Shins has in common with the 'hyperliterate prog-rock' (to borrow a phrase from Stephen Colbert) of the Decemberists. And virtually none of these groups can be considered 'Portland bands' since, with very few exceptions, they all moved to town after gaining some level of fame. They all just kind of live here. Which is why it's often quipped that Portland is the place where hipsters go to retire."

This last line is particularly telling. There must be something about Portland that inspires musicians to move there. Clark concludes that the most plausible explanation for the city's influx of rockers is the same one that draws people like Gwenn Seemel—its openness and creative vibe, its affordable real estate and aesthetic character. "You can venture into public dressed like a convicted sex offender or a homeless person, and no one looks at you askew," Clark writes. "It's lush and green. Housing is affordable, especially compared with Seattle or San Francisco. The people are nice. The food is good. Creativity is the highest law. . . . It might not be enough to lure the glitterati, but Portland's combination of affordability, natural beauty, and laid-back weirdness is an independent artist's dream."

Diversity extends beyond attire, ethnicity, and even sexual orientation, and involves social inclusion. Erin Lynch found hyperexpensive London to be different and better on that score than North America.

> There is a great "vibe" or energy in London. I love feeling like the world is at my doorstep. I felt that anything I could possibly want to do was available in London. I also felt like London was this great mix of interesting people. All walks of life came together to live there in a way that made the city feel alive and creative, almost artistic, whether or not you were directly involved with the arts. I have also felt that this might be due to the way London is organized. There are many council flats (government subsidized housing) all over London. The best neighborhoods will have council flats in them. This mixes everyone up a bit more, instead of having people confined to certain areas.

Openness—a communal sense of tolerance and acceptance of diversity—is the third-ranked factor in the Place and Happiness Survey. The survey probed openness through the following questions: "How would you rate your city or area as a place to live for the following kinds of people?":

- Families with children
- Racial and ethnic minorities
- Gay and lesbian people
- Immigrants from other countries
- Senior citizens

- People living below poverty
- Young, single people
- Recent college graduates looking for work

When communities showed tolerance to these groups, the overall happiness in the community increased. Twenty-three percent of the respondents to the Veolia urban lifestyles survey reported "diversity of the population" to be among the factors they liked most about their city.

This is not because we value diversity in the abstract. Many people are drawn to open communities on the assumption that they can be themselves there. This conforms to the research of Ronald Inglehart, whose detailed World Values Survey of more than fifty countries has found the value of individual expression to be a defining element of today's society.[12]

In this regard the Place and Happiness Survey generated another surprising finding. When people rated their city's openness to various groups, guess which group came in at the bottom of the list? Not immigrants. Not racial or religious minorities. Not gays and lesbians. At the very bottom of the list, alongside "people living below the poverty line," are recent college graduates looking to enter the job market. That's right. Educated young people looking for work. Nearly 45 percent of survey respondents said that their communities were either "bad" or "very bad" places for recent college graduates, while just 7.3 percent said they were "very good."

I find this amazing. All around the country and around the world, I hear community leaders, mothers and fathers worried about losing their young people. When I lived in Pittsburgh, people often bemoaned the fact that the region's biggest export was no longer steel but its talented youngsters. Mayors and chambers of commerce are all too eager to recruit them back after they have spent some time away, getting some skills or sowing their oats, and are ready to settle down and raise a family.

There are several reasons for this seemingly bizarre finding. Young college graduates bring new skills into the job market, which can make current workers nervous. They're single, stay up late, and like to have fun. To some people, that means noise and mischief. To others, it means changes in the status quo. That kind of mindset can easily be detected by young people. I heard this in the focus groups I conducted with graduating college seniors and graduate students in the early 2000s. And it's echoed in detailed studies by consultants Rebecca Ryan, Carol Coletta, and Joe Cortright, whose focus groups and interviews similarly find that young college graduates look for communities that will accept them for who they are. They look for lots of other young people, signals of casual dress and energetic lifestyles, and, importantly, a diverse population that includes gays and lesbians.

Openness is a key factor in community satisfaction and in overall happiness, but unfortunately, many communities aren't experiencing much of either. Many survey respondents reported significant obstacles facing some of these groups.

Nearly 45 percent of survey respondents said that their communities were "bad" or "very bad" places for gays and lesbians. Some 40 percent said the same about immigrants. And more than half said that their communities were "bad" or "very bad" places for people living in poverty.

Manchin's European survey asked respondents whether or not their city "is a good place for residents of EU countries." Dublin topped the list with 45 percent of respondents saying so, with London second (39 percent), falling off to about 30 percent in Barcelona (31 percent), Madrid (28 percent), and Helsinki

(29 percent); and about 20 percent in Rome (23 percent) and Berlin (22 percent).

The survey also asked to what extent "foreigners are well integrated." Dublin again topped the list, though with less than 1 in 5 respondents (18 percent) saying so, and London with 14 percent. In Madrid, Barcelona, and Rome, roughly 1 in 10 residents said their city was doing well at integrating immigrants, a figure which drops to 6 percent or less in Helsinki (6 percent), Paris (4 percent), Berlin (4 percent), and Stockholm (3 percent).

Clearly, cities around the world need improvement in regard to openness and diversity. It's not just about tolerance for its own sake. As my earlier research has shown, intolerant places do not grow. And as the Place and Happiness Survey confirms, residents of intolerant places are less happy and less fulfilled than those in tolerant and open-minded ones.

Safe and Secure

Economic and physical security is the fourth dimension we examined; it includes the overall condition and direction of the economy, the nature and direction of the job market, and social conditions such as general safety. These are deep-seated characteristics that cannot be altered easily or quickly, and are not amenable to direct public or private action. Economic and physical security play an important role in community satisfaction, according to the survey findings, and are only slightly less influential than openness.

Being physically secure and safe from crime is key, especially in large urban centers. A large share of respondents to the Place and Happiness Survey, 57 percent, reported feeling safe or very safe in their communities, while only 9.1 percent reported feeling very unsafe in their communities. But while 20 percent of respondents to the Veolia urban lifestyle survey reported personal and property safety to be among the things they like most in their city; nearly a quarter (24 percent) said a "lack of safety" was among the things they most disliked about their city. And safety was ranked first when survey respondents were asked about the key priorities for encouraging "future generations to stay in the city." Geneva, Oslo, Stockholm, Sydney, Copenhagen, Melbourne, Montreal, Helsinki, Vancouver, and Brussels rate as the world's safest cities, according to the Anholt City Brands Index (Figure 10.5).

Economic security also matters to community happiness. Overall, more respondents to the Place and Happiness Survey reported that economic conditions were good than bad—40 percent said good or very good, while 29 percent rated them bad or very bad; the other 40 percent fell somewhere in between. Nearly a quarter of the respondents to the Veolia urban lifestyle survey reported "economic dynamism" to be among the things they like most in their city.

In his book *The Moral Consequences of Economic Growth,* Harvard economist Benjamin Friedman shows how economic growth makes people more conscientious, less likely to commit crimes, more tolerant, and more generous.[13] Increased levels of happiness are also a by-product of such growth, while prolonged economic stagnation or decline can lead to the reverse.

Leaders or Squelchers

Leadership is one of society's great intangible goods. Countless books have been written on the subject, but it remains hard to distill exactly what defines good leadership, how to

FIGURE 10.5. PERCEPTION OF SAFETY IN GLOBAL CITIES

Geneva	1	Bangkok	51
Oslo	2	Moscow	52
Stockholm	3	Mumbai	53
Sydney	4	Lagos	54
Copenhagen	5	Rio de Janeiro	55
Melbourne	6	Cairo	56
Montreal	7	Manila	57
Helsinki	8	Mexico City	58
Vancouver	9	Nairobi	59
Brussels	10	Jerusalem	60

Note: Respondents were asked: "How safe would you feel in the city?"

Source: Anholt City Brands Index, 2nd ed., 2006.

fully distinguish it from bad leadership, and how to accurately gauge its effect on organizations, nations, and communities.

The Place and Happiness Survey probed the effects of leadership on general community happiness by asking residents for their approval ratings of the local leadership in their area. The correlation between leadership and community happiness, while significant, was on average the lowest of the five major categories.

Not surprisingly, the survey findings indicate that people are happier in cities with positive and forward-looking leaders and an emphasis on ethics and integrity. But the survey also found a sizable split in resident perceptions of leadership. While 60 percent of the survey respondents approved of the leadership in their communities, a staggering 40 percent disapproved. This may well reflect the partisan nature of today's society, in which voters appear to be more polarized than ever before.

Jane Jacobs once told me that communities everywhere are filled with creative vigor, but some of them are run by squelchers. Squelchers are control freaks who think they know what's best for their city or region, even as their leadership (or lack thereof) causes a hemorrhage of bright, talented, and creative people. Squelchers, she said, are leaders who use the word "no" a lot and constantly block community energy and initiatives. I've seen firsthand how these squelchers drain the life and energy from their communities. They respond to new ideas with phrases like "That's not how we do things here"; "That will never fly"; or "Why don't you just move someplace you'll be happy?"

I often wonder what our world would look like if all the squelchers in our communities were to be suddenly—and magically—exposed and immobilized. Perhaps then we could finally unleash the positive energy that real civic engagement both inspires and needs.

Smart, Safe, and Green

My friend and colleague, the Dutch urban planner Evert Verhagen, likes to tell communities there is a new formula for success in today's world. Where it was once enough to be "safe and smart," prosperous communities today need to be "smart, safe, and green." I'd add "fair" to his list.

John Trenouth says it's the combination of natural beauty and diversity that makes Vancouver a great fit for him and his partner.

> Between us, we've lived in twelve cities and five countries, so we've experienced a lot. We knew what we wanted and what we didn't want. Recently we left Southern California to settle back in Vancouver. Physically, Vancouver is stunning. Mountains, ocean, beaches, even rain forests are all within the city itself. The air is clean and smells of evergreen.

Downtown is rich and dense. You don't really need a car. In a short walk you can go from seedy urban underbelly, to a vibrant Chinatown that's not just for tourists, to towering skyscrapers filled with suits, to hip high-rise lofts filled with yuppies in yoga pants, to intimate old tree-lined residences and cozy hangouts. The streets hum with people—lots of different people. Chinese, Indian, Persian, Russian, Australian, and British faces and accents all mix together on the streets. Many are second or third generation. Many carry their original cultural identity along with little bits of each other's. Yet all seem to have a certain unmistakable Canadian flavor.

This racial and cultural confluence means that there are also many people of mixed race. My girlfriend is half Chinese. One of her favorite things about Vancouver is that it's one of the only places she sees faces like hers. But it's not just the face, it's the recognition that these people share the experience of growing up in the friction between two very different cultures.

Great places do many things well. Our analysis of the Place and Happiness Survey identifies seven factors that are critical to community satisfaction: a good place to raise children, a good place to meet people and make friends, a place with physical beauty, good schools, parks and open space, a safe place, and a good place for entrepreneurs and new businesses.

These factors are additionally confirmed by a statistical factor analysis that Tinagli conducted on all twenty-six dimensions of community satisfaction in the Place and Happiness Survey. Her analysis identified three clusters of factors that are key to our being happy in our communities.

The first cluster includes things that make a community smart and vibrant—local universities and colleges, arts and culture, vibrant nightlife, job opportunities in one's field, opportunities to meet people, and opportunities for young college grads, singles, entrepreneurs, artists, and scientists. The second revolves around aesthetics and livability and comprises physical beauty; parks, open space, playgrounds, and trails; climate and air quality. The third boils down to equity and includes affordable housing, manageable traffic patterns, and living opportunities for senior citizens and the poor.

We've come to expect our communities to meet our basic needs as a matter of course. We take for granted that our tap water flows when we turn the handle, our trash will be picked up when we put it on the curb. Most of us feel safe when we're walking down the street, and confident that our kids are receiving a good education.

But for better or worse, the bar has been raised. To be truly fulfilled and happy, we want and need more. And at the top of the list are two additional needs: aesthetics and openness. And they are needs, not just "frills." They are what we've come to expect from our communities.

That's what residents of New Orleans told us when they responded to the first version of the Place and Happiness Survey implemented just before Hurricane Katrina struck. At the top of their list was the "beauty and physical setting of the city" and the "availability of parks and green space." Churches and religious institutions also proved to be especially critical in the Big Easy. Sixty-one percent of New Orleanians said they spend time in worship, prayer, or meditation every day, and an astounding 56 percent said they had attended church in the past seven days—a higher frequency than in any other city surveyed. Second to churches and religious institutions, residents felt the "quality of colleges and universities" was their most important consideration.

New Orleans is known for its quixotic mixture of decadence, southern charm, and innocence, all reflected in the city's nightlife, one of the Big Easy's most important assets. Although there is more to New Orleans than Bourbon Street, these cauldrons of musical innovation, joyful celebration, and community allow people to be themselves and—alongside the neighborhood churches—play a critical role in weaving the intricate fabric of "third places" outside of work and home where people meet, congregate, and connect.

As I write this, the city is still far from recovery. Rebuilding one of our country's most unique and historic cities is no easy task. But the Place and Happiness Survey—which clearly shows what New Orleanians value most (and now likely miss) about their city—should give urban planners an idea of where to start. In their haste to focus on buildings and infrastructure—reinforcing the levees, rebuilding the central business district, and constructing housing—public and private leaders so far have virtually ignored the critical social infrastructure of New Orleans, which is the key to bringing residents back. As a conduit to the myriad of other jazz clubs, neighborhood bars, and taverns, and as a major source of tourism income, the French Quarter is part of this infrastructure. But it's not the whole story. New Orleanians want and need to connect with each other through core neighborhood institutions—churches, taverns, bars, parks, and schools. They want their personal lives and community relationships back.

Places that rank high in aesthetics and openness level the playing field for all their residents, even in a city like New Orleans, which is divided along racial and socioeconomic lines.

The aesthetics of a place—its physical beauty and natural amenities—are public goods that we can all use and enjoy. A great park is open to every social and demographic category—white, black, Asian, and Hispanic; single and married, gay and straight; rich and poor. As long as there is room, my using the park does not exclude you from using it too. In most cases, the park gets better, safer, and more exciting when more runners, cyclists, roller-bladers, strollers, dog walkers, young parents with children, picnickers, and volleyball players of every sort and persuasion congregate together.

Places that are open let us freely express ourselves and be part of a bigger picture, a larger whole. They provide us with the space necessary for personal discovery and self-actualization—for realizing our potential and dreams, for building and raising the family we truly desire. They enable us to be part of a whole and to be ourselves, adding real meaning and fulfillment to our lives.

These survey findings are meant to be guides to what dimensions of a place make the greatest positive impact on an average resident's happiness. But as our same findings illustrate, not all people want the same thing out of their community, nor do they desire the same things at every stage of life. Ultimately, being happy with one's place comes down to figuring out what best complements one's lifestyle and core values. But that's what makes this interesting. Otherwise we'd all find ourselves competing for space in the same massive city.

11

CITIES HAVE PERSONALITIES TOO

―――――――

IT IS ALL WELL AND GOOD TO KNOW THAT PLACE AFFECTS happiness, that the happiest communities tend to be open-minded, vibrant places where people feel free to express themselves and cultivate their identities, and that these communities tend to foster creativity. But fulfilling the first part of the equation—actually finding a place that makes us happy—is not always so simple.

The key to finding our happy place largely depends on identifying what it is we most want out of it. As the old adage goes, "different strokes for different folks." Not all people want or need the same things. Knowing what matters most to you—what your priorities and needs are—is a key part of the battle.

The play between our psychological wants and needs and what our community can offer is what I call *fit*.[1] My wife, Rana, who writes a syndicated relationship advice column with her three sisters, compares the search for a place of one's own to

finding the right mate. She says you have to look inward and figure out what makes you tick in order to choose a place that will
allow you to grow and develop. And remember, if it turns out
that you aren't happy, there's no shame in moving on.

A young graduate assistant compares relocating to dating.
She's already moved plenty of times in her young life, and has
had different relationships with each place. She hasn't ever
committed to one location; instead, she's dated a few that
seemed to fit at various stages of her life. There is one special
city she's gotten to know pretty well. She lived there in graduate
school and thinks it might be her true love. But for now, she's
thousands of miles away and enjoying where she is.

But for many people, the fit isn't right. According to the Place
and Happiness Survey:

- About two-thirds (67 percent) of people are happy with
  where they live, rating their community satisfaction a 4
  or 5 on a 5-point scale.
- That leaves more than a third of respondents who are
  ambivalent (24 percent rated their communities 3 out of
  5) or unhappy (10 percent gave their communities a 1 or
  2 out of 5).
- When asked how they think their communities will fare
  in five years, 43 percent said they are either ambivalent
  (26 percent gave their communities a 3 out of 5) or
  pessimistic (14 percent gave their communities just 1 or
  2 out of 5).
- And when asked if they would recommend their
  community to a relative or friend, 40 percent responded
  ambivalently (21 percent rated their communities 3 out
  of 5) or negatively (17 percent gave their communities 1
  or 2 out of 5).

Think for a minute about what happens if we pick the wrong place—perhaps this has happened to you or someone you know. As with the wrong job or the wrong life partner, the fallout can be profound and depressing. It takes a lot less time and effort to recognize a potential poor fit up front than to move again later.

One person I interviewed said that after moving his family to a new city, he immediately sensed it was wrong. He found it hard to resonate with people there. His neighbors were nice enough and about the same age. That wasn't the problem. They just didn't share his attitudes and values, likes and dislikes. The place just didn't feel right. He began to feel negative and angry. Nothing about his environment—despite the nice house and good job—really excited him. He analogized it to feeling like a visitor in his own skin. It took him a while to put it together, but ultimately he realized that he was not somewhere he felt free to be himself and realize his dreams.

He's not the only one. I've heard similar stories from many other people. First they tell me they start getting negative or even angry at their community. They may not even realize the reason for their mood swings, or they think it comes from something else. Eventually they begin to realize that for some reason they don't really fit in where they live. Being in the wrong place is a theme that appears in the greatest literature and slapstick entertainment—mined for comedy and terror and everything in between.

The Big Five

The question of psychological fit plays a big role in our place happiness. After writing *Rise of the Creative Class*, I began to suspect that in addition to the more conventional economic and sociological factors behind our decisions, there may also be psychological ones. My interest was piqued in the spring of 2006, when Will Wilkinson, policy analyst at the Cato Institute and managing editor of its online monthly magazine, asked me about it after reading an early draft of my book.[2] He wanted to know if I had ever considered how different kinds of personalities might be attracted to and thrive in different kinds of places. Is there a fit between individual personality and community? Are people happier when they find a community that fits them? What happens when someone's personality is different from that of his or her community?

Psychologists say that there are five basic dimensions to personality.[3] The first type is openness to experience. Open types have a tendency to enjoy new experiences, especially intellectual experiences, the arts, fantasies, and anything that exposes them to new ideas. People high in openness tend to be curious, artistic, and creative.

The second type is conscientiousness. Conscientious types work hard and have a great deal of self-discipline. They are responsible and detail oriented, and they strive for achievement. Psychologists find that people high in conscientiousness tend to be better than average workers on almost any job, completing tasks competently and efficiently. The third type is extroversion. Extroverts are outgoing, talkative, gregarious, assertive, enthusiastic, and excitement seeking. They enjoy meeting new people and tend to maintain a fairly stable, positive mood under most circumstances.

The fourth type is agreeableness. Agreeable types are warm, friendly, compassionate, and concerned for the welfare of others. They generally trust other people and expect other people to trust them.

The fifth type is neuroticism. Neurotic types are emotionally unstable, more likely to experience anxiety, hostility, depression, self-consciousness, and impulsiveness.

While it is tempting to think of people as one or another—we all know people who are extroverts and others who are introverts—most people fall somewhere along a spectrum. And while most people have dominant types, everyone possesses some level of each of the five traits. A psychologist might describe Woody Allen as low in extroversion (he seems quiet and reserved), low in agreeableness (aloof and distant), somewhat conscientious (he gets his movies made), high in neuroticism (he's self-absorbed and nervous), but very high in openness to experience. After all, he's a creative, innovative, and artistic filmmaker.

Personality psychologists have empirically verified the five-factor model in scores of research studies, and have found that its five basic traits are rooted in biology, are stable over time, and are consistent across cultures. Psychologists who specialize in business and organizations have examined the links between personality type and work. For example, extroverts are found to perform better in sales jobs. Agreeable types do best in jobs that require teamwork. Conscientious types excel at jobs that call for standard tasks. People who are open to experience perform well in creative endeavors and jobs that require flexibility and innovation.

But research on the relationship between people's personalities and their home or work environments hasn't examined the relationship between personality type and the places people choose to live. I felt so inspired by the idea of connecting place and personality that when I was invited to deliver the keynote speech to the Gallup International positive psychology summit in fall 2006, I decided to center my remarks around it. At the conference I felt somewhat out of my element. After all, what did I know about psychology? So I attempted to make light of my being an outsider. I noted that many of the people I had interviewed for my research said they were drawn to places with "energy."

"At first," I said, "I didn't know what to make of this. Bear in mind, when we economists talk about 'energy,' we're usually referring to a physical resource." Could it be, I joked, "that all of those people were simply attracted to places with low gas and electric prices?"

Over time, I explained, I began to understand what they meant. My colleagues and interviewees were talking about energy in a psychological sense. They were describing places with vibrant rhythms, lots going on, and other high-energy people.

Fortunately the joke worked.

I knew my lecture had been a modest hit when afterward, three of the leading positive psychologists in the world—Martin Seligman of the University of Pennsylvania, Christopher Peterson of the University of Michigan, and Mihaly Csikszentmihalyi, the leading authority on the psychology of creativity—approached me and asked if we could all get together.

At the meeting, Seligman zeroed in on the notion of energy. Energy, he explained, is a concept that cuts across biology, physics, and chemistry, and is evident in everything from brain scans to heart rate monitors. "The human body is an energy system, and indeed life itself is based on energy processes, insofar as living things must constantly consume and burn energy."

Think about this stunning fact, he continued. The human brain constitutes only 2 percent of the human body mass, but typically consumes about 20 percent of its total calories. "A good day," he told me, "starts with high energy, positive feelings, and an excited mood. Bad days are marked by low energy and the sluggish, discouraged, and overwhelmed feeling that it brings."

If you want to find places of energy, particularly high-level creative energy, Csikszentmihalyi chimed in, look for concentrations of people who exhibit high levels of curiosity—a point I will return to later in this chapter.

Then Seligman added a clincher: "Biographies of great achievers often note their subjects' remarkable levels of energy, far more crucial to their success than any raw ability."

I asked them, What about place? We know that periods of high achievement, creativity, and innovation have tended to occur in certain cities. Is it possible that these cities have been able to attract and energize certain types of personalities?

We agreed to look into this. Seligman and Peterson offered me full access to detailed data drawn from hundreds of thousands of responses to their Values in Action (VIA) personality assessments.[4] Because each entry included the respondent's address and zip code, it could be used to look for a significant correlation between place and personality.

Around the same time, I came across a blog post about a study on the connection between musical taste and personality. The study was by Sam Gosling, a psychologist at the University of Texas who had become famous for his work on animal personalities, and Jason Rentfrow, a young psychologist at Cambridge University.

Perusing Gosling's website, I was captivated by their studies of personality. Gosling and Rentfrow found that they could identify basic personality types simply by asking people what kind of music they like, or by observing the arrangement and decoration of their dorm rooms or offices. Their findings were intuitive, and they were borne out by the data. How we decorate our homes and offices, which books we buy, the CDs we own, the movies we watch, the clothes we wear, the way we arrange our personal space—none of this is random. We base these decisions on who we are, who we want to be, and how we want to be perceived.

Intrigued, I shot off a note to Gosling asking if he knew of anyone who might have undertaken similar work on the relationship between personality and location. Are certain kinds of personalities more likely to move than others? Could it be that cities and regions take on collective personalities of their own, which over time attract certain kinds of people?

Gosling responded within minutes. He and Rentfrow were already knee-deep in such a project. Their initial study, entitled "The Geography of Personality," examines the geographic clustering of basic personality traits.[5] Surveying past literature, they note a long-standing interest in cross-cultural personality differences that dates back to the pioneering anthropological studies of Margaret Mead and Ruth Benedict in the early twentieth century.[6]

Since then, the emergence of modern personality studies and the five-factor model of personality have reignited interest in and research on the geography of personality. A 1973 study found that people living in the northeastern, midwestern, and West Coast regions of the United States had significantly higher "creative productivity"—characterized by high levels of creativity, imagination, intelligence, and unconventionality—than those in other regions.[7]

Drawing on this study and others, Rentfrow and Gosling utilized a large database of personality traits from Internet surveys of more than half a million people to explore the distribution and clustering of personality by state.[8] Their results confirmed that certain states are high on openness, others on agreeableness, others on neuroticism, and so on. These personality dimensions are also associated with key social and economic outcomes. Openness to experience, for example, was highest in the northeastern and West Coast states and was related to the proportion of artists and entertainers working in a state, percentages of votes cast for liberal candidates in presidential elections, support for same-sex marriage, and patent production.

Rentfrow and I met in Washington, D.C., in the spring of 2007 and decided to combine forces. His research with Gosling identified a connection between place and personality at the state level. Our hunch was that people tend to sort and cluster in specific regions, communities, and neighborhoods.

What Color Is My City?

Since those who completed the personality survey also provided their zip code, we were able to link a personality to a location. Thus we could generate maps from the hundreds of thousands of individual personality profiles across the United States. The first set of maps, generated by my colleague Kevin Stolarick, covers all the zip codes in the United States with thirty or more responses. There is one for each of the five major personality types (Figure 11.1).

The patterns in these maps are striking. Each of the five personality types shows up in distinct locations. As the maps show, four of the personality types are regionally clustered. But open personalities are spread out across the Northeast, southern Florida, and the West Coast, indicating that open people are most likely to reside in large urban areas. They are likely to seek out and cluster in specific regions that offer new and exciting experiences. Conversely, conscientious and agreeable types, who are less adventuresome and tied more closely to traditional relationships, will tend to spread out from their existing locations.

For this new, global edition of the book, my team and I combed through individual personality data for more than one hundred global cities, charting the personality clusters for all locations with thirty or more responses. Figure 11.2 maps personality types for more than one hundred cities worldwide.

FIGURE 11.1. PERSONALITY MAPS

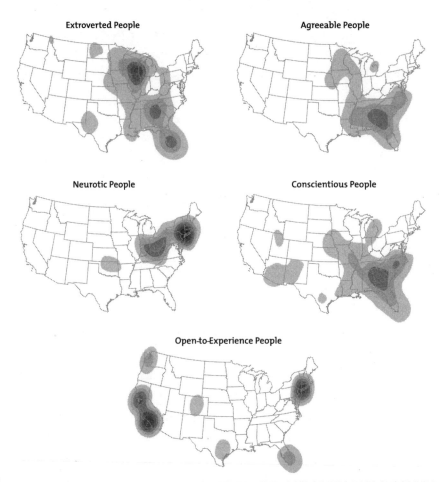

SOURCE: DATA FROM JASON RENTFROW AND SAM GOSLING;
ANALYSIS BY KEVIN STOLARICK; MAP BY RYAN MORRIS

- Copenhagen tops the list on conscientiousness, with Dublin, Vancouver, and Sydney all showing above average concentrations of conscientious personalities.
- Vancouver and Dublin score highest on agreeableness with Bangkok, Antwerp, Utrecht, Kulala Lumpur, Toronto, and Manila showing high concentrations of agreeable personalities.
- Antwerp and Utrecht top the list for extroverts, with Vienna, Dublin, Madrid, Melbourne, and Vancouver also showing above average concentrations. On the flip side, Hong Kong, Manila, Toronto, Kuala Lumpur, Brisbane, Valparaiso, Bangkok, Flanders, New York City, and Montreal appear to be more introverted places.
- Buenos Aires, Flanders, Singapore, Valparaiso, Beirut, Vienna, Manila, and Hong Kong top the list of neurotic places, outdoing even New York City, with Perth and Montreal not far behind. Conversely, Dublin, Adelaide, Utrecht, Vancouver, Melbourne, Copenhagen, Bangkok, and Sydney appear to have higher concentrations of emotionally stable personalities.
- Madrid, Copenhagen, Montreal, and Buenos Aires top the list of open-to-experience locations, all of which rank ahead of New York City and Los Angeles. Utrecht, Vancouver, and Toronto also have relatively high concentrations of open types.

Obviously regions aren't made up of just one personality type but are home to millions of people with different combinations of personality traits. Thus if Woody Allen, as a prototypical New Yorker, is low in some traits and high in others, wouldn't New York City follow suit too? In addition to having a large concentration of open-to-experience personality types, what combination of personality traits define its overall regional personality?

188

FIGURE 11.2. GLOBAL PERSONALITY

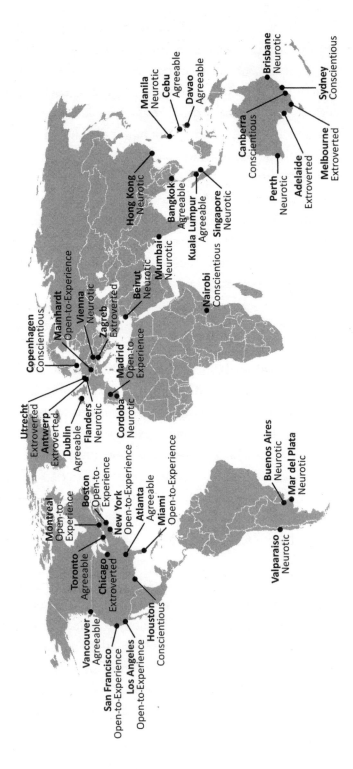

SOURCE: JASON RENTFROW AND KEVIN STOLARICK. MAP BY PAULO RAPOSO

How does New York's or London's personality differ from that of smaller cities? Are there specific configurations of regional personality types that we can identify? If so, can we develop a way to match people to the regions that best fit their psychological profiles?

To get at this, Stolarick undertook factor analysis—a powerful statistical matching technique—on the hundreds of thousands of data points in the personality survey to identify the main clusters of regional personality types across the United States. His analysis found that all U.S. metropolitan regions break down into three main categories.

The first cluster I call outgoing regions. Scoring high in extroversion, regions in this cluster are low in neuroticism, conscientiousness, openness, and very low in agreeableness.

Outgoing regions, Rentfrow comments, would likely be a good fit for people who are sociable and outgoing, like group activities and functions, play team sports, and like to be around other people. They are unlikely to appeal to people who prefer very close ties or community involvement, as those preferences are more common among highly agreeable individuals, or to those who need multiple options or enjoy trying new things, which are preferences more common among people high in openness.

The second cluster I call conventional or dutiful regions. Regions in this cluster score high on agreeableness and conscientiousness as well as extroversion, but low in openness and neuroticism.

Dutiful regions, Rentfrow suggests, would be a good fit for people who are hardworking, friendly, trusting, helpful, and compassionate. In some respects, these regions seem perfect for model citizens. They are places for people who want to fit in and are more conventional or traditional in their outlook and values; those who value the status quo, obey the rules, and don't typically step out of line. They are places where people trust one another, tend not to challenge authority or each other, are diligent at work and in life, and do what is expected of them. If outgoing regions are good places for people who like to socialize with lots of people, people in dutiful regions prefer to socialize with a relatively small number of close friends and family. Dutiful regions will be a poor fit for those who are artistic and creative and constantly try out new and different things.

Experiential regions form the third cluster. Places in this cluster score highly on openness and neuroticism, but low in conscientiousness, extroversion, and agreeableness. Experiential regions are a good fit for people who do not need to be around other people, question authority, and quest after intense experiences—intellectually, creatively, emotionally, and even physiologically. What's interesting about this cluster, Rentfrow suggests, is that such regions are likely to be a good fit for people who are creative but perhaps also lost in their own world, socially isolated, aloof, even cantankerous, or thrive on stress, anxiety, and instability. Experiential regions are a poor fit for people who like to meet new people and make friends easily, have conventional values, are status quo oriented, and prefer to work in stable jobs and on standard tasks.

Regions, like people, have distinct personalities. While opposites sometimes attract and unusual matches can work, most people will feel happier and more fulfilled in regions that match their personalities. Since Rentfrow's data included questions on happiness and well-being, we were able to examine the connection between personality, place, and happiness. Were people happier in places with higher concentrations of personality types like themselves? Yes. Given the psychological forces at work behind individual migration patterns, people will benefit from keeping such geographic personality clusters in mind when contemplating where to live.

Of course, it is always possible to seek out a well-suited neighborhood, even in a region that does not perfectly mirror your tastes and preferences. And some people can and do thrive in places where they are outside the norm, especially those who like to see themselves as unconventional. As Rentfrow explained in an email:

> In a place like Austin, where the norm is to be open and creative, it's not enough to drink coffee and beer, to smoke American Spirit cigarettes, and listen to Miles Davis. If you're truly open and creative, and desire to be seen as such, it's important to demonstrate this by adopting preferences and habits that are not the norm. After all, being creative and innovative means being unconventional. Furthermore, I think that this group of ultra-creatives, in their efforts to portray themselves as such, may acquire preferences that are not only different, but require a certain degree of commitment; things that require repeated exposure before they can be tolerated and appreciated (it's sort of like a rite of passage). The need to be unique may also be an important determinant of relocating.

But what accounts for the clustering of personality types and the emergence of distinct regional personalities? The first thing that crosses my mind, given my background as an economic geographer, is the historical imprint of economic and industrial structure. Agreeable and conscientious personality types are heavily concentrated in old industrial regions, where rule-driven mass production industry took root, or in more traditional regions outside major cities. These industries require agreeable and conscientious people and often orient their hiring accordingly. Extroverted types are concentrated in cities like Chicago and in Dublin or Madrid where lots of sales headquarters and high-level services have located. Open-to-experience types are clustered in larger cities, especially on the coasts or near ports, historically home to diverse economic structures, immigrant populations, and long-standing artistic and bohemian quarters.

While it is admittedly hard to identify what came first—was it an initial concentration of personality types that drew industry or the historical impact of industry structure that shaped and selected for personality?—the overlay between the two is clear. This overlay between personality type and economic structure may pose additional obstacles for older industrial regions. While those regions grew by attracting and mobilizing the agreeable and conscientious personality types that were required to perform standard manufacturing (and in many cases even higher-level service tasks), globalization means that many of those functions have been shifted offshore. Manufacturing has moved to economic centers like Shanghai and other regions in China, and standard services has moved to regions in India, for example.

The status quo orientation and don't-rock-the-boat values of those regions may damp down creativity and innovation in those regions as well as encourage an out migration of the open types who tend to be the source of new creative energy and innovation. Thus the longer-run issues facing these regions may have as much to do with their psychological makeup, or what Rentfrow calls their "psychosocial environment," as their business climate and economic structure.

There are several other reasons why personalities might cluster. The first of these, as Rentfrow and Gosling explain, has to do with the physical environment. It is widely acknowledged that physical environments shape cultures and societies. In his book *Guns, Germs, and Steel*, Jared Diamond points out the physical attributes that shaped the propulsive growth of northern Europe. Jeffrey Sachs, director of the Earth Institute at Columbia University, has shown that coastal locations have consistently higher rates of economic growth than those inland.[9]

Rentfrow and Gosling argue that physical factors such as climate and environs can similarly affect our personalities. Residents of places with cold climates and dark winters exhibit a higher incidence of seasonal affective disorder, depression, stress, and anxiety. Other studies have found that people who live in warmer climates commonly display more aggressive behavior. Rentfrow's own research has found a positive correlation between neuroticism and average yearly rainfall.

Social factors also come into play. Political scientists and sociologists have long noted the effect of values and culture on work and economic life. Max Weber famously attributed the growth of capitalism to the "Protestant work ethic." Ronald Inglehart's research on more than fifty nations illustrates the relation between places that value individual self-expression and high income and sustained economic growth.[10]

We know that values, beliefs, and attitudes cluster geographically and are sustained over time through social interaction—that's what defines culture. Sooner or later, Rentfrow and Gosling argue, these places (and their inhabitants) will also assume certain personality traits. They refer to these as "social founder effects." That is, people come to acquire personality traits that reflect their practices, lifestyles, and beliefs. Places that tolerate or encourage openness to experience will ultimately attract people who seek environments in which they can feel free to express themselves in whatever way they choose. Even people who are not initially open-minded may, to some extent, internalize some of those values and preferences over time. Eventually large segments of the population may end up embodying these traits.

Another factor is what Rentfrow and Gosling call "selective migration." Geographic differences in personality, they write, "could have emerged as a result of immigrants selectively migrating to places that satisfied and reinforced their psychological and physical needs." According to the theory, these initial groups establish personality traits that are then passed down to subsequent generations—a notion, Rentfrow and Gosling point out, that is supported by ample evidence. Dubbing this "genetic founder effects," they argue that the migration of like-minded people to certain areas may reduce the amount of variation in the gene pool over time, thereby increasing the proportion of people who possess particular traits.

These effects are reinforced by social pressure and social influence. Clearly, certain kinds of personalities are more attracted to certain kinds of places. We seek out places to live that reinforce and reflect aspects of who we are and who we want to become.

Of course, migration may well be psychologically motivated in the first place. It's not necessarily surprising that certain kinds of personalities would be predisposed to being mobile. People who are open, Rentfrow and Gosling write, "may attempt to escape the ennui experienced in small-town environments by relocating to metropolitan areas where their interests in culture and needs for social contact and stimulation are more easily met." People who display high levels of openness to experience are by nature the most adventuresome and mobile. Thus it makes sense that they will flock to places that offer lots of exciting experiences and stimuli and eventually (if unwittingly) cluster around one another. As this process occurs, more conventional regions are gradually drained of open people, which reinforces their nonopen personality types while encouraging more open people to leave.

The need to be challenged, to excel, to be the best, can also play a role. Rentfrow writes:

> The fact that my musician friends who had successful careers in Austin have since moved to NYC and LA is not some random coincidence; those are the places to be if you really want to excel. It's not easy. On the contrary, there you're competing with the professionals. But that's just it. The people I know who moved there were up for that challenge. Austin was no longer a challenging place for them, so they moved to places where they're forced to rise to the occasion.

Rentfrow uses musicians as his example, but the same can be said of investment bankers who are drawn to New York and London, fashion designers to Milan or Paris, or young techies and entrepreneurs who move to Silicon Valley.

The effects of personality on mobility hit me one day as I was addressing the top marketing team at Dewar's. They had read my book *Rise of the Creative Class* and wanted to break the image that all scotch drinkers are sixty years old, affluent, white, and male. They had found that young creative types, whom they dubbed "urban independents," clustered in creative and bohemian neighborhoods that had developed a taste for scotch whiskey. Dewar's began reaching out to their budding clientele, keeping track of their predilections and preferences.

During our meeting, I asked the marketing team a series of questions: Did the scotch drinkers like loud music and live performance? Did they prefer espresso to lattes?

The answers that came back surprised even me. Yes, the team said, these younger scotch drinkers preferred black coffee and espresso, liked loud music, and favored straight whiskey over mixed drinks.

This all hit a chord. Certain personality types seem to require more intense stimulation. They are drawn to extreme experience—complex music, intense tastes, exciting places, and eccentric people. It's not by chance that people with these qualities happen to cluster in highly stimulating places, I thought. They are inclined, if not programmed, to seek them out.

Analyze This

Since personality types cluster geographically, might they also play a role in regional innovation, talent, and economic growth?

Seeing the strong clustering of personality types and learning more about the relationship between psychology and place was causing a subtle but profound shift in my thinking. As an economic geographer, I look at how social and economic factors shape the world. I'd never really been into psychology—never thought about how personal proclivities might affect innovation or economic development. But now it was dawning on me that psychology plays a central role.

For years I had sought to develop better and more refined measures of what economists refer to as human capital or skill. My own measures of the creative class and creative occupations were my attempts to add the kinds of work people do to economists' emphasis on human capital or level of education.

But what if skill is more than education and more than work? Rentfrow suggests that personality involves the capacity to acquire and perform certain tasks competently and effectively. The type of skill economists are interested in, he writes, "implies something that can be acquired with proper training, talent, motivation, and resources." But, he adds, "it's more consistent with personality theory to argue that personality traits predispose people to acquire certain skills. For example, highly conscientious people have a disposition to be detail oriented, plan ahead, or stay organized. Openness influences people's ability to acquire new skills relatively quickly."

Obviously some people are more creative or more ambitious or more motivated than others. What separates Steve Jobs or Bill Gates from most people is not their level of education or even the work they do; it is this something else. What if this something else is rooted in psychology and personality? Any mother will tell you (mine surely did) that her children came out of the womb with their personalities intact. What if personality itself is a key driver in our capacity to seek out new connections, mobilize resources, innovate, and achieve?

For years I've tried to make out why technology-based growth took off around MIT and Stanford but not around Carnegie Mellon, where I taught for nearly twenty years. It's surely not the warm, sunny weather. It seems that there really is something to the old joke: Q: How do you make the next Silicon Valley? A: Take one part great university, add two parts sunshine and three parts venture capital and shake vigorously.

What if Silicon Valley succeeds not just because it is a magnet for highly skilled people but because it attracts those who are also highly motivated, highly ambitious, highly curious, and highly open? The same is true of the people who migrate and succeed in finance in New York or London or in other leading talent centers around the world.

And what about the mobile and the rooted discussed in Chapter 5? For years, I've researched the migration of the young, highly educated, and highly skilled. But what if it's not just educational background, job skills, or financial resources that shape one's tendency to move? What if the people who move have a different personality makeup than those who stay put? What if the means migration discussed in Chapter 6 is more than the movement of the educated and the talented? What if it is the relocation of certain personality types? And what if these are the same types that are most likely to tolerate risk, try new things, create new innovations, and start new businesses?

It began to dawn on me. Perhaps the same types of people who are most likely to move are also the ones most likely to innovate and start new firms. As more and more people leave their place of birth and cluster together, the population concentrations become hotbeds of creative endeavor, innovation, start-up companies, and economic growth. The sorting we are witnessing is not just that of education and skill but also of basic personality types.

To get at the effects of this personality sorting on innovation and economic growth, my research team and I matched our datasets on innovation, human capital, and economic growth to Rentfrow and Gosling's data on personality types and Seligman and Peterson's data on psychological strengths. We then conducted a series of statistical analyses (including a rather advanced set of Bayesian linear estimation techniques) to sort out the relationships between personality, innovation, human capital, the creative class, income, and economic growth. The results were so striking that they shocked us.

First off, we found that the personality variables are indeed capable of explaining a significant portion of the variance in innovation, human capital, income, housing values, and other factors. Of the five personality factors, openness to experience is clearly the most important. It shows consistently significant statistical relationships with each of these factors. But before turning to it, let's take a look at the other four personality types.

Neuroticism is negatively associated with top talent in the form of human capital or the supercreative class. In more advanced models, it also turns out to be negatively associated with the creative class, high-tech industry, and wages. In other words, regions with high concentrations of highly educated and ultracreative individuals tend to be more emotionally stable, less volatile, and more resilient. This suggests, among other things, that these are places where people may be more likely to take risks because they're less concerned about failure.

Agreeableness is associated with jobs in management and health care. Although it is positively associated with innovation, high-tech industry, wages, and income in our more advanced models, the effects are quite small. This could mean that the ability to work well with others contributes, albeit slightly, to innovation. Extroversion is significantly correlated with management and sales jobs, but it too has no effect on human capital overall, high-tech jobs, or regional income.

Conscientiousness is an important characteristic to success in many fields and industries. A management consultant I know likes to say that for every open and creative person who comes up with a new idea, a company needs ten or twenty conscientious ones to carry it out. Psychologists have found that entrepreneurs possess a mixture of openness and conscientiousness, particularly stick-to-itiveness—the ability to persevere in the face of adversity. But as our statistical results show, conscientiousness is not a big factor in regional growth. In fact, it turned out to be negatively associated with innovation, wages and income, and housing values. Then again, as Rentfrow suggested, conscientious individuals tend to be rule followers; give them a clearly defined task and they will develop the most efficient procedure for completing it. But when the task is not clearly defined and requires creative thought, someone who is highly conscientious but not very open will struggle to create something original. The way I see it, conscientiousness alone is not enough to power regional growth. However, it may play a role in combination with other factors, say, in places where conscientious personalities mix with open ones.

Openness to experience is the only personality type that plays a consistent role in regional economic development. It is highly correlated with jobs in computing, science, arts, design, and entertainment; with overall human capital levels, high-tech industry, income, and housing values.

And when we ran Rentfrow and Gosling's personality measures against Seligman and Peterson's strengths inventory, it turned out that openness is correlated with two particular factors. One is beauty, which helps to explain the strong pull of aesthetic factors we saw in Chapter 10. The other is curiosity—the factor Csikszentmihalyi initially told me would be the best possible predictor for concentrations of creative people and creative energy. Peterson's independent analysis of his strengths data and my own creativity measures found a direct relationship between character strengths—such as appreciation of beauty, creativity, curiosity, and a love of learning—and creativity index for cities.[11] However, Peterson found a negative relationship between creative cities and strengths that connect people to one another—such as modesty, gratitude, spirituality, teamwork, kindness, and fairness. Creative cities may have higher concentrations of people whose basic personality makeup is doing their own thing. This jibes with my research team's findings which show that regional creativity and innovation are related to diversity and openness, but not to social capital of the sort Robert Putnam has written about. Putnam's most recent research has also found that diversity hinders social capital.[12] This is troubling news for our sense of community and social cohesion. The very strengths that make places diverse and creative seem to damage our social capital and community commitment.

The role of personality in regional economic development became even clearer when we ran more advanced statistical tests. Openness to experience had the biggest positive coefficient estimate in every case and was involved in at least eight of the ten top models for every variable. Furthermore, it was the only variable to be positive and statistically significant in every equation.

Out of sixty top models generated, openness was a factor in more than fifty.

But the strongest results by far were those that looked at my Gay and Bohemian Indexes and openness to experience—literally off the chart. The finding for openness and the Gay Index was the strongest of our entire analysis. This makes me think that my earlier measures of gay and bohemian concentrations are really proxies for regions with large concentrations of open-to-experience people.

When the *Globe and Mail* wrote a story on my impending move to Toronto in July 2007, a reader commented:

> I just don't see the "gay" component as being all that central to this urban conversion; at least not until well into the later stages. Now, open mindedness indeed is central! I think we could all agree that open mindedness is a key personality trait of any creative person. But one could easily say that the people who "paved" these places were open minded to many things . . . living outside social norms; an alignment to alternate expectations in life . . . I guess, I'm just wondering why "gay" has been elevated in his thesis.

While I would phrase it differently, this reader has a point. It's not gay and bohemian concentrations in and of themselves that drive regional concentrations of creativity and innovation, but the broader, underlying regional environment of openness to experience that those two measures actually reflect.

The more I consider these results the more I am convinced that the clustering of open-to-experience personalities is a driving factor in regional innovation and economic growth. Openness is a key factor in the ability to attract and capitalize on diversity. At bottom, regional economic growth requires two dimensions—depth and breadth. Depth comes from specialization and deep experience in certain key fields. Breadth comes from diversity and the open-mindedness required to accept, generate, and convert new ideas. Places that are innovative and can sustain themselves over the long run—places like London, New York, or the San Francisco Bay area—are those that can constantly develop and capitalize on breadth. Their resilience stems from more than the level of education, skill, or technology in those areas. It is part and parcel of their personality profile—their ability to attract and to mobilize open-to-experience people.

Personality plays a significant role in connection with cities, regions, migration, and economic growth. And the interplay between the two—personality and place—is key. "The ways in which personality manifests depends, in part, on the situation one is in," Rentfrow writes. Clearly personality affects which situations and environments people approach and which ones they avoid. "But sometimes we find ourselves in situations that we didn't choose. I think it's this aspect that's especially interesting to consider at the regional level," he adds. "If we broaden the situation to include the neighborhoods and cities within which people live, then we can begin considering how the social climate, economic conditions, and available resources in a place interact with the personality traits of the region to affect regional growth."

What does this all boil down to? For cities and regions, it means that their leadership—political, business, and otherwise—must be aware of the powerful role psychology plays. Places really do have different personalities. Those personalities stem from their economic structure and inform and constrain their future. It's a lot easier to go out and attract a new company or even build a new stadium than it is to alter the psychological makeup of a region. Regional leaders must become more aware of how their region's collective personality shapes the kinds of economic activities that it can do and the kinds of people it can attract, satisfy, and retain.

For each of us, the key is to find the right fit—to think strategically in order to identify our priorities and choose the place that best fits us. As we will see in the next part of the book, such priorities change as we age and pass various life milestones.

PART IV

WHERE WE LIVE NOW

12

THE YOUNG AND THE RESTLESS

M<small>Y FIRST BIG MOVE CAME ON THE HEELS OF MY</small> P<small>H</small>D,
when I became an assistant professor at Ohio State
University. I rented a Rent-a-Wreck truck and drove from New
York City to Columbus, Ohio, where I took a small apartment in
German Village and started to build a life.

Today, many young people have much broader horizons than
I did. Recent college grads are considering, exploring, and moving to locations across the country and across the world. Many
undergraduate students have told me they are seeking jobs and
life experiences not just in the United States or Canada, but also
in Europe, South America, Africa, or Asia. A good number have
friends and ready-made networks in a number of places abroad.

After moving from Italy to Carnegie Mellon University in
Pittsburgh to work on their graduate degrees, my collaborator
Irene Tinagli and her husband Marco moved to Paris, where he
took his first academic job.

When my husband finished his PhD and had to send out job applications we sat down and made a list of all the places that would allow both of us to live and work pleasantly/rewardingly. This ruled out most of those good universities located in remote and small places. We ended up with a list of "large cities" worldwide we both liked. The job offer in Paris was the first to come in and we didn't wait for others. We were both very happy about it.

What I like about Paris is that it has all the offerings of a large city, but with lots of things you would find in a small community: open markets, neighborhood life, small stores, etc. Paris is beautiful and "walkable." I never use the car, I don't need to. Subway, trains and buses are great; though I almost never use them because it's so nice to walk I walk everywhere! Also, since I mostly move/work internationally, flight connections are important to me—and Paris has flight connections to everywhere. I'll finish my PhD shortly and I will look for a job globally, so we're both ready for a new international move. But the last two years in Paris were so wonderful that I'm hoping to find something there.

Freedom

The freedom to live where we choose—oceans and borders notwithstanding—is a relatively recent phenomenon. Before the late twentieth century, most people stayed fairly close to home. That's not to say that young people didn't go away to college, but even those who attended college farther away tended to return home after graduation. Those who did move away generally settled in one place and stayed put. Some of this reflects changes in marital trends. In the 1950s and 1960s, people married young and moved out of their parents' home to their own place, where many stayed for life. For example, my parents bought their small two-family house in North Arlington, New Jersey, in 1959 and never left.

These days, more and more people are postponing marriage until their late twenties or thirties, and some choose not to get married at all. The upshot of this is a much longer period of being unmarried, with additional flexibility and in some cases the necessity to find a place that fits.

Young people are the most likely to move of any demographic group. The likelihood that one will move peaks at around age twenty-five and then declines steeply until forty-five and continues to trail off into retirement and old age. A twenty-five-year-old is three times more likely to move than a forty-five- or fifty-year-old, according to a 2005 study.[1]

The odds of moving also increase with level of education. According to the National Longitudinal Survey of Young Adults, 45 percent of people with advanced degrees end up leaving their home state, compared with only 37 percent of people with a bachelor's degree and just 19 percent of those with a high school diploma.[2]

For young people, this imparts a simple lesson. Because the ability to move (and the likelihood of moving) slows down so significantly with age, the place we choose to locate and settle after college can have a huge effect on our future.

For cities and regions, it means that places which attract young people win the nationwide competition for talent. This does not bode well for cities and regions that count on re-attracting young people who have moved away for fun and adventure once they hit their thirties and decide to settle down and start families. The numbers simply don't add up. Places that lose young people will never be able to recoup, since moving slows down with age. The winning places are the ones that establish an edge early on, by attracting residents in their mid-twenties.

These places gain a long-lasting advantage; those that lose out find it all but impossible to catch up.

To date, the most comprehensive analysis of where singles live and why comes from a study by Joe Cortright and Carol Coletta, *The Young and the Restless*.[3]

Cortright and Coletta conclude that while economic growth is important, highly educated young adults place a "higher priority on quality of life factors." Furthermore, their findings show that well-educated young people are "more likely to move to a place with slower job growth than the place they left almost 60 percent of the time."

The Mating Market

But there's another big reason behind these moves—one so basic and obvious it is hard to imagine why so many people ignore it: the basic need to be in a place where you can find a life partner. I call it the mating market.

Let me put it this way: which of these two factors do you think has a bigger impact on your life—finding the right job or finding the right significant other?

Getting married may not be everyone's goal in life. But for many of us, finding that special someone is as important as, if not more important than, what we choose to do for a living. While marrying the girl or boy next door is an endearing ideal, it is less and less common in today's society. Where we live has more effect on our chances of meeting our life partner than ever before.

An intriguing study entitled *Sex and the City* by Columbia University economist Lena Edlund found that young women outnumber young men in most urban areas throughout the industrialized world. Since cities offer better labor markets for highly skilled workers, urban job markets should attract more men than women, or at least equal numbers of both. Edlund found, however, that while men out-earn women at all ages, young women in the twenty-five to forty-four age range live in more affluent cities. Her explanation lies in what she calls the "asymmetries in the marriage market." Men, she writes, "pay women for marriage," that is, for the relatively higher costs women incur in having and raising children.[4]

As places become more specialized, not just in the jobs and careers they offer but also in the kinds of people they attract and cater to, our odds of meeting that special someone become significantly better in some places than in others. Certain locations have far more single people, as well as more amenities and more activities that bring single people together. And among these favored places, the divergence of urban personalities means that any one person will find many more attractive people in some mating markets than in others. In short, the places to find a mate, like everything else, are clustering.

The Singles Map

I didn't know just how true this was until I posted a rather mundane entry on my blog in April 2007. It was a map, originally published in *National Geographic*, with no text or discussion, entitled "The Singles Map."[5] On it were red dots for places where single women outnumber single men, and blue dots for those where single men outnumber single women. The blog, which I started in 2006, had been puttering along with some thousand or so visitors a day. But within hours after I posted that map, the number of hits surged to more than 200,000, and it was linked to a huge array of the most popular Internet sites. Clearly people were very interested in seeing which places had the best ratios for their own purposes. My team and I redid the analysis using a broader definition of singles, including in it those who had never been married, as well as those divorced or widowed, across all sexual orientations, ages 25 to 64 (Figure 12.1).

When the map was included in an earlier form of this book, it again aroused a great hoopla. But this time, a series of bloggers and commenters developed their own versions of the singles map, creating single ratios by dividing by population, ranking places with the highest levels of gays and straights, highly educated people, and members of various racial and ethnic groups.[6]

In any event, the U.S. region with the largest surplus of single women is greater New York, where single women outnumber single men by more than 200,000. Single women outnumber single men on the East Coast in Washington, D.C., Baltimore, Philadelphia, and Miami as well as Chicago and Detroit in the Midwest. Conversely, the region with the best numbers for single women is greater Los Angeles, where single men outnumber single women by nearly 90,000. Single men outnumber single women in West Coast regions like San Francisco, Seattle, Denver, Dallas, and Phoenix.

The singles map generated a huge number of emails and comments. Some tried to explain the pattern, while others were personal or even confessional. One commenter wrote the following:

> I'm a single male who moved to San Francisco half a year ago. Coming from Chicago, I can speak with personal conviction to the effects of this graph. When I was in Chicago, it was never long between dates. I moved out here for the new tech boom, jumping head-first into the gold-rush mentality that's driving so many other young single men out here as well.
>
> When I'm hanging out with friends, oftentimes in a large room with few if any women, we routinely turn to the topic of how the dating scene sucks. One of my female friends

FIGURE 12.1. THE SINGLES MAP

Circles are sized to reflect how many more singles there are in each metro area, by gender.

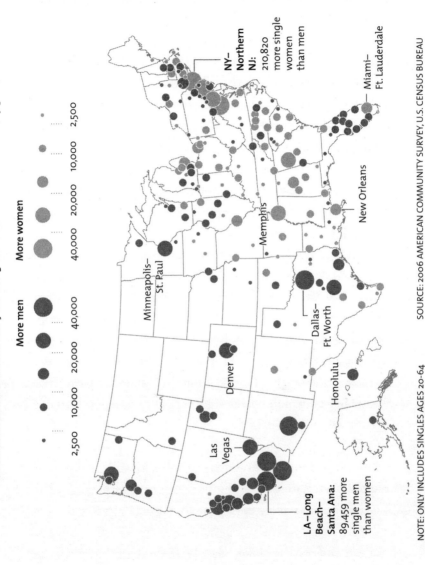

NOTE: ONLY INCLUDES SINGLES AGES 20–64

SOURCE: 2006 AMERICAN COMMUNITY SURVEY, U.S. CENSUS BUREAU

who's also new to the city says that she's never received so much attention from men in her life. Perhaps this explains why most online dating sites got started in Silicon Valley.

Then there's Farhan Thawan, a high-tech professional who moved to Austin during the dot-com boom after graduating from the University of Waterloo. While he liked the city a great deal, the dating scene was a challenge. Upon returning to Toronto he felt the odds turn in his favor.

> Austin was amazing, and while it's the most liberal city in Texas, you're still among Texans. The dating scene was a bit dismal for someone who likes to date Indian women, even though it was rated one of the best places in the U.S. for single people. So after 3 years I made the decision to move back to Toronto at 27 years old. I headed to Singapore for the winter of 2004 to setup an offshore software development team. I applied to Rotman as I had concluded that Toronto was definitely the place for me after living away from home again. Oddly enough I started dating the woman who would become my wife after a shared birthday party within a week of moving back to Toronto.

A few comments offered hypotheses based on deeper economic or social patterns. A regular commenter played off the locations of two hit cable television shows:

> *Sex and the City* takes place at the hub of the #1 female surplus region—New York. Perhaps their frustrations are a reflection of the large single female surplus.
>
> *Entourage* on the other hand is explicitly about young men from Queens, NY migrating to Hollywood, the hub of

the #1 male surplus region, Los Angeles, and I believe is based on Boston native Mark Wahlberg's experience.

I agree that the West still holds a "Gold Rush" mentality for young men, and on top of the "Hot Babe" and other beach/surfer dude-oriented aspect of it all, you have the whole Silicon Valley Type-A nerd culture to draw young men from the East. I think it's also part of the West being the least rooted part of the nation. A young single male who wants to totally throw off his familial and social bonds for more cosmic pursuits would probably like the West better.

I'm not so sure what Texas holds for these young men, but it could be a combination of big oil in Houston, big funkiness in Austin, and just plain big money in Dallas. San Antonio seems to have not joined this club yet. I'm surprised the Southeast is such a female-surplus region, but I supposed their young men migrate West, too. Maybe it's the South's sometimes excessive "rootedness" that pushes the most ambitious young men to flee West.

I met my wife, Rana, at a speaking event in Lansing, Michigan, a university community outside Detroit. She says the high female-to-male ratio there is simple to understand: young men have a greater tendency to move to economic opportunity, while young women stay closer to family.

Demography Is Destiny

Behind this singles map lies a deep and fundamental shift in demographics and family structure. During the 1950s, for example, approximately 80 percent of Americans lived in households headed by married couples. Today that number is just less than half—49.7 percent.[7] That's 55.2 million of the nation's 111.1

million households, according to the Census Bureau. Just a quarter live in a nuclear family, defined as a married couple with kids at home.[8]

The fact that the concept of "family" is so diversified poses a problem for some. Until recently, being single into one's late twenties or thirties was seen as odd or worse. In 1957, 80 percent of Americans considered an unmarried woman to be "sick," neurotic, or immoral. As late as 1986, 38 percent of Americans thought that being single was not a fully acceptable lifestyle. The 1988 edition of the *Handbook of Sociology* uses the phrase "untraditional dyadic relations" to describe all people not part of traditional husband-wife-children families.[9]

I lived through the shift, so I understand how challenging it can be. I grew up with a large extended family. I had ten aunts and uncles on my mother's side, and there were twelve cousins. All of us would gather at my grandmother's house in Newark every Sunday for dinner. I had a similar number on my father's side. Virtually everyone on both sides lived within a five- to ten-mile radius of Newark. North Arlington, where I grew up just five miles away, was a family-oriented town. All the kids knew each other; we participated in the same Cub Scout or Girl Scout activities and played on the same Little League teams. My childhood world included no divorced people and no single adults. Neither the concept nor the word "gay" was part of my vocabulary. In fact, I don't remember anyone who didn't have an extended family much like mine.

Times change. No matter what you call it, our notion of the family is being radically redefined—not by any particular political or ideological agenda but by people themselves. In a recent cross-national survey, 75 percent of Americans said that the main purpose of marriage was something other than having children. My parents or grandparents would have found that unthinkable. Throughout history, marriage has been first and foremost about procreating and having kids, the strong bond that held the family together. In the nineteenth and early twentieth centuries, three-quarters of all households included children under the age of eighteen. By 1960 the number had dropped to less than half; today it's roughly a quarter.

As already mentioned, people are postponing marriage until later in life. Between 1960 and 2007, the average age of marriage for men rose from twenty-three to twenty-seven, while for women it shifted from twenty to twenty-six. For women with a college degree, it's twenty-seven, and for women with a graduate or professional degree, it's thirty.

Young people today are increasingly choosy. According to the National Marriage Project, 88 percent of singles in 2001 agreed that there is a "special person," often referred to as a soul mate, "waiting for you somewhere out there." What's more amazing is that 87 percent of these never married singles believe they will find that special someone when they're ready to get married.

One consequence of this shift is that since 1960, the number of unmarried couples living together has increased by an astonishing 1,200 percent. A quarter of unmarried women between twenty-five and forty-nine are currently living with a partner, and an additional 25 percent did so at some point in the past. Living together has become a surrogate for and equivalent to a first marriage.

The advanced nations are going through a second transition, according to leading demographers. The first occurred during the early to mid-twentieth century and precipitated a golden age for marriage and family life. During that period, more people were married, divorce rates were low, and the age of first marriage for both men and women was the lowest in centuries. The second demographic transition, which began in the 1960s and has accelerated since the 1980s, is marked by declining marriage rates, rising divorce rates, falling fertility, and a sharp rise in the age of marriage for both men and women.

So where do people turn for support during the increasingly long interval between leaving their parents' house and getting married? The answer, according to Ethan Watters, is a new surrogate family, the urban tribe.[10] Watters defines it as an "intricate community of young people who live and work together in various combinations, form regular rituals, and provide the same kind of support as an extended family."

"If our tribes were maximizing our weak ties within a city," Watters writes, "might we be creating the social science equivalent of dark matter—a force that was invisible but was nonetheless critical to holding everything together?" Furthermore, Watters argues, the urban tribe is especially good at meeting members' needs for self-expression and self-actualization in ways that actual parents and siblings sometimes suppress. But these tribes are not just substitutes; on the contrary, they constitute what amounts to our real families, in ways the networks we were born into may never be. Or as a young woman from Chicago put it, "You don't get to pick your family. But you do get to pick your new family—your friends."

To Each His Own Neighborhood

People don't just choose one region over another and end there. They also have to decide on a specific community or neighborhood. Based on more than twenty years of research, I have developed a typology of neighborhoods by life cycle stage. More than anything else, this has shown me how many distinct neighborhoods and communities exist.

When I was young, there were older urban neighborhoods like the Newark my grandparents and parents were from—the kind of place Philip Roth writes about. There were high-end city neighborhoods like Park Avenue, New York. And there were bedroom suburbs and rural areas. Today, however, we have a wide array of different kinds of neighborhoods that offer a much wider variety of choices to multiple demographic groups.

For recent college graduates, one obvious choice is to stick around where you went to school, at least for a year or two. Many young graduates eventually move on, but many stay for a while—to engage in research, hang out with friends, or take advantage of a school-related job opportunity. This is what I did, and I'm far from the only one.

Roger Martin decided to remain in Cambridge for a spell after graduating from Harvard. Since he had already served as captain of Harvard's volleyball team, he jumped at the chance to stay on when the coach announced he was leaving.

Needing a better cover to offer his parents for why he would be staying on, he applied to Harvard Business School and was accepted. What started out as a year in Cambridge morphed into almost two decades. At business school, Roger, some other graduate students, and a few professors, including strategy luminary Michael Porter, decided to create a new consulting firm. In the mid-1980s they launched the hugely successful Monitor Company, and the rest, as they say, is history.

An even greater trend among young grads is to head for the big city. Between 2000 and 2005, the number of New York City residents with at least a bachelor's degree increased by about 285,000, according to an August 2006 *New York Times* story.[11] Other magnet regions for young graduates are London, Tokyo, Stockholm, Amsterdam, Beijing, Shanghai, and various large cities around the world.

Within cities and metropolitan regions, many young singles gravitate toward downtown areas. "All parts of New York City became more educated," the *New York Times* story reports, "but Manhattan and Brooklyn stood out. In Manhattan, more than 57 percent of all residents had at least a bachelor's degree."

Without children to worry about, singles are drawn to the density and connective tissue of urban centers, where they can walk or take public transit to work or go out at night, where owning a car is not a necessity, and where there are vibrant mating markets—saturated with places to meet, mingle, and have dates.

According to Cortright and Coletta's research, young singles between twenty-five and thirty-four were 33 percent more likely to live in a close-in neighborhood (within three miles of the city center) than were other demographic groups. Half of all singles who responded to a Yankelovich survey said that they would consider living in a downtown neighborhood; 67 percent said they would consider living close to downtown; and 69 percent said they would consider living in another urban neighborhood outside of downtown. Only 33 percent of respondents said that they would even consider living in a distant suburb.[12]

Young people cluster in several kinds of urban neighborhoods. One increasingly popular option is what I call the *urban mosaic*. A diverse in-city neighborhood, it bears some resemblance to the classic urban neighborhood that Jane Jacobs wrote about, with a twist. It offers cheap space, ethnic restaurants with cheaper meals, and dense streets, but may have a higher crime rate, less shopping, and less nightlife and open space. Once a magnet for immigrants, working families, and the older poor, they are now attracting twenty- and thirty-somethings drawn mainly by proximity and housing prices. Unfortunately urban mosaics, almost by definition, are neighborhoods in flux. They teeter between poverty and disrepair on the one hand, and total gentrification, which eliminates their diversity, on the other.

Another option is one I call the *hipster haven*. With just the right combination of city grit and posh, hipster havens tend to attract a relatively affluent crowd—that doesn't want to appear too affluent. Music scenes, nightclubs, and coffee shops pop up everywhere in their wake, as older residents either cash out or are pushed out. Hipster havens also attract the bridge-and-tunnel crowd on the weekends—people from the suburbs who can't quite stomach city life during the week but like to visit from Friday through Sunday. They come for the small, colorful shops and stay for the sidewalk cafés and the hustle and bustle of a center city neighborhood.

Not all young people aspire to be hip urban dwellers. Many prefer suburban life, though some will admit that they like older suburbs, which have many of the amenities typically found in cities.

Older suburbs can appeal to young people for these reasons. Some are located on subway or mass transit lines that make commuting easier. All in all, they offer younger residents safety, amenities, and access to a mating market without some of the risks of living in the urban core. These types of neighborhoods also fit the needs of many young professionals in their thirties, whether single or coupled, many of whom have decided to remain in one place for a while.

But for those whose income tempts them into high-end living—or for those who just want to live as if they had a lot of money (even if they don't)—there is a pricier kind of city neighborhood: *designer digs*. These places feature upscale condos, renovated town houses, organic markets, posh grocery stores, and niche boutiques. Wine bars and high-end restaurants are the equivalent to the ethnic eateries in an urban mosaic or the dive bars in a hipster haven.

I've lived in two such neighborhoods. When I took my first academic job at Ohio State University, I lived in Columbus's strikingly beautiful German Village—a picturesque place lined with small, elegant brick houses built by German brewers in the late nineteenth century and dappled with tiny cobblestone streets and amazing shops that with strong community support had been saved time and time again from the wrecking ball.

German Village taught me how important historical preservation is to neighborhoods. I loved living there and made fantastic friends.

In 1987 I moved to Carnegie Mellon in Pittsburgh and settled in Shadyside, an area filled with great historic houses and a vibrant commercial strip. I watched it change from an academic and hippie neighborhood filled with bookstores, head shops, delis, old-man bars, and antique shops into an upscale retail district.

There are many such places across the major cities of the world. Designer digs can be lovely places, and many once were. But development pressure, rising rents, and the invasion of chain stores have made them far more homogeneous than they were a decade ago. Designer digs offer wonderful buildings, clean streets, and terrific architecture and renovations, but real estate prices are through the roof, and diversity—particularly economic diversity—is lacking.

Giant Sorting Sound

What we are witnessing, for better or for worse, is the growing stratification of communities, countries, and the world at large, which Bill Bishop dubs the "big sort."[13] Various ages, economic affiliations, cultures, and political affiliations once lived in proximity to one another. Now, more and more, we are segregating across virtually every economic and social dimension. It's not just rampant gentrification and the "blanding" of our cities that worry me, it's that the big sort is wreaking havoc on our social fabric, dividing and segregating societies across class lines.

For every young person who moves into an urban mosaic or a hipster haven, it is likely that a lower-income family has been driven out. For every young professional who finds him- or herself living the good life in a designer digs community, many more lower- and working-class households struggle to find affordable rental housing that will allow them to raise their families and make ends meet. City neighborhoods are a perfect microcosm of the rooted versus mobile phenomenon. And its implications are starkest for low-income people.

Many have argued that our society's growing economic divide is not born out of outsourcing, immigration, or even wage gaps. While all those things play a role, the real culprit is the divide in human capital and education. "The return for a college education, in percentage terms, is now about what it was in the Gilded Age in the late nineteenth century," the economics professor and blogger Tyler Cowen writes. Starting around 1950, the relative returns to education began to rise. Since 1980 they have skyrocketed. Furthermore, "evidence suggests that when additional higher education becomes available, it offers returns in the range of 10 to 14 percent per year of college, at least for the first newcomers to enroll."[14]

Where we live affects how we grow up, how we spend our free time, the educational opportunities available to us, and the people we meet. Being stuck or rooted in place bears on one's financial success and overall happiness. But clearly, for many, being rooted has graver implications. It means being trapped in a place where options are limited and means to get out and move up become ever sparser.

13

MARRIED WITH CHILDREN

F OR MOST OF US, OUR SECOND BIG MOVE COMES WHEN
we have kids. At that point certain trade-offs become
clear—schools versus restaurants, safety versus edginess, abundant space to play versus a great music scene. As already noted,
lots of young married couples, even with children, continue to
live in the same neighborhoods they did when they were single.
But once the kids are ready to start school, most people bite the
bullet and move somewhere that can accommodate their emerging needs.

In the past, most people chose to move to nearby suburbs, as
my parents did when they made the five-mile jump from
Newark to North Arlington. Longer moves were generally cor-
porate transfers. But today, people are looking at their options
through a wider lens. With flexible careers not so closely tied to
any one employer, they are considering places across the country and even across the world.

A growing number of families pursue multiple global locations, often by necessity and sometimes by choice. Like Kim Tan and her family.

> With our immediate families still living in Malaysia and Singapore, and after fourteen years of bone-chilling winters, we decided to move from Toronto to Australia when my husband was sponsored by the bank he worked for part-time during his student days. After seven years in Melbourne, my husband obtained an expatriate posting to Hong Kong and we were supposed to return to Australia after three years. However, when the time came, our younger daughter (who did not want to move to Hong Kong in the first place!) decided she wanted to stay on to finish her high school. So my husband found a job with a local bank, and we are now in our 13th year in Hong Kong. The children of course returned to study at the University of Toronto and are now living in Toronto and New York. There are lots of expatriates living in Hong Kong who will tell you the same story—how they came out for a few years to the Far East and are still here 20 yrs later!

Rise of the Strollerville

When most people think of family-friendly communities, they imagine a sylvan setting in a small town or upscale suburb—a place with big houses and big yards. But in fact families live happily in a wide variety of urban neighborhoods. A 2006 Yankelovich survey found that young married couples with children are as open to moving to urban neighborhoods close to downtown (51 percent) as to small towns (52 percent) or far suburbs (54 percent). On balance, it's true that most young families (73 percent) prefer to reside in older suburbs close to the city.[1] Forget *Leave It to Beaver.* There are many kinds of family-friendly neighborhoods (with and without cul-de-sacs).

One such option for young families is a place I call *strollerville.* This is a neighborhood full of urban holdovers—young families who never tired of city life. Every city has them. My brother is raising three kids in Hoboken, New Jersey; the abundance of strollers in the city's small parks amazes me each time I visit. The same can be said of Capitol Hill in Washington, D.C., or Toronto's Cabbagetown, where strollers and children line the streets.

New York City neighborhoods that used to be singles haunts or even drug bazaars now teem with young mothers and nannies out with their babies. In March 2007 the *New York Times* reported that "Manhattan, which once epitomized the glamorous and largely childless locale for *Sex and the City,* has begun to look more like the set for a decidedly upscale and even more vanilla version of 1960s suburbia in *The Wonder Years.*"[2] Roberts points out that since 2000, the number of children under age five living in Manhattan has increased by nearly a third (32 percent).

The story profiles David Bernard and Joanna Bers, who own a management and marketing consulting business. Despite growing up in suburbia, they now live with their twin toddlers on Fifth Avenue. "I like the idea of raising them in the city because they're prepared for pretty much anything. The city challenges you," Bernard told the *Times.* "It prepares you for life." Bernard and Bers defended New York City as a melting pot, despite the recent boom of white babies: "We were just at the Children's Museum, and I didn't see a lack of diversity there at all," Bers said, before adding, "We have every intention of sending our kids to P.S. 6. New York is a wonderful place to raise children, especially if there are more of them and more resources devoted to them."

Of course, there is plenty about New York City that would deter many parents from raising a family there. A nice two-bedroom apartment in Manhattan costs $2 million or more. And while P.S. 6 is a public school, it is one of only three on the Upper East Side rated acceptable by the Parents League of New York.

But strollervilles, despite their convenience and urbanity, lack spontaneity when it comes to child raising. A friend comments that he and his wife could never just send their kids outside; they had to take them out. The kids could never just casually drop by a friend's house—something I was doing by age four. He or his wife had to make a play date and then go over and chat with the parents until it was time to go home. A steady routine of supervising their children's play can be exhausting for the parents, and it's one reason many of the women pushing the strollers in strollerville are not mothers at all but nannies—which in turn is another reason why living there is so very expensive.

And this is to say nothing about what the lack of unsupervised time does to children's creative development. I spent much of my childhood without an adult in sight, which is far less true of kids today. Ironically, today's creative-class parenting styles may actually stunt children's creative growth.

Strollervilles can also reduce the diversity that parents are trying to achieve for their children. White children now constitute the majority among Manhattan's white, black, and Hispanic children—and as of 2005 their parents' income averaged $284,208 a year. By contrast, the average income among other households in Manhattan with toddlers was $66,213 for Asians, $31,171 for blacks, and $25,467 for Hispanics.

But what's the point of living in a city whose demographics increasingly resemble those of the suburbs?

Urban Family Lands

American cities differ strikingly from other cities around the world in that families feel they have to leave the city when their children reach school age. Many U.S. urban areas suffer from lackluster (to put it euphemistically) schools and relatively high rates of violent crime. A growing number of industry leaders, academic experts, parents, and kids agree that our current school system is, to use Bill Gates's term, "broken."[3] More than 1 in 10 U.S. high schools are "dropout factories" where no more than 60 percent of freshmen make it to their senior year, according to a 2007 study by Johns Hopkins University researchers.[4] For these reasons, all but the truly wealthy and the most ardent urbanophile families move to the suburbs. The demography of urban America resembles a "barbell" with young singles and empty nesters whose kids are out of the house—relatively devoid of children.

Cities in Europe, Asia, Canada, Australia, New Zealand, and elsewhere in the advanced world are different. Public schools are quite good, and there is much less of a differential between urban and suburban schools. Urban centers are more family-friendly across the board than in the United States.

My collaborator Charlotta Mellander, who is a mother in Sweden, says that her country is a "place where society takes a larger responsibility for the family as a whole." She notes her community's good day care centers: "I don't pay more than $200 per month to have my two kids there forty hours a week, including meals." A safe environment, she adds, means "kids can have their own interests early on. Seven-year-olds go to their own sports activities. They go to the park with their sleds in the wintertime—without their parents. I'd say that the kids can have more freedom, without depending on the time of their parents."

Parents in Europe and Scandinavia, as well as other parts of the world, accept smaller yards for the proximity as well as the diversity and cultural capital these urban centers offer to children and families, as Lynn Jolliffe and her family discovered when they moved to Europe:

> Nine years ago, by absolute fluke, a business partner asked me if I had ever thought about living in Europe, to which I replied, "Often." My family and I were on a plane to Brussels two and a half months later. It was the best experience of our lives, well at least mine and one of my sons. The multicultural milieu of Brussels in particular and Europe in general was intoxicating. I loved every minute of it. The history, the people, the language—all were amazing. Over the seven years we were there, we traveled all over Europe, Africa, Middle East, and Australia. The boys went to an International School and all of their best friends were from everywhere but the U.S. They became bilingual and my husband learned French to deal with the trades and tennis and general living. I improved my French and learned some Flemish. We lived for three years in a French area, which was where we could find a place to rent in a week. We then decided to buy in a Flemish area where we had friends as well as being closer to my office and to the school. We loved the house and it was affordable. It was all very sad when I was asked to move to Orange County, California.

Here's one more story for you. In the fall of 2006, I was discussing the question of where we choose to live with students, many of whom are from foreign countries, in my graduate seminar at George Mason University near Washington, D.C. When I asked those from abroad where they thought they might eventually settle, I was shocked by their answers. Most said they wanted to get their degrees and establish their careers in the United States.

But once they married and had children, they expected to return home. Whether they were from East Asia, India, Latin America, Europe, or Africa, they all wanted to raise their children outside the United States. The educational systems were better, they said; their societies were less materialistic; and there was less pressure to work and far more time and consideration for family. And, they added, they would leave the United States even if it meant giving up money and long-term career prospects. There is a veritable world of options out there for people looking for a great place to raise their families.

I am struck on a daily basis by how many kids of all ages live in Toronto. Not just kids of affluent parents living in posh neighborhoods and going to private schools. Middle-class kids using public schools, ethnic kids, kids of every race, nationality, and family structure.

Our neighborhood in Toronto is a mile and a half from the university and less than two miles from the downtown core. It has great public as well as private schools, and is filled with families with children. The suburbs-versus-city trade-off does not really exist here. As Roger Martin explains:

> In Boston, we lived in the lovely Wellesley Hills. Even though it was an upscale neighborhood, with large single-family houses, we wouldn't have considered letting our seven-year-old son or ten-year-old daughter walk six or seven blocks to a friend's house—or let our twelve-year-old son walk four blocks down to the shopping district on Route 16. It would have felt like being a bad parent.
>
> In Toronto, our youngest has been biking to school since he was thirteen years old—and school is about a

twenty-minute bike ride along one of the main north-south streets of the city—without inducing even a mild concern. We simply do not worry about their personal safety here.

How many American parents can still say that? In our old neighborhood in Washington, D.C., every child was in private school. Not only were the public schools not up to snuff, the surrounding community was extremely dangerous. We got a feeling for this one day when we came across a map of D.C.–area crime in the *Washington Post*. Our neighborhood was a veritable island on this map surrounded by huge swaths of dots showing murders and other violent crimes all around us.

And safe cities are just as important for families with teenagers as they are for families with small children.

Toronto's family friendliness was driven home to us during our first Halloween. I gave it a name, the Trick-or-Treater Index, on my blog. During our time in Washington, D.C.—in a solid neighborhood in the city's northwest quadrant—not a single kid came to our door in three years. But on Halloween night in our neighborhood in Toronto, which is closer to the city core and considerably denser than our D.C. neighborhood, our house was mobbed by a mosaic of races. A person wrote a comment on my blog, pointing out that Catherine Austin Fitts, a former assistant secretary of Housing and Urban Development, came up with a similar index—the Popsicle Index—which she describes as the percentage of people in a community who feel that a child can leave home safely to buy a Popsicle. As if that wasn't enough, the day after Halloween the U.S. Census Bureau released a study which found that nearly 50 percent all children in the United States live in places where their parents fear that neighbors may be a bad influence, and more than 20 percent of children are kept indoors because they live in dangerous neighborhoods, a number that rises to 34 percent for African Americans and 37 percent for Hispanics.

Living in urban neighborhoods enables children to benefit from the cultural capital that comes from diversity. A Toronto blogger, Metro Mama, sees living in the urban core as a key element in the development of her daughter, Cakes:

> It's important that Cakes lives somewhere where she'll meet people of varying backgrounds. I want her to have an open mind. I want her to speak more than one language. I want my daughter to be colour blind. There are several children on our street and she is the only white one. Cultural diversity has many other benefits, a huge one being food. We're so lucky to have so much fabulous and authentic food to enjoy, from dim sum in Chinatown, to curries in Little India.

Some even choose their city based on what's good for their kids. At a speech in Toronto during winter 2008, I ran into a high-powered Canadian consultant I used to know back in Pittsburgh. When I asked him why he moved back to Toronto, he answered simply that he and his wife had been thinking about where their kids would be likely to stay when they grew up. When they ran through the options, Toronto was a no-brainer.

Family-friendly cities are particularly good places for teenagers. They provide the freedom where teens can explore, discover, and express themselves. Kwende Kefentse was able to do just that growing up in Mississauga but spending time in Toronto.

> My parents immigrated to Toronto in the second Caribbean diaspora during the '60s. As I got older and more into music, all of the record stores and concerts were downtown

but moreover the aficionados who were into the hip-hop music and culture the way that I was were all drawn downtown. I was frequently commuting downtown myself, traveling through the city and the surrounding areas encouraging random encounters, going to shows, meeting people, and taking in what the city had to offer us, which for me was something vital.

Ethnic Enclaves

Another kind of neighborhood is the *ethnic enclave*, primarily immigrant communities built around specific religious or cultural or ethnic identities. Often its streets give the impression of a foreign country—the groceries, restaurants, churches, and shops all retain a specific cultural character. Toronto, where we live now, is filled with them. Ethnic enclaves now dot the suburban landscape too. They are especially popular with families who want to immerse their children in the customs and languages of their home country. Such communities are often fraught with tension, as they endeavor to preserve their culture in the face of competing ways of life; they also tend to be extremely family focused, viewing children as the important legacies of their culture.

My wife, Rana, is Jordanian and grew up in Troy, Michigan, near a huge Middle Eastern enclave. After graduate school she took a job as director of public relations at the Detroit Zoo. Her cousin Suha works as an elementary school teacher in the Detroit public schools, teaching bilingual classes to new Arab immigrants.

On a spring day several years ago, Rana and her cousin arranged for the class to visit the zoo. For weeks, Suha had told her students about her younger cousin. When the class finally arrived, Rana came zipping out to greet them on her zoo-issued golf cart, wearing a miniskirt and heels, her long hair flowing behind her.

When Suha introduced the class in their burkas and traditional Arabic dress, they started to giggle and tease their teacher: "That can't be your cousin." The students didn't know any members of their community who dressed and looked like Americans.

Similarly, as young people flood into ethnic enclaves, these communities are seeing their ethnic character fade.

For parents who want some semblance of urban amenities but in a less congested setting, there is the *boho-burb*. These are older suburbs, typically dating from before the great postwar suburban building boom. Often they are on old streetcar, railroad, or subway lines and contain busy commercial strips with cafés, restaurants, boutiques, and shops. Boho-burbs offer proximity, historic buildings, and teeming retail corridors, but they also share some of the problems of strollervilles: the real estate prices are sky high, and children often cannot play outdoors unsupervised.

Suburbia remains the classic family choice in the United States, filled with soccer moms, patio men, bouncing babies, manicured backyards, and giant gas barbecue grills.

But suburbs often lack diversity. Commutes can be long and arduous, and the architecture can be mundane. Schools and churches tend to be the nodes that tie these communities together; people socialize in backyards, at private clubs, or behind closed doors, with the implication that if you're not invited, you may never even know what kinds of groups exist. The lack of a physical town center is often mirrored in the lack of a social center.[5]

Others want to live even farther out. They want a bigger house with a bigger yard in a more traditional suburb. These people gravitate to *edge cities*, identified by Joel Garreau.[6] Garreau explains that the population of an edge city increases at 9:00 A.M. on weekdays, meaning that more people arrive to work than leave to work, as would be the case in a traditional residential suburb. Edge cities have huge shopping malls and commercial complexes that, to the chagrin of some and the delight of others, serve as their centerpiece. Edge cities "are so dispersed across the geography," Garreau writes, "as to challenge the definition."

Many of the fast-growing edge cities of the 1980s and 1990s are struggling today. They're congested and their malls have not aged well. Edge cities now face a number of challenges, the first and foremost being how to transform themselves into real communities. How to reduce the reliance on cars as the way of getting around? How to increase density? How to make them more pedestrian friendly and accessible by mass transit? How to transform them from subdivisions amid shopping malls to integrated live-work-learn-play communities?

Newburbia is another option. The brainchild of architects like Andres Duany and Peter Calthorpe, newburbia is a designed community with a traditional feel.[7] The houses are clustered tightly together but surrounded by lots of green space. These places are typically oriented to pedestrian traffic (they restrict the use of cars) and shaped around town centers. One of the most famous examples is Celebration, Florida, on the outskirts of Disney World. But even though they have town centers, these new urbanist communities can lack diversity. Seaside, Florida, Duany's signature project, was the community used in the movie, *The Truman Show*. Jim Carey's character is unaware that he is living in a constructed reality surrounded by fake friends and family, leading a life intended for the entertainment of those who live outside it.

All of these communities involve trade-offs. Strollervilles offer convenience, proximity, urbanity, and diversity, but they are pricey and can be difficult places for children to lead spontaneous lives. Family land suburbs and edge cities offer big yards, plenty of space for kids to play, and great schools, but may lack ethnic and racial diversity. Many who live there but work in the central city face long commutes, which psychologists now rate as one of life's least satisfying activities. While each place has something to offer, none is perfect. The key is to think through what your family's needs are and choose what best fits you.

Like Marries Like

It is often said that love is not enough for a marriage to work. Most successful partnerships are built on shared values, similar backgrounds, and comparable lifestyle preferences. In the past fifty years, women have asserted their right for these things, and the result has been an increase in what some call egalitarian marriages—relationships in which wives are just as smart, wealthy, and career-oriented as their husbands. A *New York Times* article published in the fall of 2006 called attention to a troubling implication of this seemingly progressive shift: "Are we achieving more egalitarian marriages at the cost of a more egalitarian society?"[8]

In other words, while partners have come closer to achieving parity in education and income, the rift between those couples and their less educated, less privileged counterparts has widened, reinforcing existing socioeconomic divides. College-educated men and women today are less likely to marry down—to choose mates who are less educated than they are.

According to a 2005 study by sociologists Christine Schwartz and Robert Mare, the chances of a high school graduate marrying someone with a college degree shrank by 43 percent between 1940 and the late 1970s.[9] In this decade, researchers reported in the journal *Demography*, the percentage of couples who share the same level of education reached its highest point in forty years.

It's hard to fault people for what Nobel Prize winner Gary Becker termed "assortative mating," the tendency to pair off with someone like themselves.[10] And in a world in which highly talented and highly paid people concentrate in the same handful of places, it should come as little surprise that they are marrying each other. Over time, this growing tendency of like marrying like will only reinforce clustering and geographic sorting along class lines, giving the emerging map of social, economic, and cultural segregation even greater permanence.

It stands to reason that assortative mating reflects economic inequality, but recent research also offers evidence that the phenomenon is a driving force behind disparities in wealth as well. A study by economists Raquel Fernández and Richard Rogerson, published in 2001 in the *Quarterly Journal of Economics,* concluded that increased marital sorting (whereby high earners marry high earners) "will significantly increase income inequality."[11] Likewise, a 2003 analysis by Brookings economist Gary Burtless found that increased marital sorting between 1979 and 1996 was behind 13 percent of the growth in economic inequality during that period. Burtless cautions, however, that he does not believe assortative mating is necessarily more pronounced than it used to be: men have long married women of their own social class. "Now that women who are in a position to [work or pursue advanced degrees] are attending college and graduate school and joining the professions," writes Annie Murphy Paul in the *New York Times*, "the economic consequences of Americans' assortative mating habits are becoming clearer."

Also behind increasing socioeconomic inequality is a growing gap between married couples and single people. Recent studies show that the marital prospects of rich and poor people are diverging. As already noted, marriage has declined across all income groups, but among those who do get married, highly educated couples with high incomes fare far better than couples with lower incomes. "As marriage with children becomes an exception rather than the norm," the *Washington Post* reported in March 2007, "social scientists say it is also becoming the self-selected province of the college-educated and the affluent."[12]

Class seems to be the best predictor of whether Americans will marry or cohabit, perhaps because marriage is so expensive, argues Pamela Smock, a University of Michigan sociology professor.[13] This trend is not limited to the urban poor; it affects suburban and rural areas in equal measure.

Given the simple law of compounding, the end result is easy to see. Over time, highly educated households draw from two growing incomes, while less skilled and less advantaged people struggle along with one or occasionally none. From where they meet to how they advance in our society, their location and impact are inextricably tied to our increasingly spiky world. Thus the family, like so many other aspects of our society, is subject to the same kind of sorting brought on by the clustering of like with like.

At the same time, it's getting harder and harder to draw a line between different kinds of families. While culture warriors bloviate about how "yuppies, sophistos, and gays" are undermining old-fashioned family values, the facts of the matter stand—the best places for traditional families and the best places for gay and lesbian families are often the same places. Not only is it high time to pay attention to where you choose to raise your family, it also may be time to rethink what the term "family values" actually means.

14
WHEN THE KIDS ARE GONE

WHEN MY WIFE AND I LIVED IN WASHINGTON, D.C., many of our neighbors were recent or imminent empty nesters. On summer weekends, when we would gather by the neighborhood pool, I would invariably overhear two kinds of conversations.

The first would be among our neighbors' children—twenty-somethings back home for a visit—fervently discussing the pros and cons of where they then lived and where they might go in the future.

The second would be among the parents. With their children out of the house or about to leave, they would talk about selling their large houses and moving somewhere else.

But where would they go? Some wanted to move to George-town, a mere three miles away, where they could walk to shops and restaurants. Those considering a move beyond D.C. wanted to find a similar kind of neighborhood in a dense, authentic urban center. Not once did I hear anyone mention a traditional retirement community, except with disdain.

The third big move in life often comes after the kids leave home. Many empty nesters and retirees consider nearby locations, but a large number also examine broader options. The location choices for this age group will become even more significant as more and more baby boomers—those born between 1946 and 1964—head into their sixties.[1]

If history is any guide, the baby boomers' impact will far exceed expectations. From the Beatles to Woodstock, baby boomers have redefined the lifestyle, consumption pattern, and values of each new life stage they have entered. Their location and habitation patterns are no exception. Boomers spurred the gentrification of urban neighborhoods in the late 1970s and early 1980s, the creation of edge cities in the 1980s and early 1990s, and the revitalization of inner-ring suburbs in the late 1990s and 2000s. As they age, they will certainly redefine what we used to call the retirement community. With greater wealth, higher levels of education, and more active lifestyles, the country's aging population is headed for an empty nester and retirement lifestyle different from that of any previous generation. And because of their numbers and accumulated capital, where boomers choose to locate will have an unprecedented effect on the choices open to younger generations as well.

But despite the generation's overall wealth, not all baby boomers will fare well. According to a major study by William Frey and Ross DeVol, the rise of the "yuppie elderly"—married, in good health, with substantial accumulated resources, more active lifestyle, and greater locational choices—will coincide with the rise of another group, the "needy elderly," particularly widows over the age of seventy-five who are especially dependent on families and social institutions.[2]

Generation Ageless

"When it comes to finding a place to live," the *Wall Street Journal* wrote in October 2006, "today's retirees are looking for something completely different."[3] While weather and leisure remain important, retirees are looking for a community "where they can make friends and connections quickly, whether it's a small town or a walkable neighborhood in a big city." They also want to live where they can indulge postwork passions, a second career, or a newly adopted sport, or be near their grandkids, whether in a mixed-used development, a small town, or an urban center. Empty nesters and retirees have a wide range of communities to choose from these days. Free from the constraints of full-time jobs and full-time parenting, some even find themselves with the flexibility and means to divide their time among multiple places.

After years of raising kids and taking care of large houses, an increasing share of this demographic is interested in downsizing and returning to the hustle and bustle of urban neighborhoods. "We don't want to be slaves to our house forever," is how one of my former Washington, D.C., neighbors put it. Many empty nesters find themselves drawn to the same neighborhoods that attract young professionals and many people in the gay community. One reason is the obvious: no kids. Another is a common preference for proximity and urban amenities.

A growing number of empty nesters have become re-singled, and by joining communities where they can make friends and meet other unattached people, they are able to form their own version of midlife urban tribes.

For many empty nesters and retirees, a key factor in their location choice—and in most everything they do—is proximity to their children and grandchildren. While children may return home after college or when their parents become ill, an increasing trend is for parents, especially those with means, to follow their kids. Some pick up and move everything—lock, stock, and barrel; for others, a small second home nearby suffices. In many cases, parents come to offer financial assistance or help out with young families. Some boomer parents want to share the excitement of their children's new lives in a vibrant big city—a prospect their children may regard with ambivalence!

Or how about a joint family move? When Tom Hoog retired as CEO of Hill & Knowlton in New York, he started to think about where he and his wife would move. So they held a family caucus to talk it over with their three adult children. One son lived in Colorado, where the family had originated, and another lived in Virginia. Their daughter was in Texas.

As they talked it over, Hoog says, "it made sense to reunite the entire family in one place." They chose a place in the Rocky Mountains outside Denver, close to where they had lived when the kids were growing up. So they built a new home about six blocks from their original house. Their son Michael built a home there; their daughter, Michele, and her family came from Texas; and their son Mark followed. With the grandkids all in the same age range, Hoog adds, "they play on the same Little League teams, and the girls go to the same dance studios and are best of friends."

Whatever boomers do, society listens and follows suit. Wherever they go, new kinds of neighborhoods emerge and prices rise. It's no accident that the previous two major moves in the boomer life cycle, in the 1970s and 1980s, coincided with major run-ups in real estate markets. Where boomers flock, bargains disappear, and the neighborhood butcher shop is replaced by a pan-Asian fusion restaurant and a hardware store gives way to a high-end remodeling center. Authenticity quickly acquires a sheen of self-consciousness that, to some, connotes its opposite.

Those who lived in these places before feel as if they have been invaded by an alien culture, even while some of them make a mint from selling their homes.

The recent back-to-the-city movement among boomers has already changed the dynamics of entire communities, making it nearly impossible for subsequent generations to buy in, pushing them to fringe districts or out to the suburbs. Sometimes, if I ask just the right way, my students and the younger members of my research team will tell me how they resent what boomers have done, not just by foisting "their music" on them, but by taking over whole parts of cities and pricing them out.

Are we sowing the seeds of generational conflict over location and community? Time will tell.

15
PLACE YOURSELF

W HEN I ANNOUNCED MY INTENTION TO WRITE A BOOK
that would help people choose the best place to live,
many colleagues were alarmed. "You're a serious scholar," they
said. "Academics don't write self-help books." Except that some
do. Leading psychologists, like Martin Seligman, have written
extensively on how to improve your life by working to your
strengths. Dozens of leading medical researchers and clinicians
have written useful books, sharing their insights on everything
from weight loss to general health management.

After more than twenty years of doing research on place, I
hoped to impart some information people could actually use. I
was heartened when my editor offered his usual sage counsel:
"If you really want to give advice, you have to earn it. The way
for you to earn it is to write a serious, engaging, and convincing
book on why place matters." If you've read this far, I hope you
think I've earned that right.

By now I hope you will agree that place matters even more today than it did in the past. Despite all those predictions about how new technologies—the car, the cell phone, and, of course, the Internet—would free us from the constraints of location, allow work to be moved all over the world, and enable us to live most anywhere we want, location remains a key factor in the global economy.

When we look at where innovation and economic activity occur, it turns out that only about two or three dozen places across the world make the cut. By any measure of past, present, or future economic growth—population, economic activity, innovation, location of scientific talent—these megaregions tower above their neighbors. And behind all these trends lies the great power of the clustering force: the tendency of creative people to seek out and thrive in like-minded groups, and the self-perpetuating economic edge that comes from their doing so. But place is not important only to the global economy, it is also important to your life.

I started this book by saying that most of us devote a great deal of thought to two key questions: what we do for a living and whom we choose as a life partner. All of us, regardless of the career we ultimately choose, intermittently agonize about where to work and how to best nurture and advance our career. Some of us take even more time finding the right person with whom to spend our life and create a family.

But few of us spend sufficient time strategically considering the third question: where to live. As I researched this book, it became clear to me that this third question is at least as important as the other two.

As we've seen, where we reside has great relevance to the kinds of work available to us. In a large number of professions, jobs have become geographically specialized, concentrating in certain places. What matters most to people is not unlimited job or career opportunities, but enough solid options to provide real flexibility and choice.

Where we live can determine other aspects of our economic stability too. Take buying a house, which is the single biggest financial investment most of us ever make. The performance of real estate markets—the growth and appreciation of housing investments—varies widely from place to place. This does not mean one should choose a place to live solely on the basis of potential real estate returns, which is sort of like marrying for money. But so long as housing remains one of life's largest investments, it's better to know how different markets stack up on this score.

In addition to the state of our finances and our professional life, where we live can hugely determine how happy we are. Where we live can determine whom we meet, how we meet, and whether we get to spend time with friends and loved ones.

Perhaps even more important, place can determine how happy we are with ourselves. In addition to economic and cultural specialization, the clustering force has resulted in the geographic concentration of personality types. Understanding which places best fit one's personality ought to be at the top of every person's to-do list.

So in finding the best place for you to live, it's important to weigh five key factors.

First, you need to think about how the place you live will affect your job and career prospects. As we have seen, many kinds of jobs are clustering and concentrating in particular locations. Before you settle on a place, you need to look closely at how it matches up with your short-run and long-run career goals.

Second, it's important for you to gauge how important it is to you to have close friends and family nearby, and what you will give up if you move far away. In Chapter 5, we considered a study which found that leaving close friends behind is worth as much as six figures in monetary compensation. Whether you think that number is reliable or not, it helps you focus on how your choice of place can affect your relationships with family and close friends.

Third, you need to be honest with yourself about the kind of place that best suits your lifestyle. Some of us like the buzz and energy of the big city; others like the ease of living in the sub-urbs; still others want to be part of nature and the great out-doors. What are the hobbies, activities, and lifestyle interests that bring you true joy? I'm a cyclist and would not even think about living somewhere without great road riding. If you're a skier you probably want to be close to snow-capped mountains. If you're a surfer, sailor, or beach bum, you'll want to be close to a great coastline.

Fourth, think carefully about how the place you choose to live matches your personality. If new experiences are your thing, you'll want to be in a place that provides intense stimulation. If you're an extrovert, you'll want to be around lots of other people who are easy to meet and befriend. If you're conscientious, you'll want to be around other people who take work seriously and honor their commitments.

Fifth and finally, you'll want to make sure your place fits your particular life stage. If you're single, you'll want to be in a place where you can make friends and find people to date. If you're married with children, you'll want a community that's safe and offers great schools. If you're an empty nester, you'll want a place not too far away from your kids where you can engage in interests and hobbies you really love.

Most of all, be aware of the trade-offs involved. It's vital to weigh how important each dimension is to you when narrowing down the places on your list and ultimately making your choice.

Finding a place that best fits us isn't easy—as nothing that's truly important in life is—but it can be done. To help you better assess your priorities and options, I've come up with a basic framework, some real-world tools, and a ten-step plan to help you narrow the field and make your decision.

Step 1: Get Your Priorities Straight

If you ask people what's most important to them in a partner or a job, chances are they will have a well-rehearsed response ready. Our relationship with place is no less intimate and should not be neglected, slighted, or taken for granted. Figuring out what your priorities are is the first and most fundamental step before deciding where to live.

Consider what's really important to you by asking yourself some basic questions about the place where you live or might want to live.

- What do you like most and least about where you're living now?
- Where are the places you'd most like to live? If the place you live now isn't on this list, you need to give this special attention.
- Is it important to you to find a job in a specific field, or are you thinking about a career change?
- What stage of life are you in, and does that figure into your expectations?
- What's most important to you right now—your work? Finding a mate? Your physical environment? Your family?
- How important to you are outdoor activities and the natural environment?
- To what degree do climate and weather matter?
- How much do cultural activities like access to art, film, theater, and music mean to you?

- Do you crave experience? Do you need to be around other people, or do you like being alone?
- Do you prefer a hustling city, a comfortable suburb, or a rural community? Do you want to be closer to the action or farther from the frenzy?
- What are your deal makers? Deal breakers?

Take out a piece of paper and a pen and write down your preferences in these and any other key dimensions of your life. Consider nothing too big or too trivial.

Step 2: Generate a Short List

For most people, simply giving these questions some preliminary consideration will lead to surprising revelations. But my team and I have developed basic tools that can help you identify the broad metropolitan regions that may fit you best. They are available at whosyourcity.com (or use the link at creativeclass.com).

Step 3: Do Your Homework

It would be great if you could simply push a button and be instantly matched with your perfect place, but it's not that simple. There's a ton of pertinent information about the place that's best for you that can't be crammed into any computer program.

Once you have your short list in hand, my team and I have developed a framework that will help you assess your options. It's organized around what I call the place pyramid (Figure 15.1), which reflects the research in this book.

At the base of the pyramid is opportunity. Next in line are basic services like education, health care, and so forth. Leadership forms the midpoint of the pyramid. Then come values, and on top there's the aesthetics, and quality, of places. As I demon-

FIGURE 15.1. THE PLACE PYRAMID

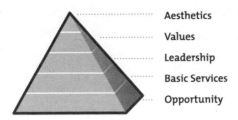

Aesthetics

Values

Leadership

Basic Services

Opportunity

strated in Chapter 11, each level is important. Most of us will be happiest in a place that meets our needs and preferences across the entire pyramid. The goal is to live in a place that fulfills your needs from bottom to top. When considering a potential move, you need to assess how your new community will stack up against your needs at each level.

For many things you need to know more about, there simply isn't any quantitative data available. You'll need to collect qualitative information—read local papers, talk to local people, and go out and see for yourself. In many cases, collecting information this way will give you deeper and better insight into the places you're considering. The real power is in the combination of both types of data—hard statistical facts and your own personal assessments. If the numbers all say a place is perfect but your gut says it's not for you, take notice. Remember that the bottom line is your happiness.

To help you collect this information, my team and I have designed a tool we call the place finder, which I've included in Appendix C. It may look simple, but, trust me, it reflects decades of research. (You can download as many versions of it as you like from whosyourcity.com or creativeclass.com.) I see it as a way to help you organize your thoughts, consider your priorities, collect and analyze quantitative and qualitative information, and ultimately compare, rate, and rank places. Fill out each box on the form using a 1 to 5 scale, with 1 as the lowest value and 5 the highest. Even after you've collected statistical information, there's plenty of room for your personal judgment. Enter the score that best reflects your assessment, your needs, your observations, and your sensibilities.

Step 4: What Do They Offer?

The first step in your assessment starts at the base of the pyramid: what economic opportunities do the places on your list offer? If there aren't any, you may not be able to afford to live there. Local newspapers and business magazines provide more detailed assessments of the local economy. Check out the local business media as well as the local chamber of commerce website. Most major cities have bloggers who write regularly on local economic conditions.

How do your places stack up in the specific job opportunities they offer? Consider the following questions: Do you want a job in the field you're in now, or do you want to change careers? Are you a risk taker, or do you like to play it safe? Do you want to work for a company, or launch one?

Don't forget the cost of living. Some places are more expensive than others, and your paycheck won't stretch equally everywhere. Make sure to calculate comparative costs so you know how far your salary will really go. There are calculators available online that will help you tally the precise cost-of-living differences among the locations you're considering. They also enable you to see what kind of salary you would need in order to maintain your current lifestyle in other places. These sites (salary.com is just one example) also give you objective, fact-based tools you can use in negotiating your salary, which is especially important if you're moving primarily for a new job.

Whether or not you're on a fast career track, access to professional development and lifelong learning opportunities is important to everyone—if only to make sure our minds remain active as we age! Studies have shown time and again that expanding your mind can add years to your life. Access to such opportunities may depend, in part, on proximity to great colleges, universities, and graduate programs. But learning outside of formal educational institutions through seminars, networks, executive training programs, and professional development offerings can be even more important.

In a similar vein, studies have also shown that people who feel disconnected or isolated age at an accelerated pace; they're also unhappier. Plugging in, building networks, meeting people, and creating support structures—these things not only further professional development but also contribute significantly to overall well-being. In this respect, as in most others, not all places are created equal. Ask yourself: Is this a place I can easily plug into, or is it the kind of place I'll run into real resistance?

Step 5: Getting the Basics Right

Next, take a long look at the quality of the community's basic services like education, safety, health care, housing, and the like. This, you will recall, is one of the most important dimensions a place has to offer. And it can vary a great deal across communities.

The quality and range of schools is critical for parents of school-age children, but it's something everyone needs to look at. The quality and proliferation of educational opportunities can indicate the quality and proliferation of other things too, including safety. I know plenty of parents who relocated for better access to high-quality public schools only to later transfer their kids to specialized private schools.

Health is another key to happiness. Access to quality, afford-able health care is critical and varies with age and life stage. Are doctors readily available? Are they taking new patients? What are the major health care centers nearby? How long are waits at the emergency room? How healthy is the community overall?

It's imperative that you have a good sense of the housing mar-ket, given the wide discrepancies out there. If you're a renter, you'll need to know if you will ever be able to buy a house in an area where you would want to live. In addition to current prices, pay attention to historical trends and future projections.

The ability to move around easily—to get to and from work or anywhere else for that matter—is significant to a daily sense of well-being. Two of the biggest stressors related to place are long commutes and traffic jams, according to psychologists who study happiness. A study by Daniel Kahneman and his collabo-rators based on detailed diaries of people's daily activities found that commuting was the least enjoyable activity in anyone's day.[1] Can you afford a house within a reasonable commuting dis-tance, or will you have to drive long distances? Is there a sub-way, a train, or other form of mass transit available? Can you live in a neighborhood where you can walk or use a bike for most ac-tivities? To get a day-to-day sense of what traffic patterns are like during rush hour, visit local websites and watch local news. And above all else, try out your potential commute in advance.

It's also important to consider transportation and connectivity in a broader sense. How accessible is your location to the world? Is there a major hub airport nearby? If travel is part of your job or lifestyle, how many direct flights are there to your key desti-nations? How easily can you—and others—get in and out? What are the lines like at security?

Don't forget about the wired world. Colleagues of mine who moved to Paris in 2006 spent more than a month there without Internet or phone service. In this day and age, and particularly in this global economy, being cut off from the wired world can feel like a death sentence.

Step 6: Does the Place Get It?

Next, assess the leadership in the places on your list. Statistical analysis and polls of resident perceptions are one way to do it. But the best way to get a feel for leadership is simply to read the local media, especially the alternative papers and local bloggers. When possible, read up on the political history of a place; past events will undoubtedly inform its present context. Who are the political and business leaders? What kind of track record do they have? How popular are they? Do they reflect the kind of diversity you want to see? Do their values and vision fit yours? Do they address issues that are important to you? Are decisions about the community discussed and made out in the open or behind closed doors? Are there opportunities for citizens to be involved? Talk to residents. How informed and engaged are they? How do they feel about their leadership? Is the leadership open-minded and inclusive, or dominated by squelchers?

Step 7: Values Check

The next step is to look closely at the prevailing values in the places on your list—things like tolerance, trust, and self-expression. Many people neglect to consider these things when moving to a new place, but as we've seen, they matter greatly to how happy you'll ultimately be.

Like people, places vary in their ability to welcome and absorb newcomers—particularly those who are different from its current residents. Some places, like New York City, London, or Toronto, have a large number of new immigrants from around the world. Others are more insular, making it harder for newcomers to fit in and feel welcome. Some are warm and friendly, others more aloof. Do you see the kinds of people you want—and need—to be around?

Trust—not only between people but also between people and institutions—is hard but not impossible to measure. There are signs everywhere. Do people make eye contact with each other on the street? Do they hide their handbags or briefcases when they sit down? Does someone's word seem to matter in every-day business transactions? Do people lock their doors when they leave their houses or cars? Do people treat each other with respect? How are children treated? What about young singles, families, the elderly, or people with disabilities? Are some groups marginalized? When we moved from D.C. to Toronto, we were amazed that people are polite, that cars stop for pedes-trians, and that virtually no one shouts or leans on a car horn.

Here again, places vary a lot. Some welcome self-expression while others are more conformist. How strong is your need to be yourself? What role does individuality play in your daily life? Is it important to you to find a place where you can be unique and reinvent yourself should you so desire? Do you see visible signs of self-expression on the street, or do people seem to be cookie-cutter versions of one another?

Step 8: Come on City, Light My Fire

Now it's time to find out whether the places you're looking at have the spark you need. To remind you, the Place and Happi-ness Survey found aesthetics and "energy" to be among the most important determinants of how happy people are with their place. Take it seriously.

All of us are drawn to beauty, but remember the old adage about beauty being in the eye of the beholder. Each person looks for something different. Some consider a gritty urban streetscape to be a pleasant aesthetic. Others prefer well-manicured parks. What do you find beautiful? How do the places on your list match your own sense of beauty? Does their appearance really excite you and make you feel alive?

In a mass-produced and mass-marketed world, many people crave authenticity. If you're one of them, ask yourself the following: How authentic is the place? Does it have unique neighborhoods and shops, or is everything generic? What gives it true soul? How does it value and promote its history, uniqueness, physical structures, and culture?

Places are not just about work. What are the things you really love—arts and culture, music or theater, spectator sports or participant sports, running or cycling, rock climbing or fishing? Is it a place that allows you to do the things that matter most to you? And what about things you might want to do, someday? An avid cyclist may one day choose a different form of exercise. People in their twenties who like clubs and nightlife may become symphony or jazz buffs in their thirties, or find themselves coaching soccer when kids come along. Do you see people doing the things you love? I can tell a place is for me if I see lots of cyclists buzzing along in their riding gear.

Every city has its own energy level or buzz. Are you inspired by high energy and lots of activity, or do you prefer a slower speed? What is the energy of the place? Does it jibe with your own ideal pace? Does its energy level match your own?

Step 9: Tally It Up

Now that I've reminded you of all the things you need to consider and why, it's important to remember: no place is perfect. Don't drive yourself crazy by seeking the ultimate match.

Now tally your score and compare your places. Use your score to weigh the pros and cons of each place. There are no right or wrong answers here: the objective is to find the place that fits you best.

Step 10: Go There

Few of us would ever make an important decision like taking a job or getting married purely based on what someone—or something—told us to do. Deciding where you'll live is no different. I'm always shocked at the number of people I meet who tell me they relocated without visiting first. Would you take a job before assessing how you might get along with your superiors and peers? Would you marry someone before going out together?

Don't get me wrong. I know there are exceptions to this rule. For that matter, I know someone who swears that the longer you date someone, the less likely you are to marry!

But there's no good reason not to take better precautions if you can. According to a Yankelovich survey published in 2006, people highly value the information they get from friends or family who live in a community.[2]

And then go visit. My personal rule of thumb is to visit at least three places on your list before making a final decision. According to the same Yankelovich survey, a weekend visit is by far the best means to a useful assessment. Actually, you should consider taking more than just a weekend—spend enough time to get to know the place. Believe me, you owe it to yourself, your family, and your future.

While you're there, make sure to consider how you would feel about the community in future stages of your life. Visit a neighborhood you might like to live in now, and a neighborhood you might like to live in ten years from now.

Above all, if a place doesn't feel right for any reason while you're actually there, don't hesitate to reject it based on your gut feeling. Realize that your intuition is telling you something important. It's how you feel about the place—and how it makes you feel.

Finally: Choose

Now that you've done your homework, collected more information than you ever thought existed, compiled all your scores, talked to people, and made your visits, it's time to pick your place. Take a deep breath. Where you choose to live is one of the top three decisions, if not the single most important decision, you'll ever make.

It's a lot to think about, for sure. But if you do it right, finding the best place for yourself will vastly improve every facet of your life.

Choose wisely.

ACKNOWLEDGMENTS

ABOOK LIKE THIS IS TRULY A TEAM EFFORT. I AM fortunate to have a team of research collaborators who are second to none. First and foremost, I thank my longtime collaborator Kevin Stolarick, my colleague once again at Martin Prosperity Institute, who supplied much of the statistical material and data in this book. I am also grateful to Charlotta Mellander of the Jönköping International Business School, who has worked with me on a series of research projects for this book, for her detailed comments on various drafts of the manuscript.

I also want to thank a number of others who have collaborated on research for this book. Tim Gulden developed the light emissions and megaregions data and built the maps for Chapters 2 and 3. Rob Axtell—whom I've known since my earliest days at Carnegie Mellon—built the model of emergent cities in Chapter 4. Darby Miller-Steiger helped design and implement the Place and Happiness Survey; and Irene Tinagli and David Wilson collaborated on the analysis discussed in Chapters 9 and 10. Jason Rentfrow provided the personality data and collaborated on the research reported in Chapter 11. The book has also benefited from several capable research assistants: Scott Jackson, who worked on the analysis of music scenes; Brian Knudsen; and Ryan Sutter, who worked on the personality and location research. Patrick Adler provided research assistance for the global English edition.

Two great editorial assistants made this book a much better read. Jesse Elliott worked side by side with me on the first draft of the manuscript, before moving on to record and tour with his band, These United States. Abigail Cutler took over on the second draft; her deft editorial hand improved the tone, tightened the arguments, and helped make this a much better book. Amanda Styron and Abby Liebskind worked on the references, assisted with data collection, checked over the facts, and did myriad tasks whenever asked. Ryan Morris designed the book's maps and graphics. Kim Ryan proofread the technical appendixes. Paulo Raposo prepared the new maps, and Marisol D'Andrea provided technical assistance for the global English edition.

Susan Schulman, my agent, believed in this project and helped to see it through. Bill Frucht is a terrific editor and much more. He is a collaborator and friend whose intelligence and energy make my ideas much better. Courtney Miller and Jodi Marchowsky shepherded the manuscript deftly through the production process. The entire Basic Books team is professional, effective, and a delight to work with. I thank each and every one of you.

Don Peck of the *Atlantic Monthly* helped me shape my ideas on the spiky world and the means migration. Will Wilkinson provided helpful comments on an early version of this manuscript. There are so many friends and colleagues who support my efforts in so many ways. Among them, Elizabeth Currid, Martin Kenney, and Gary Gates stand out as people I have worked with consistently over the years and whose intelligence, interaction, and comments strengthen my own thinking.

I could not imagine a better place to work than the Martin Prosperity Institute. Roger Martin is the best dean around. He is brilliant, committed to big ideas, and tireless. He came up with the idea for the institute and got it funded. I thank the entire Rotman team for their collegiality, support, and professionalism. I'd also like to thank Geoff Beattie for believing in this idea from the beginning, and our funders—particularly Premier Dalton McGuinty and the Province of Ontario, and Joseph Rotman—for their commitment to this work.

My team at the Creative Class Group (CCG) keeps me grounded in the real world. David Miller was in on the early brainstorming sessions for this book. Steven Pedigo worked on various data sets for this book and handled organizing them so that they could be turned into graphics.

I've met so many people in my travels who work tirelessly to bring change to their workplaces and their communities; their efforts keep my ideas grounded in the real world, inspire me, and give me energy. I thank Alberto Ibargüen and the Knight Foundation for supporting some of our community capacity-building initiatives around the United States.

I am fortunate to have a large extended family that is the source of great comfort and joy. My brother Robert, his wife, Ginny, and nieces Sophia and Tessa and nephew Luca; the Kozouz clan: Zak and Ruth Kozouz, and Reham, Markis, and Adiev Alexander; Dean and Ruba Alexander; Leena, Adam, Christian, Melia, and Sophia Hosler; Tarig and Anastasia, and Ramiz and Christina Kozouz; and my DeCicco cousins too numerous to mention who bring incredible joy to my life.

At the end of the day, I owe my deepest debt of gratitude to my wife, Rana. Her energy and enthusiasm are boundless; her passion for life is incredible; her quirky sense of humor keeps me in stitches. And by the way, she also runs the CCG, deals with the lawyers and accountants, the website and IT people, and manages our entire CCG team—basically giving me the time, space, and flexibility to focus on my research and writing. I am beyond lucky to have her as my life partner and soul mate.

Appendices

Appendix A: Megaregions of the World

Name (Ranked by LRP)	Population (Millions)	Population Rank	LRP ($Billions)	Innovation/Patents (Rank)	Star Scientists (Rank)
Greater Tokyo	55.1	4	2,500	2	24
Bos-Wash	54.3	5	2,200	8	2
Chi-Pitts	46.0	9	1,600	9	14
Am-Brus-Twerp	59.3	3	1,500	22	18
Osaka-Nagoya	36.0	14	1,400	7	22
Lon-Leed-Chester	50.1	6	1,200	25	10
Mil-Tur	48.3	7	1,000	34	23
Char-lanta	22.4	18	730	16	9
So-Cal	21.4	22	710	13	4
Frank-Gart	23.1	17	630	21	12
Barce-Lyon	25.0	16	610	24	20
Tor-Buff-Chester	22.1	19	530	19	7
Seoul-San	46.1	8	500	6	32
Nor-Cal	12.8	28	470	3	1
So-Flo	15.1	25	430	17	17
Fuku-Kyushu	18.5	24	430	23	19
Paris	14.7	26	380	4	16
Dal-Austin	10.4	30	370	14	13
Hou-Orleans	9.7	32	330	15	5
Mex-ajara	45.5	10	290	35	32

Cascadia	8.9	33	260	10	3
Rio-Paulo	43.4	12	230	32	32
Hong-Zhen	44.9	11	220	28	31
Sapporo	4.3	37	200	27	32
Vienna-Budapest	21.8	21	180	26	29
Tel Aviv-Amman-Beirut	30.9	15	160	31	21
Prague	10.4	29	150	12	25
Buenos Aires	14.0	27	150	33	32
Denver-Boulder	3.7	40	140	5	6
Phoenix-Tucson	4.7	36	140	11	15
Shanghai	66.4	2	130	30	32
Taipei	21.8	20	130	36	30
Lisbon	9.9	31	110	36	28
Beijing	43.1	13	110	29	32
Delhi-Lahore	121.6	1	110	36	32
Glas-burgh	3.8	39	110	18	8
Berlin	4.1	38	110	1	11
Singapore	6.1	34	100	36	27
Madrid	5.9	35	100	20	26
Bangkok	19.2	23	100	36	32

Source: Data by Tim Gulden; analysis and rankings by Charlotta Mellander. For full sources and methodology see, Richard Florida, Timothy Gulden, and Charlotta Mellander, "The Rise of the Mega-Region," Cambridge Journal of Regions, Economy, and Society, 1, 1, 2008.

Note: Ranking based on the 40 megaregions with LRP (light-based regional product) of $100 billion or more. Rankings for innovations and star scientists are adjusted for population.

Appendix B: Key Results from the Place and Happiness Survey

FACTOR	MEAN RANKING	Correlation			
		OVERALL PLACE HAPPINESS	CITY SATISFACTION	RECOMMEND TO FRIENDS AND FAMILY	OUTLOOK FOR THE FUTURE
AESTHETICS AND LIFESTYLE	3.65	.622	.581	.579	.503
Aesthetics	3.88	.560	.534	.510	.456
Beauty and physical setting	4.00	.499	.475	.463	.395
Outdoor parks, playgrounds, trails	4.06	.445	.424	.413	.355
Air quality	3.76	.389	.371	.341	.333
Climate	3.70	.373	.358	.340	.300
Lifestyle	3.35	.457	.412	.438	.367
Meet new people and make friends	3.65	.528	.486	.500	.422
Cultural offerings	3.38	.342	.309	.329	.272
Nightlife	3.08	.289	.254	.281	.233
BASIC SERVICES	3.46	.603	.545	.558	.509
Primary and secondary education	3.55	.468	.443	.427	.384
Health care	3.83	.410	.383	.380	.334
Job offerings	3.15	.401	.365	.380	.327
Faith institutions	4.23	.346	.324	.334	.265
Higher education	3.93	.321	.292	.305	.261

	Mean				
Housing	3.03	.310	.257	.278	.293
Traffic	3.33	.306	.266	.257	.299
Public transportation	2.77	.188	.161	.179	.162
OPENNESS	**3.03**	**.509**	**.455**	**.475**	**.427**
Families with children	3.75	.558	.506	.516	.466
Senior citizens	3.49	.466	.432	.418	.394
Young singles	2.94	.384	.337	.373	.310
Recent college graduates	2.69	.375	.322	.361	.314
Racial and ethnic minorities	3.19	.252	.219	.236	.218
Immigrants	3.00	.201	.177	.188	.175
Gay and lesbian people	2.75	.176	.156	.171	.140
People living in poverty	2.49	.169	.142	.153	.155
ECONOMIC AND PERSONAL SECURITY	**1.72**	**.497**	**.454**	**.441**	**.437**
Overall economic security	0.66	.440	.393	.390	.395
Economic conditions	3.24	.548	.514	.495	.458
Good time to find a job	NA	.294	.265	.267	.256
Economy getting better	NA	.256	.206	.221	.260
Personal security	3.54	.409	.394	.354	.352
LEADERSHIP	**NA**	**.432**	**.408**	**.377**	**.376**

Note: Mean score is based on 1–5 scale where 1 is the lowest and 5 the highest N=27,885.

Appendix C: Place Finder

Rate each category on a 1–5 scale where 1 is lowest and 5 is highest		Current Place	Option 1	Option 2	Option 3
OPPORTUNITY					
Economic Conditions	How are overall economic conditions?				
Job Market	Does the place offer good jobs and good salaries in your field?				
Professional Development	How available are the professional development resources that you need in your life and career?				
Networking	Do you have a professional network already established; If not, how easy is it to access and build one?				
	Subtotal				
BASIC SERVICES					
Education	Does the place offer educational options that meet the needs of you and your family?				
Health and Safety	Does the place meet your criteria for safety and healthcare?				
Housing	Does the place have housing that you like at a price you can afford?				
Connectivity	Is the place connected—locally, globally, and digitally—in the ways that most matter to you?				
	Subtotal				
LEADERSHIP					
Politicos	Do political leaders inspire your trust and confidence?				
Business	Are business leaders the type you admire and have confidence in?				
Diversity	Is leadership diverse — by gender, race, age, ethnicity, sexual orientation and other factors?				
Access and Engagement	How open and inclusive is the decision-making process?				
	Subtotal				

		Current Place	Option 1	Option 2	Option 3

VALUES

		Current Place	Option 1	Option 2	Option 3
Tolerance	How are people of different races, ethnicities, religions, and lifestyles treated?				
Trust	Do people generally trust one another?				
Self-Expression	Can you be yourself there?				
People Climate	How does the place value people?				
	Subtotal				

AESTHETICS AND LIFESTYLE

		Current Place	Option 1	Option 2	Option 3
Physical Beauty	How do you rate the physical and natural beauty of the place?				
Authenticity	Does the place have a unique character?				
Amenities	Does the place have the arts, lifestyle, and recreational amenities you need?				
Buzz	How does the "energy" of the place match yours?				
	Subtotal				

		Current Place	Option 1	Option 2	Option 3
	TOTAL				

Notes

Chapter 1

1. Books and articles on happiness are a veritable growth industry. See, for example, Darrin McMahon, *Happiness: A History*, Atlantic Monthly Press, 2006; Jonathan Haidt, *The Happiness Hypothesis*, Basic Books, 2005; Martin Seligman, *Authentic Happiness*, Free Press, 2004; Richard Layard, *Happiness: A New Science*, Penguin, 2005.

2. See Jason Schachter, *Why People Move: Exploring the March 2000 Current Population Survey*, U.S. Census Bureau, Current Population Report, May 2001. These data are updated annually and are available on the census website.

3. Veolia Observatory of Urban Lifestyles, *Life in the City*, 2008.

4. Charles Tiebout, "A Pure Theory of Local Expenditures," *Journal of Political Economy* 64, 5, 1956, pp. 416–424.

5. In particular, the work of Jane Jacobs: *The Death and Life of Great American Cities*, Vintage, 1992 (1st ed., 1961); *The Economy of Cities*, Vintage, 1970; and *Cities and the Wealth of Nations*, Vintage, 1985. Much of my own research on this subject is summarized in *The Rise of the Creative Class*, Basic Books, 2002.

Chapter 2

1. Thomas Friedman, *The World Is Flat*, Farrar, Straus & Giroux, 2005.

2. The original article is Frances Cairncross, "The Death of Distance," *The Economist*, September 30, 1995. She later published an influential book by the same title, *The Death of Distance*, Harvard Business School Press, 2001. Also, "Conquest of Location," *The Economist*, October 7, 1999.

3. Edward E. Leamer, "A Flat World, A Level Playing Field, a Small World After All or None of the Above? Review of Thomas L. Friedman, The World Is Flat," *Journal of Economic Literature* 45, 1, 2007, pp. 83–126.

4. Urbanization data are from "World Population Prospects: The 2006 Revision Population Database," Population Division, Department of Economic and Social Affairs, United Nations 2007, esa.un.org/unpp.

5. "Q&A with Michael Porter," *Business Week*, August 21, 2006, www.businessweek.com/magazine/content/06_34/b3998460.htm.

6. Richard Florida, "The World is Spiky," *Atlantic Monthly*, October 2005.

7. Gulden used the light that is visible from space at night as a basis for estimating economic activity. He calibrated the light data using estimates of gross regional product (GRP) compiled for the lower forty-eight U.S. states. He translated this physical economic activity into standard units by renormalizing the total for each nation to agree with that nation's 2000 GDP in 2000 U.S. dollars at current market exchange rates. He then overlaid the light maps with detailed population maps from the Land-Scan 2005 population grid, developed by Oak Ridge National Laboratory. The result consistently estimates economic activity for every 30 arc-second grid cell (less than 1 square kilometer) in the world. For more on this methodology, see Richard Florida, Timothy Gulden, and Charlotta Mellander, "The Rise of the Mega-region," *Cambridge Journal of Regions, Economy, and Society* 1, 1, 2008. See also William Nordhaus et al., "The G-Econ Database on Gridded Output: Methods and Data," Yale University, May 12, 2006; Nordhaus, "Geography and Macroeconomics: New Data and New Findings," *Proceedings of the National Academy of Sciences*, March 7, 2006, pp. 3510–3517. Data on economic output or gross regional product for U.S. regions is from Global Insight, *The Role of Metro Areas in the U.S. Economy*, Prepared for the United States Conference of Mayors, January 13, 2006.

8. Gulden estimated global patents for every region in the world by combining data from the U.S. Patent and Trademark Office (USPTO), which provides the exact city location of the inventor with data from the World Intellectual Property Office (WIPO) on national patents. Because inventors from around the world file for patent protection in the United States, and the USPTO tracks the inventor's city of residence, he was able to count the number of U.S. patents for each city in the world. These data on patenting by U.S. region were developed by Phil Auserwald and his research team at George Mason University's School of Public Policy, who made them available to us. While this file provides a fine portrait of inventions in U.S. cities, it undercounts (sometimes radically) inventions in other countries because not every inventor files for a U.S. patent. Gulden compensated for that by using the USPTO data to estimate the relative importance of the cities within each country. He then took the number of patents reported to WIPO by each national patent office as granted to domestic inventors and reallocated them to cities using the weights derived from the USPTO data. He assumed that inventors who obtain patents in the United States have the same spatial distribution as inventors who patent domestically. This may overstate the importance of major cities (where access to the world patent system may be easier), but that is not a large source of bias. For more on this methodology, see Florida, Gulden, and Mellander, "Rise of the Mega-Region."

9. AnnaLee Saxenian, *Silicon Valley's Immigrant Entrepreneurs,* Public Policy Institute of California, 1999. Vivek Wadhwa et al., "America's New Immigrant Entrepreneurs: Part 1," Duke University/University of California–Berkeley/Pratt School of Engineering, January 4, 2007. See also Rafiq Dossani, *Chinese and Indian Entrepreneurs and Their Networks in Silicon Valley,* Stanford University, Shorenstein APARC, March 2002.

10. See Martin Kenney, "The Globalization of Venture Capital: The Cases of Taiwan and Japan," November 17, 2004; "A Life Cycle Model for the Creation of National Venture Capital Industries: Comparing the U.S. and Israeli Experiences," November 14, 2004; "Building Venture Capital Industries: Understanding the U.S. and Israeli Experiences," November 26, 2003; "Venture Capital Industries in East Asia," December 4, 2002. All available at http://hcd.ucdavis.edu/faculty/kenney.

11. More information on IPOs is available from the U.S. Securities and Exchange Commission. SECLaw.com has a complete IPO information center at www.seclaw.com/centers/ipocent.shtml.

12. These data may be somewhat skewed because they exclude citations in many non–English language journals. That said, the vast majority of global scientific discourse is conducted in English. Authors publishing in other languages are not likely to be cited often enough to show up on this map. See Michael Batty, "The Geography of Scientific Citation," *Environment and Planning A,* 35, 2003, pp. 761–770. An earlier version dated December 19, 2002, has more detailed data and maps. It can be downloaded from his site: www.casa.ucl.ac.uk/people/MikesPage.htm.

13. Lynne Zucker and Michael Darby, "Movement of Star Scientists and Engineers in High-Tech Firm Entry," Working Paper no. 12172, National Bureau of Economic Research, September 2006.

14. Mike Davis, *Planet of Slums,* Verso, 2006.

15. Peter J. Taylor and Robert E. Lang, *U.S. Cities in the "World City Network,"* Brookings Institution, February 2005.

16. "Magnets for Money," *The Economist,* September 13, 2007.

17. Benjamin Barber, "McWorld vs. Jihad," *Atlantic Monthly,* 269, 3, 1992. See also Barber, *Jihad vs. McWorld: How the Planet Is Both Falling Apart and Coming Together and What This Means for Democracy,* Crown, 1995.

18. Tairan Li and Richard Florida, "Talent, Technological Innovation, and Economic Growth in China," February 2006. Available at creative class.com.

19. Jonathan Watts, "Thousands of Villagers Riot as China Enforces Birth Limit," *Guardian,* May 22, 2007.

20. Tao Wu, *Urban-Rural Divide in China Continues to Widen,* Gallup Organization, March 28, 2007.

21. Rafiq Dossani, *Origins and Growth of the Software Industry in India,* Stanford University, Shorenstein APARC, September 2005. Available at http://aparc.stanford.edu/people/rafiqdossani.

Chapter 3

1. David Ricardo, *Principles of Political Economy and Taxation,* Cosimo Classics, 2006 (1st ed., 1817).

2. Jane Jacobs, *The Economy of Cities,* Vintage, 1970; also Jacobs, *Cities and the Wealth of Nations,* Vintage, 1985.

3. Jean Gottman, *Megalopolis,* Twentieth Century Fund, 1961.

4. Kenichi Ohmae, *The End of the Nation State: The Rise of Regional Economies,* Simon & Schuster, 1995. See also Ohmae, "The Rise of the Region State," *Foreign Affairs,* Spring 1993.

5. John Gapper, "NyLon, a Risky Tale of Twin City States," *Financial Times,* October 24, 2007.

6. Robert Lang and Dawn Dhavale, *Beyond Megalopolis: Exploring America's New Megalapolitan Geography,* Brookings Institution, July 2005. See also Edward Glaeser, "Do Regional Economies Need Regional Coordination?" Harvard Institute of Economic Research Discussion Paper 2131, March 2007.

7. To do this, Gulden set a light threshold that captures the essence of the geographic pattern of U.S. megaregions described by Lang and Dhavale and other researchers who use more complex methods, such as population, income, or measures of commuting patterns, to identify megaregions. He found that while these factors are critically important for understanding the functioning of a megaregion, contiguous development is a good enough proxy for economic integration that it can meaningfully be used in this context. After determining the threshold that gives the best approximation for established U.S. megaregions, he then applied the same threshold to the nighttime lights dataset for the rest of the world. This produced tens of thousands of lighted patches representing the full range of settlement sizes, from the largest megaregions covering thousands of square kilometers to small villages and other light sources that are on the order of a single square kilometer. He then closed the remaining small gaps, merging lighted areas that are separated by less than 2 kilometers. For more on this methodology, see Florida, Gulden, and Mellander, "Rise of the Mega-region."

8. "The Texas Triangle as Megalopolis," Federal Reserve Bank of Dallas, Houston Branch, April 2004, www.dallasfed.org/research/houston/2004/hb0403.html.

9. On Montreal, see Kevin Stolarick and Richard Florida, "Creativity, Connections, and Innovation: A Study of Linkages in the Montréal Region," *Environment and Planning A,* 38, 10, 2006, pp. 1799–1817.

10. Dominic Wilson and Roopa Purushothaman, "Dreaming with BRICs: The Path to 2050," Global Economics Paper no. 99, Goldman Sachs, October 1, 2003.

Chapter 4

1. Robert Lucas, "On the Mechanics of Economic Development," *Journal of Monetary Economics* 22, 1988, pp. 3–42.

2. Adam Smith, *The Wealth of Nations,* Bantam, 2003 (1st ed., 1776).

3. David Ricardo, *Principles of Political Economy and Taxation,* Cosimo Classics, 2006 (1st ed., 1817).

4. Joseph Schumpeter, *Theory of Economic Development,* Harvard University Press, 1934 (1st ed., 1911); Schumpeter, *Capitalism, Socialism, and Democracy,* Harper, 1975 (1st ed., 1942). Thomas McCraw has written an illuminating biography of Schumpeter, *Prophet of Innovation: Joseph Schumpeter and Creative Destruction,* Belknap, 2007.

5. Bill Steigerwald, "City Views: Urban Studies Legend Jane Jacobs on Gentrification, the New Urbanism, and Her Legacy," *Reason,* June 2001.

6. See the discussion of Jacobs's ideas in David Ellerman, "Jane Jacobs on Development," *Oxford Development Studies,* December 4, 2004, pp. 507–521.

7. Geoffrey West et al., "Growth, Innovation, Scaling, and the Pace of Life in Cities," *Proceedings of the National Academy of Sciences,* April 24, 2007, pp. 7301–7306.

8. Robert Axtell and Richard Florida, "Emergent Cities: Microfoundations of Zipf's Law," March 2006. Available at creativeclass.com.

9. George K. Zipf, *Human Behaviour and the Principle of Least-Effort,* Addison-Wesley, 1949; Zipf, *The Psychobiology of Language,* Houghton Mifflin, 1935.

Chapter 5

1. A comprehensive 2005 study of the subject found that wages and salaries for Americans in the middle of the national income distribution rose 11 percent between 1966 and 2001. The rise in wages and salaries for top earners was a staggering 617 percent. That means that over thirty-five years, wages and salaries rose at least as fast as nationwide productivity for only a tenth of U.S. laborers. As Cornell University economist Robert Frank pointed out in his 2007 book *Falling Behind,* the richest 1 percent of Americans saw their share of national income rise from 8.2 percent in 1980 to 17.4 percent in 2005. "More astonishing still," noted journalist Clive Crook in a 2006 article for the *Atlantic Monthly,* is that "from 1997 to 2001, the top 1 percent captured far more of the real national gain in wage and salary income than did the bottom 50 percent. And even within that highest percentile, the gains were heavily concentrated at the top." See Ian Dew-Becker and Robert Gordon, "Where Did the Productivity Growth Go? Inflation Dynamics and the Distribution of Income," presented to the Brookings Institution, September 2005.

Robert Frank, *Falling Behind: How Inequality Harms the Middle Class*, University of California Press, 2007. Clive Crook, "The Height of Inequality," *Atlantic Monthly*, September 2006, pp. 36–37.

2. Herbert Muschamp, "Checking into Escapism," *New York Times*, November 2, 2002.

3. Greg Spencer and Tara Vinodrai, "Where Have All the Cowboys Gone: Assessing Talent Flows between Canadian Cities," ISRN Annual Meeting, May 2, 2008.

4. Bethan Thomas and Danny Dorling, *Identity in Britain: A Cradle-to-Grave Atlas*, Polity Press, 2007. See also Lucy Ward, "Where You Live Can Be Crucial to Your Future," *Guardian*, September 8, 2007.

5. See Nattavudh Powdthavee, "Putting a Price Tag on Friends, Relatives, and Neighbors: Using Surveys of Life Satisfaction to Value Social Relationships," *Journal of Socio-Economics*, 2008.

6. Albert O. Hirschman, *Exit, Voice, and Loyalty*, Harvard University Press, 1970.

Chapter 6

1. "The World Goes to Town," *The Economist*, May 3, 2007.

2. Alfonso Hernandez Marin, "Cultural Changes: From the Rural World to Urban Environment," *United Nations Chronicle*, November 4, 2006.

3. Kenneth Jackson, *Crabgrass Frontier*, Oxford University Press, 1987; Robert Bruegmann, *Sprawl: A Compact History*, University of Chicago Press, 2005.

4. Joel Garreau, *Edge City*, Anchor, 1992.

5. Alan Ehrenhalt, "Trading Places: The Demographic Inversion of the American City," *The New Republic*, August 13, 2008.

6. David Brooks, *Bobos in Paradise*, Simon & Schuster, 2001; Brooks, *On Paradise Drive*, Simon & Schuster, 2004.

7. Edward Glaeser and Christopher Berry, *The Divergence of Human Capital Levels Across Cities*, Harvard Institute of Economic Research, August 2005.

8. Richard Florida, "Where the Brains Are," *Atlantic Monthly*, October 2006, p. 34.

9. Joseph Gyourko, Christopher Mayer, and Todd Sinai, "Superstar Cities," National Bureau of Economic Research, Working Paper no. 12355, July 2006.

Chapter 7

1. Dan Pink, *Free Agent Nation,* Warner Books, 2001.

2. Peter Drucker, *Post-Capitalist Society,* Harper Business, 1993; Drucker, "Beyond the Information Revolution," *Atlantic Monthly,* October 1999, pp. 47–57; Drucker, "The Next Society," *The Economist,* November 1, 2001, pp. 1–20. Fritz Machlup is often credited with the term "knowledge worker" from his 1962 book *The Production and Distribution of Knowledge in the United States,* Princeton University Press, 1962.

3. See Richard Florida, *The Rise of the Creative Class,* Basic Books, 2002. Data updated by Kevin Stolarick.

4. "The World's Richest People," *Forbes,* March 8, 2007.

5. Richard Florida, Charlotta Mellander, and Kevin Stolarick, "Inside the Black Box of Economic Development: Human Capital, the Creative Class, and Tolerance," *Journal of Economic Geography,* 8, 5, 2008.

6. The correlations between occupation and per capita income are as follows: computer and math (.659); business and finance (.549); arts, entertainment, and media (.511); sales (.480); engineering and architecture (.472); science (.393); law (.390); and management (.358).

7. The correlations with regional income are as follows: health care occupations (.052); education occupations (.055).

8. See for example, Alfred Weber, *Theory of the Location of Industries,* University of Chicago Press, 1929 (1st ed., 1909).

9. Michael Piore and Charles Sabel, *The Second Industrial Divide,* Basic Books, 1984.

10. Alfred Marshall, *Principles of Economics,* Cosimo Classics, abridged ed., 2006 (1st ed., 1890).

11. Michael Porter, "Clusters and the New Economics of Competition," *Harvard Business Review,* November-December 1998; Porter, "Location, Clusters, and Company Strategy," in Gordon Clark, Meric Gertler, and Mayrann Feldman, eds., *Oxford Handbook of Economic Geography,* Oxford University Press, 2000; and Porter, "Location, Competition, and Economic Development: Local Clusters in a Global Economy," *Economic Development Quarterly* 14, 1, February 2000, pp. 15–34.

12. Joseph Cortright and Heike Mayer, *Signs of Life: The Growth of Biotechnology Centers in the US,* Brookings Institution, Center for Metropolitan Policy, 2001.

13. Pui-Wing Tam, "New Hot Spot for High Tech Firms Is the Old One," *Wall Street Journal,* October 5, 2006.

14. Ann Markusen and Greg Schrock, "The Distinctive City: Divergent Patterns in Growth, Hierarchy, and Specialization," *Urban Studies* 43, 8, July 2006, pp. 1301–1323.

15. Maryann Feldman and Roger Martin, "Jurisdictional Advantage," *National Bureau of Economic Research*, October 2004.

16. Dan Fitzpatrick, "Extreme Commuters at PNC Raise Eyebrows," *Pittsburgh Post-Gazette*, August 7, 2005.

17. Robert D. Putnam, *Bowling Alone: The Collapse and Revival of American Community*, Simon & Schuster, 2000.

18. Andrew Hargadon, "Bridging Old Worlds and Building New Ones: Toward a Micro-sociology of Creativity," in Leigh Thompson, ed., *Creativity and Innovation in Groups and Teams*, Erlbaum, 2007.

19. AnnaLee Saxenian, *Regional Advantage*, Harvard University Press, 1994.

20. Mark Granovetter, "The Strength of Weak Ties," *American Journal of Sociology* 78, 6, May 1973, pp. 1360–1380.

21. Richard Caves, *Creative Industries: Contracts Between Art and Commerce*, Harvard University Press, 2002. See also Elizabeth Currid's detailed analysis of the interweaving of design, music, and art scenes in contemporary New York, *The Warhol Economy*, Princeton University Press, 2007.

22. See Terry Nichols Clark, "Making Culture into Magic: How Can It Bring Tourists and Residents?" *International Review of Public Administration*, January 12, 2007, pp. 13–25. Also see Terry Nichols Clark, Lawrence Rothfield, and Daniel Silver, eds., *Scenes*, University of Chicago, 2007. Also see Richard Lloyd and Terry Nichols Clark, "The City as an Entertainment Machine," *Research in Urban Sociology: Critical Perspectives on Urban Redevelopment* 6, 2001, pp. 357–378.

23. Richard Florida and M. Scott Jackson, "Sonic City: The Evolving Economic Geography of the Music Industry." *Journal of Planning Education and Research*, forthcoming, 2009.

24. "Jack White Leaves 'Super-Negative' Detroit," *USA Today*, May 25, 2006.

Chapter 8

1. The data on housing trends here are from the U.S. Bureau of the Census, American Community Survey, www.census.gov/acs/www.

2. Peter Coy, "The Richest Zip Codes–and How They Got That Way," *Business Week*, April 2, 2007.

3. Knight Frank, *2008 Annual Wealth Report: Prime Residential Property*, Knight Frank UK, 2008.

4. Joseph Gyourko, Christopher Mayer, and Todd Sinai, "Superstar Cities," National Bureau of Economic Research, Working Paper no. 12355, July 2006.

5. Robert Shiller, "Superstar Cities May be Investors' Superstardust," *Shanghai Daily*, May 22, 2007, www.taipeitimes.com/News/editorials/archives/2007/05/20/2003361715.

6. Robert Shiller, *Historic Turning Points in Real Estate*, Yale University, Cowles Foundation for Research in Economics Discussion Paper no. 1610, June 2007. Available at http://cowles.econ.yale.edu/P/cd/d16a/d1610.pdf. Detailed data from the Case-Shiller Home Price Index are available at http://macromarkets.com/csi_housing/sp_cases hiller.asp. See also Shiller, *Irrational Exuberance*, Princeton University Press, 2005; Shiller, *The Subprime Solution: How Today's Global Financial Crisis Happened, and What to Do About It*, Princeton University Press, 2008.

7. Roger Lowenstein, "Pop Psychology," *New York Times*, March 18, 2007. For an interesting perspective on bubbles in general, see Daniel Gross, *Pop! Why Bubbles Are Great for the Economy*, Collins, 2007.

8. Ryan Avent, "Are Superstar Cities Super Investments?" *The Bellows*, May 22, 2007. Available at www.ryanavent.com/blog/?p=403.

9. Richard Florida and Charlotta Mellander, "There Goes the Neighborhood: How and Why Artists, Bohemians, and Gays Affect Housing Values," 2007. Available at creativeclass.com.

10. John D. Landis, Vicki Elmer, and Matthew Zook, "New Economy Housing Markets: Fast and Furious—But Different?" *Housing Policy Debate* 3, 2, 2002, pp. 233–274.

11. Jennifer Roback, "Wages, Rents, and the Quality of Life," *Journal of Political Economy* 90, 6, 1982, pp. 1257–1278.

12. Edward Glaeser, Jed Kolko, and Albert Saiz, "Consumer City," *Journal of Economic Geography* 1, 1, 2001, pp. 27–50; also Glaeser and Joshua Gottlieb, "Urban Resurgence and the Consumer City," *Urban Studies* 43, 8, 2006, pp. 1275–1299.

13. Maya Roney, "Bohemian Today, High-Rent Tomorrow," *Business Week*, February 26, 2007.

14. Ann Markusen and Greg Schrock, "The Artistic Specialization and Economic Development Implications," *Urban Studies* 43, 10, 2006, pp. 1661–1686.

15. Tim Harford, "Undercover Economist: On the Move," *Financial Times*, March 9, 2007.

16. Andrew Oswald with David Blanchflower and Peter Sanfey, "Wages, Profits, and Rent-Sharing," *Quarterly Journal of Economics* 111, 1, February 1996, pp. 227–252.

Chapter 9

1. Daniel Gilbert, *Stumbling on Happiness,* Knopf, 2006.

2. Edward Diener and Martin E. P. Seligman, "Beyond Money: Toward an Economy of Well-Being," *Psychological Science in the Public Interest* 5, 1, 2004, pp. 1–31.

Betsy Stevenson and Justin Wolfers, "Economic Growth and Subjective Wellbeing: reassessing the Easterlin Paradox," Wharton School, University of Pennsylvania, May 9, 2008, http://bpp.wharton.upenn.edu/jwolfers/Papers/EasterlinParadox.pdf.

3. Also see Angus Deaton, "Income, Aging, Health, and Wellbeing Around the World: Evidence from the Gallup World Poll," Center for Health and Wellbeing, Research Program in Development Studies, Princeton University, August 2007.

4. Nick Paumgarten, "There and Back Again," *New Yorker,* April 16, 2007.

5. Robert Manchin, "The Emotional Capital and Desirability of European Cities," Gallup Europe, presented at the European Week of Cities and Regions, Brussels, October 2007.

6. The correlation coefficients between overall happiness and various factors are as follows: financial satisfaction (.369), job satisfaction (.367), place satisfaction (.303). Compare with income (.153), homeownership (.126), and age (.06). The regression coefficients (from an ordered probit regression) are as follows: financial satisfaction (.342), place satisfaction (.254), job satisfaction (.254). Compare with income (.039), age (–.06), and education (–.09).

7. The overall correlation between income and community satisfaction is relatively weak (.15).

8. Veolia Observatory of Urban Lifestyles, *Life in the City* (Paris), http://www.observatoire.veolia.com/en, 2008.

9. Mihaly Csikszentmihalyi, *Flow: The Psychology of Optimal Experience,* HarperCollins, 1990; and Csikszentmihalyi, *Finding Flow: The Psychology of Engagement with Everyday Life,* Basic Books, 1997.

10. See Teresa Amabile et al., "Affect and Creativity at Work," *Administrative Science Quarterly* 50, March 2005, pp. 367–403.

Chapter 10

1. Abraham Maslow, "A Theory of Human Motivation," *Psychological Review,* 50, 1943, pp. 370–396; Maslow *Motivation and Personality,* HarperCollins, 1987 (1st ed., 1954). For more, see www.maslow.com.

2. See Robert Manchin, "The Emotional Capital and Desirability of European Cities," Gallup Europe, presented to European Week of Regions and Cities, Brussels, October 2007. Veolia Observatory of Urban Lifestyles, *Life in the City,* 2008.

3. See Simon Anhlot, Anholt City Brands Index, 2nd ed., 2006; and Mercer Human Resources Consulting, Worldwide Quality of Living Survey, 2007.

4. Virginia Postrel, "Why Buy What You Don't Need: The Marginal Appeal of Aesthetics," *Innovation,* Spring 2004; Postrel, "The Economics of Aesthetics," *Strategy and Business,* Fall 2003; Postrel, *The Substance of Style: How the Rise of Aesthetic Value Is Remaking Commerce, Culture, and Consciousness,* HarperCollins, 2003. More is available at www.vpostrel.com.

5. Michèle Bhaskar and Jeroen van de Ven, "Is Beauty Only Skin Deep? Disentangling the Beauty Premium on a Game Show," Discussion Paper, University of Essex, Department of Economics, January 2007.

6. James Rojas, "A Messy, Inspiring Urbanism," *National Post,* October 18, 2007, www.canada.com/nationalpost/news/toronto/story.html?id=4e82b4f5–941a–421ea50c–18bd1d6dbff8&k=1731.

7. Miller McPherson, Lynn Smith-Lovin, and Matthew E. Brashears, "Social Isolation in America: Changes in Core Discussion Networks over Two Decades," *American Sociological Review* 71, 3, June 2006, pp. 353–375.

8. Ethan Watters, *Urban Tribes: Are Friends the New Family?* Bloomsbury USA, 2004.

9. Richard Lloyd and Terry Nichols Clark, "The City as an Entertainment Machine," *Research in Urban Sociology: Critical Perspectives on Urban Redevelopment* 6, 2002, pp. 357–378.

10. Mercer Human Resource Consulting, Worldwide Health and Sanitation Ranking, 2007.

11. Taylor Clark, "The Indie City: Why Portland Is America's Indie Rock Mecca," *Slate,* September 11, 2007, Slate.com/id/2173729.

12. Ronald Inglehart, *Modernization and Postmodernization: Cultural, Economic, and Political Change in 43 Societies,* Princeton University Press, 1997. For more detail on the World Values Survey, see www.worldvaluessurvey.org.

13. Benjamin Friedman, *The Moral Consequences of Economic Growth,* Knopf, 2005.

Chapter 11

1. Psychologists have found that three main factors shape the fit between people and their environment. The first they call "selection." People seek out social and physical environments that satisfy and reinforce their psychological needs. The second is "evocation." People unconsciously elicit reactions from their social and physical environments that are a result of their psychological makeup. And the third is "manipulation." People essentially adjust and tailor their environment to reinforce and express their psychological qualities. See David Buss, "Selection, Evocation, and Manipulation," *Journal of Personality and Social Psychology* 53, 6, 1987, pp. 1214–1221.

2. Will Wilkinson, "In Pursuit of Happiness Research: Is It Reliable? What Does It Imply for Policy?" Cato Institute Policy Analysis, April 11, 2007, www.cato.org/pub_display.php?pub_id=8179. For more information and his blog, see http://willwilkinson.net.

3. For more on psychologists' five-factor model of personality, see Lewis Goldberg, "An Alternative Description of Personality: The Big-Five Factor Structure," *Journal of Personality and Social Psychology* 59, 1990, pp. 1216–1229; Goldberg, "The Development of Markers for the Big-Five Factor Structure," *Psychological Assessment* 4, 1992, pp. 26–42; Paul Costa and Robert McCrae, *Revised Personality Inventory (NEO-PI-R) and NEO Five Factor Inventory (NEO-FFI) Professional Manual,* Psychological Assessment Resources, 1992. See also www.centacs.com/quickstart.htm.

4. For more information on Seligman's and Peterson's Values in Action survey, see www.authentichappiness.sas.upenn.edu/questionnaires.aspx.

5. Peter J. Rentfrow, Sam Gosling, and J. Potter, "The Geography of Personality: A Theory of Emergence, Persistence, Expression of Regional Variation in Personality Traits," *Perspectives on Psychological Science,* 2008.

6. Margaret Mead, *Sex and Temperament in Primitive Societies,* Morrow, 1935; Ruth Benedict, *The Chrysanthemum and the Sword: Patterns of Japanese Culture,* Houghton Mifflin, 1946.

7. S. E. Krug, and R. W. Kulhavy, "Personality Differences Across Regions of the United States," *Journal of Social Psychology* 91, 1973, pp. 73–79.

8. If you are so inclined, you can take the test or just have a look at it. See www.outofservice.com/bigfive.

9. Jared Diamond, *Guns, Germs, and Steel*, Norton, 1997; Jeffery Sachs and Jordan Rappaport, "The United States as a Coastal Nation," *Journal of Economic Growth* 8, 1, March 2003, pp. 5–46.

10. Max Weber, *The Protestant Ethic and the Spirit of Capitalism*, Dover, 2003 (1st ed., 1905); Ronald Inglehart, *Modernization and Post-modernization: Cultural, Economic, and Political Change in 43 Societies*, Princeton University Press, 1997.

11. Peterson analyzed data for the fifty largest U.S. cities, those with populations of 300,000 and above, giving him a sample of 203,000 people. The highest positive correlations for cities ranking high on my creativity index measures and his character strengths were for curiosity (.43), love of learning (.36), appreciation of beauty, and creativity (.29). Conversely, the highest negative correlations were for modesty (–.65), spirituality (–.59), gratitude (–.59), teamwork (–.57), perseverance (–.52), hope (–.50), kindness (–.49), and fairness (–.48). The correlations between the creativity index and meaning were negative (–.39) for presence of meaning and positive (.30) for search for meaning. See Christopher Peterson and Nansook Park, "Why Character Matters," prepared for the International Positive Psychology Summit, October 6, 2007.

12. See Gary Gates, "Racial Integration, Diversity, and Social Capital: An Analysis of Their Effects on Regional Population and Job Growth," Williams Institute, UCLA School of Law, April 2003. Brian Knudsen et al., "Bridging and Bonding: A Multi-dimensional Approach to Regional Social Capital," Carnegie Mellon University, 2005. Robert Putnam, "E Pluribus Unum: Diversity and Community in the Twenty-First Century," *Scandinavian Political Studies* 30, 2, 2007, pp. 137–174.

Chapter 12

1. See Joseph Cortright and Carol Coletta, "The Young and the Restless in the Knowledge Economy," CEOs for Cities, December 2005.

2. National Longitudinal Survey of Young Adults, Bureau of Labor Statistics. Available at www.bls.gov/nls.

3. Cortright and Coletta, "The Young and the Restless."

4. Lena Edlund, "Sex and the City," *Scandinavian Journal of Economics* 1, 107, 2005, pp. 26–44.

5. "Singles Map," *National Geographic*, February 2007.

6. El Valiente did single men and women with bachelor's degrees: http://elvaliente.files.wordpress.com/2008/04/creativemappng.png. Half Sigma did a whole series of maps by race, age, and ethnicity: www.halfsigma.com/2008/04/the-unmarried-m.html; Huffington Post's 23/6 even did a parody: www.236.com/news/2008/04/04/boston_globe _locates_americas_5637.php.

7. Sam Roberts, "In the United States, the Married Are in the Minority," *New York Times*, October 15, 2006.

8. Much of the statistical data in this section is drawn from the National Marriage Project at Rutgers University. See, for example, "The State of Our Unions," Rutgers University, 2007, and a wide range of other studies, data, and information available at http://marriage .rutgers.edu.

9. Neil J. Smelser, *Handbook of Sociology*, Sage, August 1988.

10. Ethan Watters, *Urban Tribes: Are Friends the New Family?* Bloomsbury USA, 2004.

11. Patrick McGeehan, "New York Area Is a Magnet for Graduates," *New York Times*, August 16, 2006.

12. The Segmentation Company, a division of Yankelovich, "Attracting the Young College-Educated to Cities," CEOs for Cities, May 11, 2006, www.ceosforcities.org/rethink/research/files/CEOsforCitiesAttractingYou ngEducatedPres2006.pdf.

13. Bill Bishop, *The Big Sort*, Houghton Mifflin, 2008.

14. Tyler Cowen, "Incomes and Inequality: What the Numbers Don't Tell Us," *New York Times*, Economic Scene, January 25, 2007.

Chapter 13

1. The Segmentation Company, a division of Yankelovich, "Attracting the Young College-Educated to Cities," CEOs for Cities, May 11, 2006, www.ceosforcities.org/rethink/research/files/CEOsforCitiesAttracting YoungEducatedPres2006.pdf.

2. Sam Roberts, "In Surge in Manhattan Toddlers, Rich White Families Lead Way," *New York Times*, March 23, 2007.

3. Bill Gates, "Prepared Comments for the National Education Summit on High Schools," February 26, 2005, www.gatesfoundation.org/ MediaCenter/Speeches/CoChairSpeeches/BillgSpeeches/BGSpeechNGA –050226.htm.

4. According to the study, 1,700 high schools, 2 percent of all U.S. high schools, are places where no more than 60 percent of entering freshman make it to their senior year. Nancy Zuckerbrod, "1 in 10 Schools Are Drop Out Factories," Associated Press, October 29, 2007, www.huffingtonpost.com/huff-wires/20071029/dropout-factories.

5. See James Howard Kunstler, *Geography of Nowhere: The Rise and Decline of America's Man-Made Landscape,* Free Press, 1996.

6. Joel Garreau, *Edge City: Life on the New Frontier,* Anchor, 1992.

7. See Andres Duany, Elizabeth Plater-Zyberk, and Jeff Speck, *Suburban Nation: The Rise of Sprawl and the Decline of the American Dream,* North Point Press, 2001.

8. Annie Murphy Paul, "The Real Marriage Penalty," *New York Times,* November 19, 2006.

9. Christine Schwartz and Robert Mare, "Trends in Educational Assortative Marriage from 1940 to 2003," *Demography* 42, 4, November 2005, pp. 621–646.

10. Gary Becker, *A Treatise on the Family,* Harvard University Press, 1991.

11. Raquel Fernández and Richard Rogerson, "Sorting and Long Run Inequality," *Quarterly Journal of Economics* 116, 4, November 2001, pp. 1305–1341. See also Feng Hou and John Miles, "The Changing Role of Education in the Marriage Market: Assortative Marriage in Canada and the United States since 1970," *Statistics Canada,* May 2007, www.statcan.ca/english/research/11F0019MIE/11F0019MIE2007299.pdf.

12. Blaine Harden, "Numbers Drop for the Married with Children: Institution Becoming the Choice of the Educated, Affluent," *Washington Post,* March 4, 2007.

13. Pamela Smock, "The Wax and Wane of Marriage: Prospects for Marriage in the 21st Century," *Journal of Marriage and Family* 66, 4, 2004, pp. 966–973. See also Sarah Avellar and Pamela Smock, "The Economic Consequences of the Dissolution of Cohabiting Unions," *Journal of Marriage and Family* 67, 2, 2005, pp. 315–327.

Chapter 14

1. See Leonard Steinhorn, *The Greater Generation: In Defense of the Baby Boom Legacy,* St. Martin's, 2007.

2. William H. Frey and Ross C. DeVol, "America's Demography in the New Century: Aging Baby Boomers and New Immigrants as Major Players," Milken Institute Policy Brief, March 2000.

3. Pete Lydens, "Forget Golf Courses, Beaches, and Mountains," *Wall Street Journal,* October 2, 2006.

Chapter 15

1. Daniel Kahneman et al., "Survey Method for Characterizing Daily Life Experience: The Day Reconstruction Method," *Science,* December 3, 2004, pp. 1776–1780.

2. The Segmentation Company, a division of Yankelovich, "Attracting the Young College-Educated to Cities," CEOs for Cities, May 11, 2006, www.ceosforcities.org/rethink/research/files/CEOsforCitiesAttractingYoungEducatedPres2006.pdf.

Index